A Practical Guide
to Social Service Evaluation

Also Available from Lyceum Books, Inc.

Advisory Editor: Thomas M. Meenaghan, *New York University*

Evidence-Based Practices for Social Workers: An Interdisciplinary Approach, by Thomas O'Hare

Using Statistical Methods in Social Work Practice with SPSS, by Soleman H. Abu-Bader

Clinical Assessment for Social Workers: Qualitative and Quantitative Methods, 2e, edited by Catheleen Jordan and Cynthia Franklin

Therapeutic Games and Guided Imagery for Children, Adolescents, and Their Families, by Monit Cheung

Advocacy Practice for Social Justice, by Richard Hoefer

Using Evidence in Social Work Practice: Behavioral Perspectives, by Harold E. Briggs and Tina L. Rzepnicki

Modern Social Work Theory: A Critical Introduction, 3e, by Malcolm Payne, foreword by Stephen C. Anderson

Ethics in End-Of-Life Decisions in Social Work Practice, by Ellen Csikai and Elizabeth Chaitin.

Understanding Substance Addictions: Assessment and Intervention, by Sophia Dziegelewski

A Practical Guide
to Social Service Evaluation

Carl F. Brun
Wright State University

LYCEUM
BOOKS, INC.

Chicago, Illinois

© Lyceum Books, Inc., 2005

Published by

Lyceum Books, Inc.
5758 S. Blackstone Ave.
Chicago, Illinois 60637
773+643-1903 (Fax)
773+643-1902 (Phone)
lyceum@lyceumbooks.com
http://www.lyceumbooks.com

ISBN 0-925065-82-x

10 9 8 7 6 5 4 3 2 1

Library of Congress Cataloging-in-Publication Data

Brun, Carl F.
     A practical guide to social service evaluation / Carl F. Brun.
        p. cm.
     Includes bibliographical references and index.
     ISBN 0-925065-82-X
     1. Human services—Evaluation. 2. Evaluation research (Social action
programs) I. Title.
HV40.B874 2005
361.3′2—dc22

                                                                2005009030

CONTENTS

ILLUSTRATIONS

Preface

I once observed the words "ASK QUESTIONS" spray-painted on the brick building that housed the education department of the university where I obtained my doctorate. Two days later, those words were crossed out and replaced with the response "WHY?"

Both expressions of intellectual graffiti were removed before anything else was added. I have since imagined the following dialogue as it relates to evaluation:

> Evaluate.
> *Why?*
> Because evaluation leads to better knowledge.
> *Why?*
> Because knowledge is power and can be used for change.
> *Why?*
> Because you deserve to know. Hold people accountable for their actions.
> *Why?*
> Because evaluation helps us make better decisions.
> *Why?*
> Because it's the law.
> *Why?*
> Because I said so.
> *Why?*
> Why not evaluate?
> *Because evaluations don't make a difference. People have already decided what is going to happen to this program.*
> Why not evaluate?
> *Because it's too hard to evaluate the impact of multiple interventions.*
> Why not evaluate?
> *Because I value certain things that can't be evaluated.*
> Why not evaluate?
> *Because laws are meant to be broken.*
> Why not evaluate?
> *Because I said so.*

Social work practice cannot exist without evaluation. Yet many beginning social workers resist evaluation, for some of the reasons listed above. Many beginning social workers are not prepared to integrate evaluation into everyday social work practice. In this book, I combine my experience as a social work practitioner, administrator, educator, and evaluator to provide the reader with an understanding of how agency politics, professional and personal values, diversity, theory, and research methods shape the evaluation decisionmaking process. The reader is encouraged to rely on the values, skills, and knowledge learned in social work practice and research courses and embrace the rewards of evaluation rather than resist the unavoidable reality that evaluation is here to stay.

This book on social service evaluation bridges the knowledge, value, and skill of social work practice, planning, evaluation, and research. It can help social work students and beginning social workers achieve the following objectives, mandated in the Educational Policy and Administrative Standards (EPAS) of the Council on Social Work Education (CSWE; see CSWE, 2003, pp. 33–34):

Apply critical thinking skills within the context of professional social work practice. Readers are encouraged to constantly question how theory, values, and data-collection methods drive evaluation decisions that will ultimately help social service workers improve service delivery. Definition, purpose, and activities must be clarified for each new evaluation. No two evaluations are identical. The concepts in this book can be applied by social work students at both the undergraduate and graduate levels, especially as they apply the concepts to the field practicum setting. This book can also be used by social service workers, both those with evaluation experience and those without.

Understand the value base of the profession and its ethical standards and principles, and practice accordingly. Social work values are discussed throughout the entire book. In chapter 3, there is a more detailed discussion of ethical guidelines for evaluation following the National Association of Social Workers (NASW) Code of Ethics and the American Evaluation Association's Guiding Principles for Evaluators. Additional social work values emphasized are adherence to the strengths perspective, cultural competency, and assessment of multiple systems impacts on desired results for clients.

Practice without discrimination. Very clear suggestions exist to guide social service workers to practice and evaluate without ignoring the cultural backgrounds of the participants and key stakeholders in evaluations. Guidelines for culturally competent evaluations are discussed in depth in chapter 3.

Apply the knowledge and skills of generalist social work practice to systems of all sizes. This is a book about the knowledge and skills that all generalist social service workers can implement. The learning outcomes outlined at the beginning of each chapter can be applied to evaluations of interventions with individuals, families, groups, organizations, and communities. The Evaluation Decisionmaking Model applied in this book conceptualizes evaluation, practice, and policy as a circular rather than a linear process. Parts of the model are described in each chapter. Planning and practice examples are provided throughout the book.

Use theoretical frameworks supported by empirical evidence. Chapter 4 discusses the use of literature reviews to learn how specific interventions have been explored, described, and tested in previous research. Readers should be critical of how evaluations build and test theories that are relevant to social service practice. Additionally, each chapter offers suggestions for further reading. The use of logic models to connect theory, intervention, and evaluation is also covered in chapter 4. Logic models help social service workers identify the goals, activities, and expected results of interventions and programs.

Evaluate research studies, apply research findings to practice, and evaluate practice interventions. The primary goal of this book is for readers to be able to apply research findings in the development and implementation of evaluations of their own practice interventions. Evaluation is described in chapter 1 as having program improvement and knowledge-building functions. Evaluations help agency workers make important decisions to improve practice and to be accountable to clients to deliver services competently. Evaluations are guided by research findings from other settings and contribute to knowledge that can be used by other social service workers. Case examples are given to demonstrate the use of qualitative, quantitative, and mixed data-collection methods in evaluations. Chapter 5 is devoted solely to research methods. A theme of this book is that data-collection methods are just one component driving evaluation decisions. Key stakeholders' adherence to values and theory also drives evaluation decisions.

Function within the structure of organizations and service-delivery systems and seek necessary organizational change. Actions of individual social service workers have implications for the entire social service agency. Policies of agencies affect how social service workers interact with clients. Chapter 2 gives attention to the role of negotiating the scope, purpose, and activities of an evaluation with key stakeholders.

AUDIENCE

This book emphasizes the integration of practice and research skills. An undergraduate or graduate social work student with a beginning understanding of the social work research process can utilize it to apply theory, values, respect for diversity, and research methods in practice courses settings. For example:

Readers can understand the issues that underlie social service evaluation.

They can plan an evaluation of an intervention discussed in a practice course working with individuals, families, groups, or organizations.

They can also plan ways to evaluate the application in a practicum setting of a theory learned in a human behavior and social environment (HBSE) course.

They can propose evaluations to test the impact of a state, federal, or local policy on worker and client behavior.

Community organization courses can apply this text when discussing the role of conducting needs or strengths assessment in planning communitywide interventions.

This book can be used for a capstone course that helps students utilize evaluation as a means to integrate all the content areas learned across the curriculum.

Readers can use this text to design an evaluation at their agency practicum site.

Social service workers embarking on evaluation can also utilize this book. For example:

Readers can use it to develop a beginning evaluation plan as part of a request for proposal (RFP).

Several workers from the same agency can use it to guide planning, practice, and evaluation decisions.

Several workers from collaborating agencies can use it to arrive at agreement on the scope and activities of a specific evaluation.

Agency administrators can utilize some of its suggestions to create an environment that encourages and supports staff evaluation activities.

Readers can use the numerous lists contained in this book to concentrate on sections of the Evaluation Decisionmaking Model that apply to a given evaluation. All sections of the book will not necessarily apply to all evaluations.

Readers can use the book to develop evaluation contracts that specify the evaluation focus and the tasks of each person involved in the evaluation.

PLAN OF THE BOOK

Evaluation is both a process and a product. This book is about clarifying the components of an evaluation while at the same time helping the reader do an evaluation. Planning, implementing, and evaluating an intervention are interconnected steps. Social service workers do not always have the time to separate these three activities. The discussion in this book shows how the process of key persons agreeing on evaluation decisions greatly shapes the evaluation activities.

This book is organized according to the set of decisions (listed below) that all social service workers need to answer during an evaluation:

What is the scope and purpose of the evaluation (chap. 1)?

Who are the stakeholders that decide on the scope of the evaluation (chap. 2)?

What are the values and ethics that drive the evaluation (chap. 3)?

What are the theories that drive the evaluation (chap. 4)?

What are the data-collection methods that drive the evaluation (chap. 5)?

What is documented in the final report to show the connection between all the steps of the evaluation (chap. 6)?

While the evaluation process can begin at any of several points, the chapters in this book are organized in the order in which I myself prefer to conduct an evaluation. I believe that the scope of the evaluation as determined by key persons invested in the evaluation should be the beginning point, but, in reality, the scope may already have been determined before those key persons become involved. Similarly, in some situations, the expectation to follow certain values (e.g., focusing on client strengths) may be considered as an afterthought during the data-collection stage. Clarifying the program theory or logic model of an intervention will lead naturally to the expected outcomes that can be measured in an evaluation, but some persons may be expected to measure certain outcomes without having a clear logic model. The appropriate data-collection method can be selected more accurately after the previous components have been clarified, even though many evaluations start by stating a method that should be used (e.g., a survey or focus group). The final report then becomes the written documentation that confirms the decisions made from beginning to end of the evaluation.

Each chapter has the following structure:

Learning outcomes for the reader begin the chapter.

Case examples are given to illustrate the main points.

Evaluation decisionmaking tips are given to help the readers arrive at decisions on key issues in each chapter.

A "Further Readings" section provides readers with a list of other books and Web sites that give more detail about the key topics discussed.

Reflective journal activities help the reader become aware of subjective reactions to the material that may become an obstacle to completing an evaluation.

Procedural journal activities focus on the key evaluation decisions for the component of evaluation discussed in each chapter.

Chapter 1, "Why Evaluate? The Scope and Purpose of Evaluation," begins with the different ways that evaluation can enrich social service practice. The definition of *evaluation* used throughout the book is given, emphasizing that readers should clarify the definition that is being applied in their own situations. The other aspects of the evaluation scope are discussed:

How will the evaluation improve practice and program planning?

How will the evaluation build knowledge?

How do exploratory, descriptive, and explanatory questions lead to different types of evaluation activities?

Chapter 2, "Negotiating with Stakeholders: The Politics of Evaluation," discusses the many different persons who have a stake in evaluation. These include funders, agency administrators, direct-care staff, clients, the general community, and the evaluators. The differences between internally and externally driven evaluations are discussed. Tips are given on how to develop an evaluation stakeholder plan that contains the following:

the persons authorizing the evaluation;

the persons advising the evaluation;

the persons responsible for conducting the evaluation;

the reports expected from the evaluation; and

a time line for meeting the expectations of the evaluation.

Chapter 3, "Value-Driven Evaluation Decisions," begins by helping the reader understand the influence of personal, agency, community, and professional values on the evaluation process. Specific attention is given to ways in which the following SCREAM values can be respected during each evaluation:

assessment of evaluation participants' *strengths;*

respect for stakeholder and evaluation participants' *culture;*

conducting evaluation feasibly within one's *resources;*

administration of *ethical* evaluation procedures;

reaching a written *agreement* among stakeholders on the scope and activities of the evaluation;

measuring *multiple* systems results.

Chapter 4, "Theory-Driven Evaluation Decisions," covers two tools, literature reviews and logic models, that can help social service workers connect theory to planning, practice, and evaluation. Theory is a description or explanation of the relationship between a social service intervention or program and desired results for clients and consumers of the services. Theories help social service workers answer the question, Why do you plan to use, or why are you using, that intervention? The literature review provides a partial answer to the question by helping the social service worker learn from written accounts of successful interventions and be able to provide the answer, Because this intervention has been shown in the literature to be effective. The logic model is a clarification of intervention goals, activities, and desired results and helps workers answer the above question by providing the answer, Because this is the best intervention to meet our goals and desired results. Theory learned through literature reviews and data-collection methods described in chapter 5 helps workers develop logic models. Theory and logic models become important tools for evaluating the planning and implementation of social services.

Chapter 5, "Data-Driven Evaluation Decisions," begins with a discussion of how evaluations transform information in an agency into data that are relevant to answering the evaluation questions. The purpose of this chapter is to familiarize the reader with the issues related to data collection. Differences in open-ended, qualitative and closed-ended, quantitative data-collection processes are compared. Qualitative narrative data analysis and quantitative statistical analysis are discussed. Finally, methods for ensuring the credibility and trustworthiness of qualitative data and methods for ensuring the validity and reliability of quantitative data are covered. References at the end of this chapter should be consulted when carrying out specific data-collection methods.

Chapter 6, "Reporting Evaluation Decisions: Coming Full Circle," aids the reader in documenting decisions relevant to each of the previous chapters. The final evaluation report is, thus, the reader's justification for the decisions made and agreed on by key stakeholders during the give-and-take negotiation that all evaluations entail.

AUTHOR'S BACKGROUND

Evaluation has been my tool for bridging academe and the practice setting in my role as first an assistant and then an associate professor of social work for over ten years at Wright State University. I am a social worker. My baccalaureate, master's, and doctoral degrees are all in social work. I also have educational training in psychology, sociology, education, women's studies, cultural studies, and urban affairs. My social work practice has been in the fields of child welfare, mental health, and family violence prevention. I now make it my profession to influence future social workers through my teaching of micro- and macrocontent in undergraduate social work courses. I also mentor students completing social work honors theses and graduate theses in applied behavioral sciences, psychology, and the humanities. Social work values, knowledge, and skills related to practice, planning, and evaluation are infused into every class I teach and every thesis committee on which I serve.

The case examples that I provide throughout the book range from evaluations initiated by social service workers or students in agencies with a small staff (five or fewer) and a small operating budget ($100,000 or less) to statewide evaluations of county-implemented programs with large operating budgets (in the millions). The case examples cover different purposes (planning, implementation, and research), answer different types of questions (exploratory, descriptive, and explanatory), and were intended for different uses (continue, improve, create, or discontinue the evaluated interventions).

My involvement in all the case examples was connected to my university affiliation, which meant that all data-collection activities needed approval by an institutional review board (IRB), which is discussed in chapter 3. The SCREAM values that I describe in chapter 2 are followed to different degrees in the case examples. Some case examples utilized a logic model to guide evaluation decisions. Some examples required that the evaluated programs implement evidence-based practices. Other evaluations helped social service workers articulate the program theory that they followed, sometimes without empirical research to support the theory and agency activities. Qualitative and quantitative data-collection approaches are illustrated, sometimes in the same case example. Finally, actual reports derived from case examples are provided, including journal articles, conference presentations, annotated bibliographies, and evaluation manuals.

My role as educator, facilitator, change agent, supporter, and mediator varied across the different evaluations. In some evaluations, I was a member of an outside evaluation team that had little or no contact with the persons implementing the evaluated programs other than collecting data from them. In other evaluations, I met with the direct-care staff or planners often, in order, for example, to teach them about evaluation methods, to inform them of the theory most relevant to their service delivery, and so on.

I provide the case examples as a way to help the reader engage knowledgeably in the evaluation process. In all the examples, I was an evaluator. The reader too can learn evaluation tasks. Minimally, readers should be knowledgeable about what to expect from those persons hired to evaluate their programs. The case examples, evaluation decisionmaking tips, and further readings sections provide the applied tools that will help readers understand and successfully conduct evaluations of their practice interventions.

In each evaluation, I applied the same social work processes as I did when I was a child welfare social worker. To quote the Council on Social Work Education social work practice standard, I "engaged clients in an appropriate working relationship, identifying issues, problems, needs, resources, and assets; collecting and assessing information; and planning for service delivery" (CSWE, 2003, p. 35). Just as I did with practice clients, I wanted evaluation clients to know the potential consequences of decisions that were being mutually made. The evaluation process, like the practice process, is itself a learning tool for all persons involved. Much of the knowledge gained from the evaluation examples in this book came from the process as much as from the outcomes measured.

I conclude this preface with these catchphrases that readers should remember as they apply this book to ensure that evaluations are conducted *with* social service workers and clients rather than *on* them:

1. Clarify, clarify, clarify. It is worth everyone's time to be clear about the purpose and expectations of an evaluation. The time spent to clarify in writing with key stakeholders the important components of the evaluation reduces the amount of time spent blaming persons for doing the evaluation the "wrong" way.

2. Practice, practice, practice. Learn while doing. Try some of the ideas in this book on a small scale before applying them to an entire evaluation.

3. There is no perfect evaluation. Some stakeholder will always be critical of evaluation decisions because there are always many different options in evaluations. Keep a journal during evaluations to document the decisions made, noting those persons who agreed and opposed those decisions.

4. SCREAM as often as you can. Measure client *strengths*. Respect the *cultural* backgrounds of all stakeholders. Work within the means of the available *resources*. Treat all participants *ethically*. Expect stakeholders to reach an *agreement* on how to conduct the evaluation competently to the best of one's abilities. Measure results of *multiple* systems (i.e., individuals, families, agencies, and communities). These are values that most social services advocate in their daily interventions. The same should be true for evaluations.

5. Do not go out there alone. Form an evaluation support group to help you get past writing blocks or stakeholder blocks or the logic model blues. Others can help you see the value of moving forward even when you seem to be spinning your wheels.

ACKNOWLEDGMENTS

I could not have completed this book without the support and patience of my wife, Karla, who understood when I spent hours, weeks, and years in the upstairs office. She genuinely applies evidence-based interventions to deliver occupational therapy to special needs children. My parents, siblings, and friends have given me much encouragement to finish this book at times when I got lost in the chapters. I thank all the colleagues in the Social Work Department: Anita Curry-Jackson, Marjorie Baker, Theresa Myadze, Marita Rogers, Phil Engler, Bela Bognar, Susan Allen, and Bob Nelson. I thank all the social service workers and clients who taught me about evaluation through their questions and active participation in the evaluation process.

A theme of this book is that evaluation bridges practice and research. The following mentors and colleagues have helped me bridge all the different influences that created this book. Thank you Drs. Patti Lather, Laurel Richardson, and Mary Catherine O'Connor for your hands-on teaching and modeling of qualitative methods and constructivist, naturalistic approaches. Thank you Dr. Elsie Pinkston for teaching me the value of writing measurable behavioral outcomes and valid and reliable observation protocols. Thank you Drs. Nolan Rindfleisch, Karen Harper, Beverly Toomey, Keith Rilty, and all my doctoral classmates for building my confidence as a researcher and evaluator.

Thank you to the following evaluators with whom I have had the good fortune to collaborate: Mieko Smith, Betty Yung, Cheryl Myer, Katherine Cauley, Richard Rapp, Rhonda Reagh, Carla Clasen, Jane Dockery, Timothy Sweet-Holp, and William Mase.

Thank you to Dr. Thomas Meenaghan for your critical and conceptual suggestions in the early stages of this book and to the following reviewers of the manuscript: James Dudley, Cynthia Rocha, Patricia O'Brien, Eleanor Downey, and Richard Hoefer.

Thank you to David Follmer and Amber Neff of Lyceum Books for guiding me through the long process of completing this book.

Thanks to all the persons I reference in this book, for it is your writings that helped me conceptualize evaluation as an applied tool that belongs in the hands of social service workers and their allies.

CHAPTER 1

WHY EVALUATE?
THE SCOPE AND PURPOSE OF EVALUATION

Before my discussion of the importance of evaluation and the steps in the process, I think it important to reiterate that the steps involved in evaluation do not occur in a set order and are each affected by each other. This book provides a model to help social service workers control the evaluation process. Evaluation is described in this book as a process, a necessary process if practice and planning are to be enriched and if social service workers are to remain accountable to stakeholders. Each chapter summarizes a separate but interconnected step to evaluation that is illustrated in figure 1.1. As you read and conduct your own evaluations, remember, decisions discussed in each chapter affect activities conducted in other steps of the evaluation.

This first chapter begins with a discussion of the positive ways in which social service workers can benefit from evaluation. It then goes on to emphasize the importance of clarifying the scope of a current evaluation before proceeding with the other steps of the evaluation. This material will help students understand the issues that underlie evaluation. It will help social service workers specify the scope of an evaluation.

The *learning outcomes* for this chapter are as follows:

1. Understand how evaluation enriches social service practice and planning.
2. Clarify the scope of the evaluation by
   a. Defining *evaluation;*
   b. Clarifying how the evaluation will guide program practice and planning decisions;
   c. Clarifying whether the evaluation is answering exploratory, descriptive, or explanatory questions;
   d. Clarifying how research activities for knowledge building will be used in the evaluation.

Figure 1.1.   Interactive steps of evaluation.

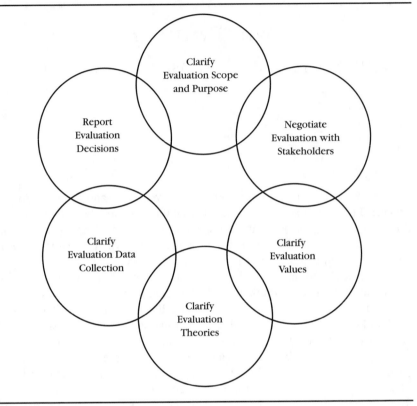

EVALUATION ENRICHES PRACTICE

Evaluation Is Social Work.   Read the case examples in figures 1.2 and 1.3. Take note of the practice skills that were necessary to collect information during the evaluations. The purpose of the evaluations guided the actions of the social service practitioners, planners, and evaluators. Interviewing skills were needed to elicit accurate and credible information. The evaluators informed participants that their participation was confidential and voluntary. The results of the evaluation guided practice and planning decisions.

Evaluation Improves Social Services.   In the example presented in figure 1.2, the Strengths-Based Case Management (SBCM) intervention for men in recovery was adapted to take account of participants' skepticism of the approach. In the example presented in figure 1.3, several reports emerged from the evaluation to help improve the implementation of the

Figure 1.2.   Case example: Evaluation of Strengths-Based Case Management.

The director of a Strengths-Based Case Management (SBCM) intervention contacted me to conduct open-ended, qualitative interviews with consumers to answer the following general descriptive question: "How do consumers experience SBCM?" The intervention was based on prior research that demonstrated the effectiveness of SBCM with persons discharged from an inpatient substance abuse rehabilitation program. Agreement on the data-collection process was reached with the three agency workers, who were also interviewed to obtain their description of the intervention. The main source of information was ten consumers, with whom one-hour interviews were conducted at three different times over a six-month period. Initially, some of the staff were nervous about how the results might affect the program. The program director assured them that all information was confidential and would be used to improve the program rather than discontinue it. My summaries and interpretations of the interviews were shared with each participant. The written report was provided to the staff and shared with them during a staff meeting. The staff benefited from hearing about client experiences of which they had not previously been aware. For example, one man reported: "I did not trust the things the counselors were saying. The only time someone in the past said something nice to me, they were lying because they wanted something from me." The staff discussed ways to deliver SBCM that incorporated knowledge learned from the information I collected, analyzed, and reported to them. The costs of this project were covered as part of the operating budget for this program, which was funded by the National Institute on Drug Abuse. The primary expenses were compensation for the participants' time ($30 for each interview) and less than 10% reallocation of my and the staff's time from other responsibilities to complete the project. All data-collection procedures were approved by my university's institutional review board (IRB) to ensure that ethical guidelines were followed in data collection.

---

family support programs. Those evaluation reports were (1) a list of commonly desired results at the child, family, agency, and community levels that could be measured across all the programs; (2) critiques of instruments to measure child health, family health, and parent involvement; and (3) a training model to help the participants conduct self-evaluations.

Evaluation Is Accountability.   Funding sources require practitioners to be accountable for producing desired results. In the example presented in figure 1.2, information from the client interviews supported positive outcomes previously reported from an evaluation of the same program. In the example presented in figure 1.3, the desired outcome of improved family functioning across participants of the community-based family support programs was not demonstrated partly because the instrument measuring family functioning that was employed may not have been the best conceptual tool for this population. Yet the individuals, local agencies, and state

Figure 1.3.   Case example: Evaluation of family support interventions.

I, along with colleagues from my and seven other universities, submitted a response to a request for proposals to conduct a statewide evaluation of thirty-eight family support interventions (FSIs) over a two-year period. FSIs were community- and school-based programs that were locally planned and implemented. Goals of the programs were to increase collaboration between families, agencies, schools, and communities to improve child, family, agency, and community functioning. Intervention strategies included assessment, referral, after-school programs, tutoring, parent education, community organization, agency outreach, counseling, advocacy, health services, and mental health services.

This $250,000 evaluation was funded by three state agencies. Our evaluation plan included conducting open-ended, qualitative site interviews during the first year to answer the descriptive question, "How do different stakeholders (administrators, direct-care staff, community representatives, and consumers) perceive success of the programs?" The results of the site interviews would help the evaluators construct a list of common desired results to measure across selected programs during the second year. At the same time, quantitative, closed-ended telephone surveys were conducted with consumers of the programs and a comparison group to test the explanatory hypothesis, "Consumers of the FSIs will significantly improve family functioning."

There were varying levels of agreement about the evaluation among stakeholders. As the primary evaluator, I had at least quarterly meetings with the state funders and often much more frequent e-mail and telephone contact. There were legal mandates on school-based FSIs to measure the student performance outcomes of proficiency test pass rates, attendance, retention, and graduation rates. Other FSIs had more flexibility to determine the best results to measure locally. Some FSIs targeted the larger community for change, whereas others targeted the family for change. This difference in program targets made it difficult to arrive at a feasible list of common results across FSIs to measure in the second year. On the basis of this information, the state funders and the evaluators agreed at the one-year point to continue the telephone survey of consumers and conduct academic literature searches to determine the best standardized instruments to measure (1) child health, (2) family functioning, and (3) parent involvement in children's education.

The following reports delivered at the end of the evaluation were made available to the state funders and local directors of the evaluated programs to assist them in future evaluations: (1) results of the statewide evaluation; (2) feedback about individual programs; (3) evaluation training material; and (4) critiques of standardized instruments that measure child well-being, family functioning, and parent involvement in children's education. The funding for this project covered 100% of my university responsibilities and about 10% of the ten faculty from other universities during the first year, telephone survey expenses, and about 10% of my and about five other colleagues' responsibilities in the second year. All data-collection procedures were approved by my university's IRB to ensure that ethical guidelines were followed in data collection.

administrators were still able to utilize the process and the results of the evaluation to improve practice and future evaluations.

Evaluation Is a Process.   In both examples, the evaluators negotiated with the key stakeholders to reach agreement on the evaluation activities, just as a social service worker develops an intervention plan with clients and other systems to help clients achieve change. In the example presented in figure 1.2, the key stakeholders were the four staff, although the director had more influence on the evaluation decisions than the three direct-care staff. The consumers' input was sought as part of the information-gathering process. There were many more stakeholders involved in the example presented in figure 1.3. The primary stakeholders were the state funders, although consultation on the evaluation plan was solicited from each director of the thirty-eight programs being evaluated.

Social Service Evaluation Is Applied Research.   In both examples, the data-collection methods were finalized only *after* the following points were clarified with key stakeholders: (1) the purpose of the evaluation; (2) whether the evaluation questions were exploratory, descriptive, or explanatory; (3) important values to be guided by in the evaluation (e.g., to measure client strengths); (4) the theory or logic model guiding the practice and evaluation; (5) preferred methods of data collection; and (6) the final reports of the evaluation.

The two case examples illustrate that social service evaluation is a process of systematically collecting and analyzing information to improve practice. In the first example, the evaluators employed qualitative, open-ended interviews with participants in a structured manner, the interview format being based on descriptive questions pertaining to the evaluated intervention. In the second example, a longitudinal, comparison group survey design was implemented to test an explanatory hypothesis related to the programs. Open-ended site interviews with key stakeholders were conducted to answer descriptive evaluation questions.

In both examples, the knowledge of specific evaluation designs (e.g., qualitative, single subject, or experimental) and data-collection methods (e.g., surveys, observation, or secondary data analysis) were then implemented on the basis of the negotiation of the factors listed above. No evaluator can master all the possible data-collection methods. The benefit of conducting the evaluation as a team, as in the example presented in figure 1.3, was the ability to utilize the skills of the different evaluators and social service staff.

In both examples, stakeholders and participants in the evaluation stated that they learned methods of self-evaluation that they could employ in the future. Clients changed destructive behavior (using substances) and increased healthy behavior (positive interaction with their children) on the basis of insight gained from the open-ended interviews. Evaluators sought out studies conducted on interventions similar to their own, located the best instruments to measure their desired outcomes, and designed self-evaluations. Administrators arranged time for practitioners to design and conduct evaluations. They also arranged training on a specific, empirically based intervention.

This book provides a model to help social service workers control the evaluation process. Evaluation is described in this book as a process, a necessary process if practice and planning are to be enriched and if social service workers are to remain accountable to stakeholders. This is not a technical research methods book. Those texts already exist. This is a book to help students, practitioners, and planners become active participants in evaluation by understanding and clarifying the terms and expectations of a given evaluation.

Social service evaluation is the systematic collection and analysis of information about one or more social service interventions and clients to improve social work practice, planning, and accountability and contribute to knowledge building. This general definition is a starting point from which to help social service workers clarify the components of the Evaluation Decisionmaking Model discussed throughout this book and summarized in appendix C.

For every evaluation, ask the questions, What do we mean by evaluation? and, Why are we doing evaluation? The second question addresses how evaluations can guide the program decisionmaking process and also guide the knowledge-building process. Each of these reasons is discussed separately because each purpose influences different, although overlapping, decisions.

EVALUATION GUIDES PROGRAM IMPROVEMENT

Why do social service workers conduct evaluations—besides because they have to? Figuring out why funders or other stakeholders require an evaluation is a good starting point for clarifying the purpose of the evaluation. Practitioners encourage mandatory and involuntary clients to clarify their own purposes and goals in and desired results from intervention. Do the same with evaluation.

Look at the list provided in figure 1.4 of possible reasons why people conduct evaluations, checking all the reasons that apply to your agency. These reasons fall into two general categories: (1) program improvement and (2) knowledge building. Evaluation is initiated for program improvement purposes when decisions to continue, change, or discontinue interventions or programs are grounded in knowledge gained from the information collected. Evaluation is initiated for knowledge-building purposes when decisions are grounded in and contribute to knowledge gained from research

Figure 1.4.   Why people evaluate.

PROGRAM IMPROVEMENT

It is required/recommended by an accrediting body.
It is required/recommended as part of an RFP.
It is required/recommended as part of receiving a grant.
It is required/recommended by the agency board of directors.
It is required/recommended by the agency director.
It is required/recommended by my supervisor.
It is required/recommended by a collaborating agency.
It is requested by an agency consumer.
I have to evaluate my staff's performance.
Other

KNOWLEDGE BUILDING

It is required/recommended in one of these academic settings:

a class in a bachelor's program

a continuing education class

a class in a master's program

a class in a doctoral program

an honors, master's, or doctoral thesis

other

---

conducted on similar interventions or programs reported in the literature. A theme of this book is that university-agency partnerships be established to promote evaluations that achieve both purposes at the same time.

Many authors define *evaluation* as the collection of data or information for the purpose of helping persons make program-management decisions (e.g., Patton, 1997; Posavac & Carey, 2003; Royse, Thyer, Padgett, & Logan, 2001; Unrau, Gabor, & Grinnell, 2001; and Weiss, 1998). A goal for this book is that persons at all levels in an agency, including direct-line practitioners, agency planners, administrators, and even consumers of services, participate in evaluation decisionmaking.

Agency workers are likely to view evaluation for administrative purposes as jumping through bureaucratic hoops. It may seem that the motivation for the evaluation comes from an outside source, such as a funder or program administrator, that is, that the evaluation is simply a program requirement. In such cases, workers are unlikely to participate in the evaluation if participation is not required. The objective of evaluation in such situations can be rationalized as helping make program decisions, whether for planning or practice purposes, a process discussed in more detail below.

Figure 1.5.   Case examples: Social service planning evaluations.

A United Way that funded services in a two-county region contacted my university to conduct a content analysis of four separate research studies conducted in the region over the previous several years. The purpose of the evaluation was to answer the question, "What are the targeted populations and interventions described in the four analyzed studies?" The results guided the selection of priority areas for funding by United Way over the next five years. I was a member of the evaluation team that provided the results of our content analysis to an advisory team of approximately fifteen agency directors and community leaders.

A local agency director contacted me to collect information to help a collaboration of agencies and community residents develop a pregnancy prevention proposal to be submitted for state funding. Information was collected by means of focus groups and surveys with teenage parents, teenagers who were not parents, parents of teenagers, teachers, religious leaders in the community, and directors of social service agencies providing services to youth (Brun & Giga, 1999).

A local agency director contacted me to collect information to help a collaboration of agencies and community residents develop a family violence prevention proposal to be submitted to a private foundation for funding. The members of the collaboration asked that I educate them about family violence prevention since I had a great deal of practical experience in the field of child welfare and domestic violence. They also wanted help constructing instruments and surveys to send to social service providers and were active in conducting literature searches. My role was as much educator, facilitator, and planner as it was evaluator.

I was a member of an evaluation team that conducted a quantitative, closed-ended survey of state mental health workers and an open-ended, qualitative focus group with key stakeholders of nine mental health facilities to answer the question, "What are the competencies expected of all direct-care mental health workers?" The results of the project were shared with stakeholders to determine priorities for developing a training program for mental health workers (Clasen, Meyer, Brun, Mase, & Cauley, 2003).

Social service planning involves the selection of the interventions that will be delivered to a group of persons to achieve desired results. Planning may involve assessing the needs and assets of those affected by the program in order to establish goals and consulting the literature and key Web sites to learn about other programs that address similar concerns in other communities. In the planning stage, information is gathered to justify implementing a new program or modifying an already existing program. During program planning, information about potential clients is also collected.

Examples of social service planning evaluations can be found in figure 1.5. In each of the examples, the evaluator stayed with the purposes established for the evaluation in question. For example, in the United Way example, the need to identify the targeted populations and interventions described in the reports analyzed was the basis of the evaluators' findings and recommendations—hence the need for the advisory group of agency directors *not* to consider other targeted populations and interventions when planning their five-year vision.

Social service practice is the actual delivery of services to a group of persons to achieve desired results. Evaluation activities include collecting information that describes or explains the relation between the intervention and desired results. In the practice stage, information can be gathered to justify continuing, changing, or eliminating the program.

The case examples presented in figures 1.2 and 1.3 were both evaluations of the delivery of social service programs. For examples of other practice evaluations, see figure 1.6. The evaluators in each of these examples reported their findings within the limitations of the evaluation questions asked.

The Government Performance and Results Act (GPRA) of 1993 mandated that both public and private agencies improve their efforts to measure results, outcomes, and other program-performance indicators. A two-year U.S. General Accounting Office study of thirteen cabinet level departments and ten independent agencies concluded that the amount of resources devoted to meeting GPRA requirements was small and varied across agencies. Interviewed evaluators stated that the "primary role of evaluation was

Figure 1.6.   Case examples: Social service practice evaluations.

A facilitator of a local support group and summer camp for children experiencing the loss of a close relative contacted me to collect information that described the activities of the interventions. The information was collected through participatory observations and interviews where I was a cofacilitator of a group and recorded observations of the other volunteers and family participants (O'Neill, 2000). The information was utilized primarily to train volunteers facilitating the support groups.

A staff person directing a county public child welfare agency's diversity committee contacted me to describe possible reasons for the disproportionate number of African American children placed in out-of-home care compared to white children. I helped the diversity team analyze national research on the same topic and develop a plan to review case records for factors hypothesized to be related to this phenomenon.

I was a member of an evaluation team that conducted qualitative, open-ended site visits in ten separate counties to answer the question, "What are the successful outreach strategies for enrolling eligible children in the Children's Health Insurance Program (CHIP)?" (Meyer, Brun, Yung, Clasen, Cauley, & Mase, 2004). The information was shared with the state and local funders to guide CHIP outreach efforts across the state.

internally focused" and aimed "toward program managers and higher-level agency officials" rather than meeting legislators' demands that program performance be improved (USGAO, 1998, p. 5).

Some of the interviewed evaluators provided the following recommendations to improve evaluation activities:

> Adapt existing information systems to yield data on program results.
>
> Broaden the range of evaluation to include less rigorous and less expensive methods.
>
> Devolve program evaluation from the federal to the local managers.
>
> Develop partnerships with others to integrate the varied forms of performance information available on the programs.
>
> Provide evaluation leadership through establishing a catalog of tested performance measures.
>
> Conduct impact evaluations to supplement the states' performance measurement information. (USGAO, 1998, p. 6)

A premise of this book is that, in order for social service workers to meet external demands to evaluate their interventions, there must be available to them internal motives and supportive resources, such as those listed above. Further, evaluation takes many shapes in addition to performance- or results-oriented models. Other types of evaluations discussed in this book include exploratory, empowerment, needs-assessment, assets-assessment, theory-driven, and evidence-based evaluations.

A 1998 Kellogg Foundation study (Patrizi & McMullan, 1998) reported the results of surveys and interviews with evaluators from twenty-one large private foundations. One study question was, "Why do foundations evaluate grantees?" Five distinct purposes were listed as "very important": (1) "improv[ing] grantee practice and implementation"; (2) "improv[ing] foundation practice and grant making"; (3) "respond[ing] to foundation board requests for evidence on benefit of grant investments"; (4) "informing public policy"; and (5) "identifying best practices in the field." Areas that were not listed as "very important" included "identifying areas for new foundation program initiatives; deciding on grant renewal or expansion; deciding on project replication; and assessing foundation program staff performance" (Patrizi & Mc-Mullan, 1998, p. 10).

The significance of the findings presented above is that there may be a disconnect between the social service staff's purposes for the evaluation and the funder's purposes for the evaluation. For example, the staff may produce information for the purpose of demonstrating performance and supplying evidence as to why the grant should be renewed when those are not the funder's goals. Rather, the funder may want the evaluation to produce data supportive of policy agendas, a purpose that might not even occur to the program staff.

It is no wonder, then, that another finding from the Kellogg Foundation study was dissatisfaction on the part of the foundation staff with the evaluation reports submitted by the grantees: "For a variety of reasons—lack of up-front agreement about evaluation purpose; too many evaluation questions being addressed; 'piling-on' of different agendas—some evaluations produce reports or products that are not focused, are too long or offer unclear conclusions or evaluative stances" (Patrizi & McMullan, 1998, p. 16).

The following recommendations were reported by foundation staff to bridge the gap between the funders and grantees related to the purposes and expected products of evaluations: "clarify the purposes of the evaluation early on"; "secure involvement from the grantee in the evaluation"; "increase the interaction between evaluators, program staff, and grantees"; and "improve the logic model of a program" (Patrizi & McMullan, 1998, pp. 17–18). All these points are reinforced throughout this book. Specific questions about the administrative purposes of an evaluation are contained in the procedural journal activities at the end of this chapter.

EVALUATION CONTRIBUTES TO KNOWLEDGE BUILDING

People also conduct evaluation for academic reasons, to learn and promote knowledge building, most often under the name *research*. Students may be required to evaluate agencies as part of a class assignment, practicum requirement, or mandatory research project. Similarly, agency workers often contact university faculty to obtain assistance with evaluations required by funders. If the evaluation for academic purposes is not conducted in such a way that the agency decisionmaking process benefits, then the staff may view the evaluation negatively, as merely an academic exercise that achieves nothing more than the completion of a class assignment.

An evaluation for academic purposes may sometimes seem to focus more on methodology and less on how the knowledge gained will directly benefit a social service worker's daily decisionmaking process. As a student, think of evaluation as an opportunity to benefit the agency. As an agency worker, think of students as a potential resource to assist with the planning and implementation of evaluation activities. Figure 1.7 gives several examples of student research projects that were utilized by social service agencies to improve service delivery.

Some authors distinguish between evaluation and research by stating that evaluation is conducted to help make program decisions whereas research is conducted to promote knowledge. This distinction between evaluation and research *can* dichotomize practitioners and academics, both in the literature and in the practice setting. It is difficult, if not impossible, to conduct an evaluation without appearing academic. Still, it is desirable not to appear academic. Research and knowledge building are necessary tools for evaluation. So are the tools of relationship building and negotiation, which

Figure 1.7.   Case examples: Student research projects benefiting social service agencies.

A master's student conducted a single system design evaluation of a behavioral modification intervention that resulted in the parents implementing reinforcement and time-out procedures that decreased hitting and fighting behaviors among their two sons. The mother of the two children gave a formal presentation to the agency staff of the changes for her family, including displaying baseline and postintervention charts of the frequency of the boys' fighting. For a thorough discussion of single-systems design, see Bloom, Fischer, and Orme (2003).

Two master's students conducted a single system design evaluation of a youth outreach intervention. The students used the Goal Attainment Scale (GAS) to measure whether the youth attained their goals. The GAS was selected because it was an unobtrusive measure that fit with the informal interactions between the youth and the staff. The results identified for staff common goals among the users of the drop-in center. For a good review of the research conducted with GAS, see Royse et al. (2001, pp. 181–91).

My doctoral dissertation (Brun, 1993) was a naturalistic, exploratory study of parents labeled at risk to neglect their child. The findings from qualitative, open-ended interviews (with questions such as, "How do parents predicted to be at risk for child abuse and neglect successfully raise their children?") conducted with six mothers were reported as six individual case narratives. The common strengths among the parents were conceptualized as the Interactive Model of Parent Strengths, which has been used to train Head Start family service workers to focus on positive parent assets (see Brun, 1997). For discussion of qualitative approaches to data collection, see chapter 5.

An undergraduate student consulted the literature and adapted a survey to measure experiences of dating violence. She administered the survey to undergraduate social work majors. The results that many participants scored high on being victims of dating violence were reported to the faculty, who incorporated more discussion of violence prevention throughout the social work curriculum.

An undergraduate student conducted a content analysis of procedural manuals written by a school district's nurse to determine how school staff should respond if children arrive at school with lice. The standard policy was for teachers to dismiss such children. The student researcher was concerned, however, because some children were missing many days of school and often no one followed up on cases to assist the parents in removing the lice and in instituting measures to prevent future infestation. The student reported to a collaborative team of nurses, social workers, and teachers that nothing in the procedural manuals indicated that children should be sent home. On the basis of the student's analysis, procedures were established for a nurse and a social worker to follow up on any reports of children having lice to reduce the number of days those children were absent from school.

ensure that the needs of the program staff and clients are met. The social work value of going where the client is guides evaluation as much as it does practice. Good social work practice is good evaluation practice.

Throughout this book the term *evaluation* is employed instead of the term *research* because the latter often implies methods of data collection rather than the entire evaluation process. Standards in many research texts focus on obtaining researcher objectivity through the use of comparison-group design and standardized instruments and the application of inferential statistical analyses. These methods are often neither feasible nor useful in all evaluations. Standards in qualitative research texts meant to ensure data credibility and trustworthiness (e.g., peer review, member check, data triangulation, journaling, and decision audits) are also labor intensive and difficult to implement completely in the practice setting. Discussion of data-collection methodology is the focus of chapter 5.

The papers collected in Hess and Mullen (1995)—papers utilizing Schön's (1983) teachings on the reflexive practitioner—illustrated that many important program decisions and opportunities for knowledge building can result from a university–social service partnership. The editors began the book by discussing ways in which social service workers and evaluators can bridge the gap between researchers and practitioners, ways that combine the practical applications of research with the knowledge gained from research. Some of the values discussed are areas of negotiation that can occur in every evaluation:

> forming working relationships with stakeholders
>
> negotiating roles and responsibilities
>
> having open, clear, and honest communication
>
> sharing power when making decisions
>
> negotiating philosophies or worldviews about the importance given to objectivity and subjectivity

For items to consider when academic research is being conducted in social service settings, see figure 1.8.

ASKING THE RIGHT EVALUATION QUESTIONS

Asking the right type of evaluation questions is probably the most important component pertaining to the scope of an evaluation that needs to be clarified. Many social work students and social service workers find data collection to be the fun part of evaluation. Social service workers like to learn and solve problems. Data collection and analysis are tools for accomplishing these tasks. But different tools are required to answer different evaluation questions.

Figure 1.8.   Evaluation decisionmaking tip: Items to consider when conducting research in the agency.

For a current agency research project, check whether each item is provided.

Verification of the requirement from the academic institution:

_____ syllabus

_____ form from professor

_____ Web-site explanation

Verification that ethical guidelines will be followed:

_____ IRB approval form (all theses and dissertations are required to have IRB approval, but class assignments may be exempt)

_____ consent forms

_____ form stating how the evaluation will be used

Verification of approval from the agency:

_____ Is there an agency evaluation advisory board?

_____ What other committee approves such activities?

Verification of how the results will be reported:

_____ to the teacher only?

_____ to a thesis committee?

_____ published as a thesis or dissertation?

_____ published as an article?

_____ presented as a paper?

Verification of how authorship will be shared:

_____ How will the agency be mentioned?

_____ Whose names will appear as authors?

Other

The open-ended interviews and observations were the best data-collection tools to answer the exploratory evaluation question, "How do parents predicted to be at risk for child abuse and neglect successfully raise their children?" (see fig. 1.7). The open-ended interview with clients was the best data-collection tool to answer the *descriptive* evaluation question, "How do consumers experience SBCM?" (see fig. 1.2). The comparison-group design and standardized instruments were the best data-collection tools to answer the *explanatory* evaluation question, "How do different stakeholders perceive success of the (FSI) programs?" (see fig. 1.3).

Exploratory evaluation questions ask clients, workers, or community members about their experiences or circumstances, the answers of which will lead to program improvement and knowledge building. Examples of exploratory questions are the following:

> What is it like to have worked in child welfare for over ten years? (Brode, 1990)
>
> What happens after families leave a homeless shelter? (Tingler, 2000)
>
> How do parents predicted to be at risk for child abuse and neglect successfully raise their children? (Brun, 1993, 1997)

The understanding of the contexts shaping participants' perceptions and experiences to be gleaned from their responses to such questions is important information that can guide social service planning and implementing.

Brode's (1990) original research question was, "How do child welfare workers overcome burnout?" Rather than study the obstacles that result in a high turnover among child welfare workers, Brode learned of the resources on which longtime workers drew to work more than ten years in an emotionally draining profession. The individual and environmental contexts surrounding each person's decision to remain in child welfare long-term can help administrators create work environments that promote longevity among the employees.

Tingler (2000) originally consulted a literature base that described the process by which homeless families become stable. Her own observations, however, were that families were returning to the shelter within a year's time. She learned that there were many factors outside families' control that prevented them from becoming stable. She also learned that families were more likely to turn to friends and informal supports rather than to formal agency services for help. She was, therefore, able to devise ways in which agencies can provide follow-up services that better support families in their attempt to become stable.

In my dissertation, I originally consulted a literature base that identified the individual and societal factors that place families at risk for abusing or neglecting their children. As I conducted open-ended interviews and observations in homes, I never heard the participants use the words *neglect, abuse,* or *at risk.* The context of being at risk was provided by outside sources. The families talked about the personal belief systems, family support, and formal supports that helped them raise their children in spite of many obstacles. While working on the dissertation, I was directed to a body of literature that described the strengths that African American families possess, the same strengths reported by the African American families that I interviewed (Brun, 1993).

Persons collecting information to answer exploratory questions must be critical of any preexisting theories that they might carry into the evaluation or research setting. In all three examples given above, the knowledge gained helped social service workers change their perception of the participants. It takes a disciplined person to remain open to multiple interpretations and, thereby, truly explore competing and complementary explanations of an intervention's intended impact.

As an exercise for yourself, think of exploratory questions related to persons in an agency setting. Write the general evaluation question in a way that does not imply a possible theory or explanation. What preexisting theories or values must you abandon to be truly open to people's description of their experiences?

Descriptive evaluation questions are questions about the demographics, attitudes, behaviors, and knowledge of clients, workers, and community members and about their interventions, the answers of which will lead to program improvement and knowledge building. Examples of such questions that we have already seen are the following:

"How do consumers experience SBCM?" (see fig. 1.2)

"How do different stakeholders perceive success of the programs?" (see fig. 1.3)

The first question was answered by collecting participants' narratives about themselves and the intervention, responses that were guided by no preconceived categories. The second question was answered partly by conducting open-ended interviews at each of thirty-eight sites with consumers, direct-care staff, administrators, and community representatives, with responses categorized according to whether the desired results targeted individuals, families, agencies, or the community.

As an exercise to test how you might categorize descriptive characteristics, go to the examples presented in figure 1.5. How would you categorize certain characteristics of the clients or interventions related to the evaluation questions in each example? Compare your answers to these solutions:

As agreed on by the stakeholders, the four reports in the United Way strategic planning evaluation were analyzed according to the categories outlined in the white paper *Vision, Impact, or Geographic Targets, Strategies, and Outcomes* (United Way of America, 1998).

A literature review was conducted to identify the pregnancy prevention programs that were shown through credible research methods to be the most effective in preventing teenage pregnancy. Those interventions were discussed in the open-ended focus groups with stakeholders. Some stakeholders valued abstinence-only interventions even though interventions that educated about both abstinence and birth control were shown to be more effective.

A literature search showed the participants of the family violence prevention plan that successful plans require the collaboration of multiple agencies, including social services, police, courts, and the government, if intolerance of abusive and violent behavior is to be reinforced.

Over one hundred competencies for direct-care mental health workers described in the literature were for the survey narrowed down to twenty-six by eliminating categories that covered the same content.

The selection of categories for descriptive questions is assisted by a review of research related to the interventions in question. The discussion of literature reviews will be covered in chapter 4. The point here is that social service workers often assume certain relationships between interventions and client change. The accuracy of such assumptions is often challenged when they are compared to the results of other social service evaluations and research.

Explanatory evaluation questions are questions posed to test whether an intervention produced the desired results for clients, workers, or members of the larger community, the answers to which that will lead to program improvement and knowledge building. The decision as to what the desired results are can be based on either evidence-based theory or program theory. Evidence-based theory is derived from previously empirically tested evaluation or research. Program theory is derived from the experience of program staff.

Explanatory questions are often posed as hypotheses or statements of expected intervention outcomes. For example, the explanatory hypothesis presented in figure 1.3 was that "consumers of FSIs will significantly improve family functioning." This hypothesis was tested by administering a standardized assessment of general family functioning to intervention clients and a comparison group at three different times over an eighteen-month period.

Two findings pertinent to the practice evaluations were that there was not a significant difference in family functioning between time 1 and time 3 and that there was not a significant difference in family functioning between the clients and the comparison group. One reason why such findings were obtained was that both the clients and the comparison group had high scores on family functioning during the first survey. Thus, there was not much room for improvement.

Another, and probably more important, reason was the assumption that family functioning would improve immediately in all interventions. However, open-ended narrative data collected through site focus groups showed that some interventions targeted change in the entire community rather than change in specific families. Also, the school-based FSIs targeted individual children, not entire families.

For a summary of the exploratory, descriptive, and explanatory evaluation questions most commonly asked by social service workers, see figure

Figure 1.9. Evaluation decisionmaking tip: Clarifying the evaluation question.

Listed below are common evaluation questions grouped as exploratory, descriptive, or explanatory. Check all that apply to an evaluation you are currently conducting.

This evaluation is being conducted to answer *exploratory* questions such as:

_____ What is it like to be a client?
_____ What is it like to be a worker?
_____ What is it like to be a resident?

This evaluation is being conducted to answer *descriptive* questions such as:

_____ What is the relationship between _____ and _____?
_____ What are the needs of _____?
_____ What are the strengths of _____?
_____ What are the program outcomes?
_____ Who are the persons who utilize the program?
_____ How many persons use the program?
_____ Are persons satisfied with the program?
_____ Which agencies in the community provide what services?
_____ Are the requirements of a grant funder met?
_____ Are the requirements of an accrediting body met?

This evaluation is being conducted to answer *explanatory* statements such as:

_____ This program resulted in the following outcomes: _____.
_____ This program achieved the following results: _____.
_____ This program had the following impacts: _____.

1.9. Data-collection methods employed to address each type of question are discussed in chapter 6.

SOCIAL SERVICE EVALUATION IS SYSTEMS EVALUATION

Following a systems perspective, social services are delivered to individuals, families, groups, organizations, and communities. The word *intervention* is sometimes interchangeable with *service, practice, program,* or even *agency* if an agency delivers an intervention, a product (e.g., money, food, or clothing) or service (e.g., counseling, referral, or support) delivered to the *client* to achieve specific goals and create desired change for the client. A **social service program** is one or more interventions delivered to achieve specified goals and desired results for identified clients. A program can be delivered by one worker, by several workers in the same agency, or by several collaborating workers from different agencies.

In some evaluations, the focus of information is the activities, behaviors, and views of individuals. Look back at the case examples presented in figures 1.2–1.3 and 1.5–1.7 and identify the different individuals from whom information was collected:

> In figure 1.2, the clients' narrative descriptions of SBCM were the primary information reported in the findings, although there also were interviews with intervention staff. In the dissertation example in figure 1.7, only narrative information collected from parents was reported in the findings. In both examples, the evaluator/researcher wanted to foreground the client's information rather than the worker's information.

> In figure 1.3, the telephone survey was conducted with clients. The site interviews were expanded to include clients, workers, and people from the community who participated in the program. Findings from the site visits were, thus, reported by comparing information collected from individuals representing different groups.

In other evaluations, the focus of information is the activities, behaviors, and views of groups and organizations. Ways in which information can be collected about groups include the following:

> In figure 1.2, the evaluator reviewed all of the SBCM forms that the group of workers used with clients: assessments; intervention plans; referral plans; and so on.

> In figure 1.3, the site interviewers asked focus group participants to share written documentation that offered evidence of program success. Documents provided to the site interviewers included annual reports, evaluation reports, media coverage of the program, and client stories.

> In the United Way planning example given in figure 1.5, the information analyzed was needs assessments and studies conducted and written by sources other than the evaluators. These sources provided information about organizational activities in the community.

> In the family violence prevention planning example in figure 1.5, one source of information was police reports of domestic violence offenses to which the county sheriff's office responded in a one-year period.

In other evaluations, the focus of information is the policies that shape the behaviors of individuals, groups, and organizations. Evaluation has a way of bringing home the point to the evaluation participants that service delivery is greatly shaped by public policy:

> In figure 1.3, participants of the school-based interventions were mandated (by state law at the time and by federal law now) to report specific student performance outcomes.

In the family violence prevention planning example given in figure 1.5, child welfare reporting laws, elder abuse reporting laws, and criminal court procedures for responding to domestic violence all needed to be reviewed.

Also in figure 1.5, many different stakeholders had a vital interest in the answer to the question, "What are the competencies expected of all direct-care mental health workers?" Those stakeholders included union representatives who influenced training policies and client advocates who demanded competent services.

The evaluation of outreach efforts to enroll eligible children in the Children's Health Insurance Program (CHIP) described in figure 1.6 revealed much information about how the eligibility requirements for CHIP were often an obstacle to enrollment. Successful enrollment interventions were conducted by agencies that found ways to overcome these obstacles, for example, by bringing portable copiers on home visits to process applications on the spot.

Evaluations of policies are relevant for planning and practice purposes. At the planning stage, persons can ask, "How *will* we show evidence that the policy or grant requirements will be followed?" At the practice stage, persons often need to justify the answer to the question, "How *did* we follow the policy or grant requirements?" Most people feel more secure having answered the former question before being asked the latter one.

One last example will demonstrate the interrelation between policy and practice in the planning, delivery, and evaluation of interventions. An evaluation advisory team was formed to evaluate the out-of-home placement patterns for African American children, as described in figure 1.6. The members of the evaluation team agreed to analyze how individual family case plans, steps taken by agency diversity committee to educate the entire staff about out-of-home placement patterns, and the state law to reduce the number of children in long-term care were all related to placement patterns for African American children.

MAJOR POINTS

Social service evaluation is the systematic collection and analysis of information about one or more interventions and clients to improve social work practice, planning, and accountability. A premise of this book is that this definition may not be agreed to by key stakeholders. Funders may require an agency to collect information for an evaluation without being clear about how that information will be used to guide future program decisions. Disagreement can arise as to appropriate evaluation questions. Service providers may ask, "Is a program effective?" Consumers may ask, "Is there a better program?" Disagreement can also arise as to what kind of information is to be collected. Service providers may argue that reporting high client satisfaction is evidence of program effectiveness, but funders may argue that only measuring positive change in client behavior is evidence of effectiveness.

In this chapter, decisions that must be made in order to clarify the scope of an evaluation were discussed. Those decisions included (1) agreeing on the definition of *evaluation* for the current situation; (2) clarifying how the evaluation will guide program planning and practice; (3) clarifying how evaluation will contribute to knowledge building; (4) clarifying whether the evaluation will answer exploratory, descriptive, or explanatory questions; and (5) understanding how evaluation demonstrates the mutual impact of policy and practice decisions on social service delivery.

In the next chapter, the discussion focuses on the key persons guiding an evaluation and how these persons can come to agreement on the scope and activities of an evaluation.

FURTHER READINGS

General Evaluation Texts

Patton, M. Q. (1997). *Utilization-focused evaluation: The new century text* (3rd ed.). Thousand Oaks, CA: Sage.

Posavac, E., & Carey, R. (2003). *Program evaluation: Methods and case studies* (6th ed.). Upper Saddle River, NJ: Prentice Hall.

Robson, C. (2000). *Small-scale evaluation*. London: Sage.

Scriven, M. (1991). *Evaluation thesaurus* (4th ed.). Thousand Oaks, CA: Sage.

Stufflebeam, D., Madaus, G., & Kellaghan, T. (Eds.). (2000). *Evaluation models: Viewpoints on educational and human services evaluation* (2nd ed.). Boston: Kluwer.

Weiss, C. (1998). *Evaluation: Methods for studying programs and policies* (2nd ed.). Upper Saddle River, NJ: Prentice Hall.

Social Work Evaluation Texts

Ginsberg, L. (2001). *Social work evaluation: Principles and methods*. Boston: Allyn & Bacon.

Reamer, F. (1998). *Social work research and evaluation skills: A case-based user-friendly approach*. New York: Columbia University Press.

Royse, D., Thyer, B., Padgett, D., & Logan, T. (2001). *Program evaluation: An introduction* (3rd ed.). Belmont, CA: Brooks/Cole.

Unrau, Y., Gabor, P., & Grinnell, R. (2001). *Evaluation in the human services*. Belmont, CA: Brooks/Cole.

REFLECTIVE JOURNAL ACTIVITIES

Think of an evaluation in which your fellow agency or practicum colleagues have been involved and answer the following questions:

1. How did staff members define the term *evaluation?* In what ways did their definitions differ? What were staff members' expectations of the evaluation? How did their expectations differ? How were those differences resolved?

2. Did staff members view the evaluation as jumping through administrative hoops? If so, why?

3. Did staff members view the evaluation as merely an academic exercise? If so, why?

4. What are your reactions to the material presented in chapter 1? How is the material different from that presented in other books you have read on evaluation or research?

5. How can evaluation improve program practice at the agency?

6. How can evaluation improve program planning at the agency?

7. Turn to figure 1.4, and check those reasons that apply to a current evaluation. If you checked more than one box, how do any of the purposes conflict with each other?

PROCEDURAL JOURNAL ACTIVITIES

1. Refer to one of the general texts on evaluation listed under "Further Readings." How does the text help clarify some of the points discussed in this chapter?

2. Answer the questions from the Evaluation Decisionmaking Model in figure 1.10 as they pertain to the scope of a past or a proposed evaluation.

Figure 1.10.   Evaluation decisionmaking model: Clarifying the scope of the evaluation.

The definition of *evaluation* for this project is: _____.

This evaluation will guide the following *practice* decisions: _____.

This evaluation will guide the following *planning* decisions: _____.

This evaluation will contribute to knowledge building about the following interventions and clients: _____.

These *Exploratory Evaluation Questions* are being asked: _____.

The following *Descriptive Evaluation Questions* are being asked: _____.

The following *Explanatory Evaluation Questions* are being asked: _____.

CHAPTER 2

Negotiating with Stakeholders: The Politics of Evaluation

This chapter can help social service workers involve key persons in the evaluation decisionmaking process. A theme of chapter 1 was that defining the scope of the evaluation leads to different evaluation decisions. A theme of this chapter is that different persons influencing the evaluation decisions will lead to different evaluation activities.

The *learning outcomes* for this chapter are as follows:

1. Identify different stakeholders influencing the evaluation.

2. Understand how external and internal stakeholders influence the decisions related to negotiating the scope of the evaluation.

3. Develop an evaluation stakeholder plan that identifies the responsibilities of key stakeholders.

EVALUATION STAKEHOLDERS

All the evaluation decisions discussed in chapter 1 can be made through negotiation with stakeholders. **Stakeholders** are those persons affected by the intervention or program and the process, results, and reports of the evaluation. Stakeholders can include funders, social service providers, consumers of services, community members, and those individuals involved in the planning, implementation, and utilization of the evaluation. An evaluation can have an impact on many people. Within a three-year period, one small multiservice program that began with only one funding source obtained four additional funding sources after the project director demonstrated success of the program through evaluation. Negotiation with stakeholders applies to evaluation decisions discussed throughout the entire book.

There is a difference between a *stakeholder* and an *evaluation participant*. Stakeholders are most often involved in advising the evaluation process. They give feedback about the purpose and manner in which information will eventually be gathered. **Evaluation participants** are those persons from whom data are gathered through interviews, surveys, observations, and documents to answer evaluation questions.

Stakeholder and participant roles may overlap during an evaluation. In one evaluation, a prominent businessperson was surveyed about her understanding of violence prevention in the workplace. On the basis of her participation in the evaluation, she eventually joined the team planning future violence-prevention programs and evaluations. In another evaluation, interviews with all members of the evaluation planning team were included in the final evaluation report. Thus, stakeholders (the planning team) were also participants, providing information for the evaluation.

Funders are those individuals who represent the source that is financing the intervention and who have input about the evaluation activities. Funders usually communicate in writing their expectations of the evaluation in the request for proposal (RFP) and grant contract. Some funders require that an evaluation plan be developed, but not necessarily carried out. Others require that a specific type of evaluation (e.g., outcomes evaluation) be implemented. Optimally, social service workers from the funded agency have ongoing face-to-face contact with the funder to clarify and gain approval of all evaluation decisions. Sometimes, the funding source may have a team of several staff members overseeing the evaluation.

Social service providers are those persons responsible for implementing the intervention. Service providers should be clear about the goals of the intervention, details of the strategies for reaching the goals, and the expected short- and long-term results of the intervention. For example, the goal of a school-based family support program was to improve the school readiness of all children in grades 1–4. The strategies included annual physical examinations and referrals, tutoring, after-school reading assistance, and assessment and referral for emotional concerns. The desired short-term results were that a specified percentage of the children be physically and emotionally healthy; have passing grades; reach grade level in spelling, reading, and comprehension; and have minimal absences from school. The desired long-term result was that a specified percentage of all children pass the fourth-grade proficiency exam.

Consumers are those persons who receive the social service intervention. Some agencies use the term *clients* rather than *consumers*. Many funding sources seek consumer input about the intervention and how to evaluate it. For example, consumers of the school-based family support intervention (FSI) described above included students, parents, and caregivers. Parents' consent is required for services delivered to children. Guardian consent must also be given for those persons who are determined unable to make the decision to participate on their own, for example, those with a severe mental illness. Consumers can be those persons with an identified concern, such as low academic performance, or persons considered at risk, such as children living in poverty. Consumers of a prevention program could all be residents of the targeted community.

Evans and Fisher (1999, p. 108) described five levels of consumers' or service users' involvement in evaluation decisionmaking. From least to most involvement of service users in the evaluation, the levels are the following:

1. Service users receive information about the evaluation.
2. Service users are consultants to the evaluation.
3. Service users participate in evaluation decisions.
4. Service users have power to veto evaluation decisions.
5. Service users control all aspects of the evaluation.

The authors provided an example of a user-controlled evaluation of a private cash-assistance program for disabled persons. A research group that included service users controlled the evaluation budget and design, served as interviewers during the data-collection process, and analyzed the interview results (Evans and Fisher, 1999, pp. 109–11).

Community members are persons who belong to a society that is affected by the intervention and evaluation. For example, family violence prevention in a school setting may include students in a class on healthy dating relationships that is part of the health education curriculum for all sophomores. In this example, community members may also include the entire school, other family members, neighbors, and other service providers.

Evaluators are stakeholders too. **Evaluators** are those persons who design and carry out the systematic collection and analysis of information to improve program practice, planning, and accountability. Additionally, most evaluators—especially those connected with a university or a professional evaluation organization—want to utilize evaluations to promote knowledge building. Thus, they can produce written reports that are used by agency workers, conference presentations, and journal articles that can be used by other social service workers not associated with the evaluated agency. An evaluator may have multiple reasons for conducting an evaluation. Discuss those reasons honestly and at the beginning of the evaluation. Do not assume that the evaluator has the same purpose as you or anyone else involved in the evaluation.

Evaluators, like social service workers, take on multiple roles in addition to that of evaluator, for example, educator, consultant, negotiator, practitioner, change agent, coach, or consoler (Fetterman, 2001; McClintock, 2003; Morabito, 2002; Patton, 1997; Weiss, 1998). Begin with your expectations of the role of evaluator, which should be directly connected to the definition of *evaluation* agreed on under the scope of the evaluation:

> Do you expect the evaluator alone to determine the merit or worth of the programs evaluated? (see Scriven, 1991)

Do you expect the evaluator to reinforce social service workers' self-evaluation of the program? (see Fetterman, 2001)

Do you expect total objectivity from the evaluator, or do you acknowledge the evaluator's influence on the evaluation setting? (see Rodwell, 1998)

There are many evaluation models, each taking a different view of the role of the evaluator. References for some of the more common evaluation models are listed in the "Further Readings" section of this chapter.

Just as social service workers can function "simultaneously as change agents and evaluators of their interventions" (McClintock, 2003, p. 95), social service evaluators can also function as change agents. With this dual role, however, come potential ethical issues. Consider, for example, the hypothetical scenario presented by Morris (2003) of an evaluator suggesting that questions about youth sexual behavior be part of a needs assessment meant to guide the planning of pregnancy prevention strategies (thereby functioning as a change agent) but facing objections raised on moral grounds (by stakeholders taking the position that the evaluator should function only as an evaluator). (The same issue arose in a similar example presented in fig. 1.5.) What should that evaluator do?

When it comes to resolving such role conflicts, the quick answer is that there is no quick answer. As Leviton (2003) made clear in responding to Morris's (2003) "ethical challenge," evaluators need to be competent, honest, and responsible. This means that they will sometimes find themselves taking positions that are in conflict with those of some evaluation stakeholders—and that the resulting role conflict must be clarified through discussion. Clarifying role conflicts begins with clarifying who the client actually is, much the same way as social service workers begin an intervention by identifying the client system.

This chapter focuses solely on ethics and values in evaluations. Further ethical guidelines for evaluators can be found in appendix A, which reprints the Code of Ethics of the National Association of Social Workers (NASW), and appendix B, which reprints the Guiding Principles for Evaluators of the American Evaluation Association (AEA).

Competent and responsible negotiation of stakeholder needs and interests related to the scope and desired activities of the evaluation takes time. This negotiation process is crucial to the success of the evaluation. For examples of the evaluator's many roles, see figure 2.1. The examples are given to help you clarify what role you want the evaluator to take during a particular evaluation, even if you yourself are the evaluator. As you read the examples, notice the time devoted to each role. Do you want the evaluator to spend time functioning as an educator or a facilitator instead of collecting information? Or perhaps your current needs are for technical assistance so that eventually you can conduct your own evaluations.

Figure 2.1.   Case examples: Negotiating evaluator roles.

All the evaluation case examples described in this book were conducted to answer exploratory, descriptive, or explanatory questions that would guide future program planning, practice, and evaluation decisions. In all the case examples, I provided findings and results based on the purpose and evaluation questions deemed important by the stakeholders. In some cases, stakeholders wanted the final report to include recommendations as well. Two additional roles requested by evaluation stakeholders are described below.

Educator

In the statewide evaluation of thirty-eight family support interventions (FSIs) described in figure 1.3, the state funders requested that the evaluators provide education and technical assistance so that the program staff could eventually conduct self-evaluations. The education component was implemented through workshops given throughout the evaluation. An evaluation manual and instrument critiques were among the final reports that the evaluator provided so that the workers could conduct future evaluations on their own.

In the evaluation of the countywide family violence prevention planning grant described in figure 1.5, the stakeholders asked me to provide one-hour presentations on practices that were effective in preventing child abuse and neglect and family violence, two areas in which I had research and practice experience.
In the statewide evaluations of the Children's Health Insurance Program (CHIP) described in figure 1.6, the evaluation team presented the successful outreach efforts to the state funders, who then disbursed the information to the participating county workers.

Facilitator

As the primary evaluator for the statewide evaluation of the FSIs described in figure 1.3, I was a facilitator of negotiations between three stakeholder groups: (1) an advisory group, consisting of at least one representative from each of the three state funders; (2) a group representing directors of the local FSIs; and (3) the evaluation team, which over the two-year evaluation period included faculty from more than seven different universities and up to thirty-five different staff persons who were responsible for collecting survey and site visit information. A great deal of time was devoted to facilitating discussion and negotiation among these different groups.

I was a member of the evaluation team described in figure 1.5 that administered a survey to stakeholders statewide to assess agreement on the competencies that all direct-care mental health workers should possess. One member of the evaluation team served on the evaluation advisory board as a cofacilitator. Also serving on the advisory board were direct-care workers, supervisors, trainers, union representatives, client advocates, and vendors that contracted for services. The final survey had to meet with the approval of this advisory board.

There were times during the family violence prevention project described in figure 1.5 that I cofacilitated advisory board meetings, although this was not my primary role. I also facilitated discussions about the scope of the grant between the funders, the directors of four other programs funded by the same grant, the evaluators hired by the funder, and the local directors. The local directors sought my advice as well in developing the final plan, which was based on the information collected both from the research literature and from needs assessments conducted over a one-year period.

It helps to sort out the different roles of evaluation stakeholders and the influence that each role has on evaluation decisions. For a list of different evaluation stakeholders and their impact on clarifying the scope of the evaluation, see figure 2.2. For an actual case example of the identification of stakeholder roles, see figure 2.3. Ask yourself these questions as you read the case example:

> Do I agree with the way in which the different stakeholder roles have been clarified?
>
> Why or why not?
>
> Have I been in a situation where there was disagreement among stakeholders about the scope and activities of an evaluation?
>
> How was the disagreement resolved?

INTERNALLY DRIVEN EVALUATION

Internally driven evaluations are those initiated by stakeholders within the agency or those connected locally to the agency, such as a board of directors or a community advisory group. The motivation to evaluate may come from external sources, but the local agencies assume control over how the evaluation will be conducted. The persons taking on the main tasks of internally driven evaluations are often employees of the agency conducting the evaluation.

Examples of internally driven evaluations given in chapter 1 are the following:

> The director of the Strengths-Based Case Management (SBCM) program wanted to describe client perceptions of the intervention to see whether those perceptions matched the intended goals of the program (fig. 1.2).
>
> The director of the children's grief support group wanted to describe the activities of the weekend camp to better understand what works and what does not in achieving the goals of the intervention (fig. 1.6).
>
> The chairs of the diversity committee of a public child welfare agency wanted to describe possible reasons why African American children

Figure 2.2.   Evaluation decisionmaking tip: Identifying key stakeholders.

Complete this form for an evaluation in your agency or practicum setting.

The following groups have a *stake* in this evaluation:

> The following *funders:*
> The following social service *providers:*
> The following *consumers* (clients):
> The following *community members:*
> The following *evaluators:*

The above stakeholders agree on the definition of evaluation for this project:
Yes _____ No _____
If yes, the definition is as follows: _____
If no, they differ on the following definitions: _____

The above stakeholders agree the evaluation will guide practice and planning decisions:
Yes _____ No _____
If yes, the evaluation will guide the following decisions: _____
If no, they differ on the following decisions: _____

The above stakeholders agree on the exploratory, descriptive, and explanatory evaluation questions:
Yes _____ No _____
If yes, the evaluation questions are as follows: _____
If no, they differ on the following questions: _____

The above stakeholders agree on the evaluator's roles:
Yes _____ No _____
If yes, the roles of the evaluator are as follows: _____
If no, they differ on the following roles: _____

---

were in out-of-home care disproportionately to white children in order to change the situations that created this disparity (fig. 1.6).

One goal of this book is for practitioners proactively to participate in internally driven evaluation activities in order to improve practice and to be accountable when externally driven evaluation activities are expected. Do you trust your practice, planning, and evaluation skills and knowledge enough to engage more in evaluations? Read the questions outlined in figure 2.4 to assess your own comfort level with evaluation.

A social service agency can be a place that supports and encourages staff to integrate evaluation into practice. One way in which to integrate evaluation into the daily operation of social service agencies is to encourage dialogue among the social service staff about evaluation. Evaluation language can become as commonplace as intervention and policy language. Dialogue about evaluation can occur informally in reading groups or

Figure 2.3.   Case example: Identifying key stakeholders.

The stakeholders identified below were involved in the family violence prevention grant described in figure 1.5 and also in figure 2.1.

The following groups have a *stake* in this evaluation:

Funders. The funder was a private foundation that funded five different Ohio county grants based on a competitive RFP. The purpose of the two-year planning grant was for each funded county project to submit a strategic plan for preventing family violence countywide. The purpose of the evaluation was to describe the process of arriving at the plan and the information collected to support the plan. The role of the evaluator could be determined by the needs of the local funded project. The role of the evaluator varied greatly across the five different funded counties. Each funded county contracted its own evaluator.

Social Service Providers. The local grant director was also the director of a county women's shelter. A steering committee that guided project decisions included representatives from the local public children's services agency and the family and children first council, schools, and a person hired as project director. These stakeholders also saw the purpose of the evaluation as describing the planning process. They asked that the evaluator serve in the role of educator on interventions to prevent child abuse and neglect and interventions to prevent domestic violence. These stakeholders also asked the evaluator to work closely with a planner hired from the same university to cofacilitate meetings with other stakeholders.

Consumers (Clients). There was at least one self-identified victim of domestic violence who served on an advisory board to the project. There were also three to five high school students on the advisory board since one proposed intervention targeted the schools. These young people actually formed a subadvisory group that worked closely with a social service provider. These consumers agreed with the purpose of the grant, which was to develop a final plan. They viewed the purpose of the evaluation as collecting the information necessary to develop that plan. They viewed the evaluator's role vis-à-vis the advisory group as a facilitator and an educator.

Community Members. An advisory board of more than twenty members met every other month for two years to develop the final plan. This board consisted of the steering committee described above as well as members of county government, representatives of the sheriff's office and the prosecutor's office, the public defender, a local business owner, a pastor, and an ombudsman. Related to the evaluation, this group approved contracting with the evaluator after he attended an advisory group meeting and submitted an evaluation plan. The group agreed that the purpose of the evaluation was to describe the planning process, help the group collect information to guide the plan, educate the group on the issues, and, at times, cofacilitate advisory group meetings.

Evaluators. As the primary evaluator, I provided to the advisory board the following principles that would guide my activities:

> The evaluation plan will follow the goals and mission of the project as set by the funders and the evaluators hired by the funders.
>
> Data will include process (how things are done) as well as outcomes (what has changed).

The county logic model will be the blueprint guiding the selection of data to be collected.

The evaluation plan and the data-collection procedures will be continually monitored throughout the project by the steering committee and the advisory board.

All evaluation reports will be reviewed by the steering committee.

The overall outcome expected at the end of the two-year period was "to create a countywide plan for violence prevention in the county" by organizing an advisory group and a steering committee that included youth. The four objectives guiding the development plan were as follows: (1) educate a diverse steering committee about family violence prevention; (2) educate and increase awareness among the general community about family violence prevention; (3) identify community needs, views, service gaps, and collaborative deficits related to the project; and (4) identify and measure key risk factors and indicators for violence potential. More discussion of logic models occurs in chapter 4.

The main point that I emphasized to all stakeholders was that I would collect process and outcome information to describe the progress of the group in reaching the four stated objectives and the final goal, the plan. I agreed to the roles of educator and facilitator to help the group meet objectives 1 and 2. There were times when I wanted more control in the construction of survey instruments to reach objective 3, but members of the steering committee wanted to help construct and conduct surveys of service providers. One reason for this decision was that, because I was not a member of the community and the steering committee felt that it would get more detailed responses to questions if the surveys were conducted by the project director, who did live in the county.

Negotiated Scope of Evaluation. I took a much more active role than did the evaluators of the other four funded grants in the development of the final family violence prevention plan by providing much education on the topic and facilitation of steering and advisory group meetings. My multiple roles and activities were approved by the funder. I was sometimes in conflict with members of the steering committee over the development of surveys and the theoretical models used to develop the plan. At the same time, I supported members' leadership role in data collection because I knew that that would help us write the plan in a timely manner and also because I knew that an effective family violence prevention plan relies on community involvement and collaboration.

---

current-research groups that meet over the lunch hour or after work to discuss research reported in the literature.

Every agency can benefit from an **evaluation advisory board,** those stakeholders overseeing the planning and implementation of an evaluation, whether it is required or not. Evaluation advisory boards can provide the following:

reinforcement of evaluation activities

guarantee of consumer representation in designing evaluations

resources, structure, and protocol for evaluations

feedback about important evaluation decisions

Evaluation advisory board members can help individuals bring their evaluations to fruition. They can also request progress reports, making available preliminary findings. In a recent study, representatives from large foundations reported their dissatisfaction with the lapse of time between data collection and data reporting (Patrizi & McMullan, 1998). Evaluation reports and other products of evaluation, whether they be verbal, electronic, tape-recorded, or videotaped, are important components of evaluation that tend to receive the least amount of attention. One reason is that evaluation reports usually come at the end of an evaluation and people are tired—too tired to polish previous notes, memos, or preliminary findings.

Discussions during formal staff, board of directors, and agency committee meetings often generate ideas about evaluation, but workers do not always devote continued agency time to carrying out evaluations. Membership on these committees can include staff, board members, and consumers of services. Some examples of how agency committees may consider evaluations to help make program planning and practice decisions are described in figure 2.5. To learn more about increasing agency capacity for evaluation, see the "Further Readings" section at the end of this chapter.

Figure 2.4.   Evaluation decisionmaking tip: Self-assessment of evaluation comfort level.

Social service practitioners, agencies, and professional organizations contain rich resources for conducting evaluations. Social service workers can begin each evaluation with a self-assessment of their own comfort level with the current evaluation by answering the questions outlined below. Think of your answers as they apply, not just to evaluations in general, but also to a specific evaluation at your agency or practicum setting.

What is my overall evaluation skill and knowledge level?

What classes have I attended on research or evaluation design and statistical analyses?

What agency training or conference workshops increased my personal integration of evaluation into daily practice?

Which of my evaluation skills were helpful in past evaluations?

Which areas do I need to improve to complete the current evaluation tasks?

Which textbooks from past classes do I need to dust off to refresh my knowledge?

Whom can I contact from past conferences as consultants for the current project?

Figure 2.5.   Evaluation decisionmaking tip: Agency committees that can support evaluation activities.

Here are descriptions of agency committees that can support evaluation activities. Check those that apply to your agency or practicum setting.

Management Information Systems (MIS) Committee. Enormous amounts of data are generated electronically by agency workers to provide funders with required documentation. An MIS committee could help ensure that the data are entered consistently by the staff. It can also generate evaluation questions that can statistically describe characteristics of programs and clients and measure whether predicted program-client relationships are present.

Quality Assurance/Peer Review/Audit Committee. Most agencies are accredited or must demonstrate accountability to some authoritative organization. The most common way in which agencies demonstrate compliance with accreditation standards is through a written audit or documentation of required standards and an explanation of the written document during a site visit. Peer review boards are established by agencies to help workers stay in compliance or prepare for an upcoming formal accreditation. The tendency is to produce the data required without further exploring the connections between the data. Great ideas are stirred up but may not be pursued once the accreditation team is gone. For more discussion of evaluation for audits, quality assurance, and accreditation, see Ginsberg (2001).

Mission/Visioning/Strategic Planning Committee. Discussions of "where we want to go" arise in staff meetings quite often because there always seems to be obstacles to implementing services in the ways in which they theoretically or practically need to be implemented. Some agencies regularly review their overall or program goals and expected results (e.g., during annual retreats) or on a semiregular basis (e.g., to develop five-year strategic plans). The clarification of goals, activities, and desired results will have an impact on evaluation.

Policy Committee. Policy analysis can be included in every social service evaluation to show the connection between policy and practice decisions, a connection that many social service workers overlook. For example, a public child welfare agency conducted an evaluation to answer the descriptive question, "What are possible reasons that there are a disproportionate number of African American children living in out-of-home care compared to white children?" The stakeholders were white and African American direct-care and administrative staff who formed the agency's diversity committee. The diversity group agreed to form a policy subcommittee to analyze the racial backgrounds of children in long-term placements because the state had instituted a policy for all county children's services agencies to reduce the number of children in long-term care (i.e., more than two years).

Public Relations Committee. Agency boards of directors often want to communicate to possible benefactors that their program works. As long as systematic methods of evaluation are employed and the full contexts of the evaluation are publicized, then it is ethical to utilize the results of evaluations when describing a program to the public. It is unethical for evaluators and stakeholders to manipulate collected information to prove one's point or cause. Negative as well as positive results of an evaluation should be presented.

EXTERNALLY DRIVEN EVALUATIONS

Externally driven evaluations are those initiated by stakeholders outside the local agency, such as state or federal funding sources. In most externally driven evaluations, the persons assigned to the tasks of evaluation do not work for the agencies being evaluated and are often hired by the public funder.

Examples of externally driven evaluations given in chapter 1 are repeated below. All the examples had an evaluation oversight committee at the state level and a separate IRB for the evaluators, all of whom were employed at a public university. The role of IRBs in ensuring ethical evaluation procedures is discussed in chapter 3. In all the examples, program results were used to guide implementation of similar programs funded subsequently:

> Three different state funders collaborated on the statewide evaluation of thirty-eight FSIs described in figure 1.3. The purpose of the evaluation was to describe the desired results across all programs and to explain the impact of the programs on family functioning.

> The state Department of Jobs and Family Services (DJFS) oversaw the statewide evaluation of county outreach programs to enroll children in CHIP described in figure 1.6. The purpose of the evaluation was to describe the successful outreach efforts and the obstacles to enrolling eligible children in the program.

> The state Department of Mental Health (DMH) oversaw the statewide study of competencies to be required of direct-care mental health workers described in figure 1.5. The purpose of this study was to describe the top five competencies agreed on by key stakeholders. These prioritized competencies would be the focus of future mandatory employee training.

In each of these three examples, the evaluators had a great deal of contact with social service workers even though staff from the local programs did not initiate the evaluations. Local social service workers were able to utilize the interaction with the evaluation team to gain a better understanding of the programs from the information being collected and analyzed. It helped social service workers to understand the objectives of the external evaluators.

The primary objective for external evaluators is to conduct an accurate and complete evaluation. The evaluator may come across as being rigid when it comes to making decisions about the evaluation design, sticking to the logic model, or implementing rigorous quantitative or qualitative approaches to data collection (all of which will be described in later chapters). The reason for this rigidity may be that the evaluator wants to complete the task competently, just as practitioners want to deliver an intervention competently. The evaluator may follow the original program logic model since

Figure 2.6.   Evaluation decisionmaking tip: What are the potential reports from this evaluation?

The entire context of the original request for proposal (RFP).

The evaluation plan in the RFP.

PowerPoint presentations of the evaluation plan.

The evaluation plan available at a project Web site.

Periodic evaluation reports.

Literature review or annotated bibliography.

Critiques of standardized instruments.

Data-collection surveys and interviews constructed for the evaluation.

Participant protocols developed for the evaluation, including consent to participate forms, procedures for recruiting participants, evaluation design, and other information required by an institutional review board (see chap. 3).

Written and electronic presentations of results, including statistical tables and narrative stories.

Photographs taken as part of the data collection (written consent—discussed in chap. 3—is required).

Training materials developed from the evaluation.

Program reports that incorporate evaluation results.

Final evaluation reports submitted to various stakeholders.

Evaluation results that are integrated into other agency publications (e.g., annual reports, brochures, or advertisements).

Conference presentations related to the evaluation.

Articles published in professional journals, newsletters, books, dissertations, or class assignments.

Other

---

that is what is stated in the RFP that funds the intervention and evaluation. Or he or she may be following specific data-collection procedures that were agreed on in the original contract. Understand that evaluators' decisions are based on their knowledge of the best ways to collect information for specific purposes. Also, view the relationship with the evaluator as you do any change agent contract. *Negotiate.* Make sure the evaluator's objectives meet your objectives. For a good discussion of the practitioner-evaluator relationship, see Hess and Mullen (1995).

A second objective for external evaluators is to disseminate the knowledge gained from the evaluation. Thus, there should be a statement in a written evaluation contract about the authorship of any publications or presentations to emerge from the evaluation. Look at the list of potential evaluation reports found in figure 2.6. Consider these questions *before* beginning the evaluation:

Whose names will appear on these reports?

Who will hold the copyright on these reports?

What permission is needed from the stakeholders in order to disseminate these reports?

A third objective for external evaluators is to ensure that ethical guidelines are followed during the entire evaluation process to protect participants' confidentiality and to identify potential conflicts of interest among persons involved in the evaluation. Roles of stakeholders often overlap in evaluations. For example, in some community-based evaluations, social service staff—because they are residents of the community or parents of children attending a community-based school program—may also be consumers of services. Clarifying any potential conflict of interest in these roles is an important part of those evaluations. Chapter 3 is devoted exclusively to upholding evaluation ethics.

Whether the evaluation is internally or externally driven, social service workers have the right to expect the following from evaluators:

1. Evaluators should seek input from funders, social service providers, consumers, and community members in designing the evaluation.

2. Evaluators should acknowledge the skills, knowledge, and underlying perspectives that they have followed in previous evaluations, both in a written résumé and, more important, in a preevaluation interview. For an example of an evaluator clarifying his perspective on evaluation to key stakeholders, see figure 2.3.

3. Evaluators should provide reports on the evaluation process, results, and recommended changes on a regular basis, such as during face-to-face meetings held monthly or bimonthly and written reports issued every three to six months.

4. Where there is an evaluation team, one person should be designated as the translator of the process. If the evaluation is being conducted through a contract with university faculty, the coordinator of the evaluation is often called the *primary* or *principal investigator.* That person has his or her name on the contract and, thus, his or her reputation on the line. Get to know that person well.

5. Evaluators should be receptive to feedback (see Scriven, 1991). They should know whether clients are satisfied with the process, results, and products of the evaluation. Meet with the evaluator on a regular basis (e.g., every three months) to discuss your feedback. Specify the grounds for discontinuing or continuing the evaluation contract, for example, your satisfaction or the availability of resources. Again, for NASW and AEA ethical guidelines, see appendixes A and B.

EVALUATION STAKEHOLDER NEGOTIATION

No evaluation happens in isolation. Evaluation activities are planned and delivered after much negotiation. Stakeholder evaluation agreement can be reached by following the seven points listed under section C, "Integrity/Honesty," of the AEA "Guiding Principles" (app. B). These seven points parallel similar expectations social service workers are taught to follow in the worker/client relationship. They are discussed below and applied to a case example in figure 2.7.

First, negotiate the scope of the evaluation with stakeholders, just as social service workers negotiate the scope of an intervention or program with clients. Discuss the fees, and agree on a budget. State the tasks that all stakeholders are expected to perform, the methods that will be used to gather information, and expected uses of the evaluation. Have the contract signed by all persons who have a financial interest in the evaluation (e.g., the funder and those people contracted to conduct the evaluation). Give all stakeholders a written statement of the purpose, time line, and activities, and obtain their approval. A statement of how the evaluation will be used should be clearly discussed during this negotiation process.

Second, stakeholders and evaluators should identify any potential conflicts of interest. Many conflicts of interest between stakeholders involve differences in personal values and worldview, differences that inevitably affect the intervention, planning, and evaluation processes. Be respectful of the views of evaluation stakeholders, just as you respect a client's right to differ with your views during an assessment and the development of a service plan. Also, in circumstances in which social service workers are involved in evaluations of their own programs, an analysis of agency weaknesses as well as agency strengths should be conducted. An evaluation that reports only agency strengths is one that has not been open to all the information collected from different critical vantage points.

Third, record all changes made to the evaluation plan and the reasons for these changes. The procedural journal can become the official document in which such changes are recorded, similar to the official case record for clients. Send a memo of any changes made to the appropriate stakeholders with a statement of when the changes were made, why, and the persons involved in approving them. In many cases, the original scope of the evaluation proposes an ambitious time line and underestimates the amount of resources needed. In order to conduct a feasible evaluation, monitor changes that need to be made to the time line and resources.

Fourth, be explicit about the interests of all persons involved in the outcomes of an evaluation. All stakeholders have something to gain and something to lose. Try to have all stakeholders in the same room at the beginning of an evaluation to state clearly their expectations, just as you might have a

Figure 2.7.   Case example: AEA principles of integrity and honesty applied during evaluation stakeholder negotiation.

The seven principles under section C, "Integrity/Honesty," of the American Evaluation Association's Guiding Principles for Evaluators (see app. B) are applied below to the family violence prevention planning example described in figure 2.3.

1. *Negotiate the scope of the evaluation with stakeholders.* Many stakeholders needed to reach agreement on the activities to create the family violence prevention plan and on the activities to evaluate the planning process. Those stakeholders included the following:

> representatives of the private foundation funding the grants, which were given to five separate awardees, each representing a different county or region in the state
>
> directors of each of the five grant awardees
>
> cross-site evaluators hired by the funder
>
> the director of the local county collaborative that received the grant
>
> members of the steering committee to the local county grant
>
> members of the advisory board to the local county planning grant
>
> the project director, the project planner, and an evaluator hired to implement the tasks of the grant

2. *Stakeholders and evaluators should identify any potential conflicts of interest.* As the evaluator, I was not directly involved in any of the stakeholder agencies. My university lay outside the county, so I also had no direct investment in the evaluation, nor was I aware of the different potential conflicts of interest among stakeholders. I did, however, have a direct investment in the focus of the project: preventing family violence. This area has been my primary practice and research area of interest. There may have been times that I advocated a little more strongly for certain approaches, such as systems collaboration, than I would normally—because of my prior knowledge and experiences.

3. *Record all changes made to the evaluation plan.* The funder required six-month reports that included the director's report and a separate evaluator's report. The original evaluation plan was contained in the first six-month report and updated in each subsequent report. The final report needed to show how the family violence prevention plan was developed from information collected through the evaluation plan and other activities of the grant. Additionally, stakeholder feedback about the evaluation plan was recorded in the minutes of the steering committee and the advisory board committee.

4. *Be explicit about the interests of all persons involved in the outcomes of an evaluation.* At the midpoint of the two-year planning grant, a "State of Family Violence" report was printed that contained a summary of the information collected locally and from the research literature. This document contained target areas for the eventual plan. The advisory board held a one-day planning meeting to discuss the report and to guide the remaining planning activities. The evidence presented in the report became the driving force behind the strategies proposed in the final plan. All the members of the advisory board had explicit stakes in the final plan because proposed strategies potentially affected the constituencies they represented.

5–6. Report results accurately, and do not misrepresent findings; and inform stakeholders if it is felt that certain procedures will produce misleading results. Each of my reports was based on the county's logic model since the funder used each local grantee's logic model as the basis for feedback. I did not try to interpret the findings beyond their application to the local county logic model. I acknowledged limitations to the information collected and reported. For example, a survey was constructed collaboratively by me and other stakeholders and distributed to local social service providers to gain their perceptions of ways in which to prevent family violence. Using a standardized instrument proven valid and reliable in previous research would in some respects have been preferable. At the same time, the networking that arose during the course of survey administration elicited much positive support from the community for the final plan.

7. Disclose to all stakeholders the financial support for the evaluation. The budget for the planning grant was made public to all advisory board members. The annual budget was approximately $100,000, with about $10,000 allocated for evaluation activities. With the agreement of the stakeholders, my contracted time as the evaluator went as much toward facilitation and education as it did toward data collection and analysis. I was asked to attend monthly meetings of the steering committee; bimonthly meetings of the advisory board; monthly cross-site meetings or teleconferences with the funders; and biweekly meetings with the project coordinator, director, and planner. The majority of the budget went toward the project director's tasks and the planner's tasks. With the agreement of the stakeholders, I consulted on some data-collection tasks such as helping construct the service provider survey. But the project director actually distributed the survey, and the planner analyzed the results. Thus, the roles of educator, facilitator, and evaluator overlapped among the primary persons coordinating the grant. The coordinator of the county grant was the director of the county women's shelter, and she spent much more time on the project than the agency was compensated for. Members of the steering committee and the advisory board also were given time off from their regular duties by their employees to participate in the grant activities.

---

family or group share outcomes and processes expected of an intervention or program. If the evaluation is external and has been commissioned by a state agency to collect information from county social service workers, ask the state funders to write statements of the purpose of the evaluation and how they will use the information collected. Also, have a meeting at a central location with contact persons from all counties to answer questions about the scope of the evaluation. In negotiations with the funders, stakeholders can make clear their own interest in the evaluation, for example, a desire to increase collaboration between the university and the community or to add to the knowledge base by submitting articles based on the evaluation for publication.

Fifth, report results accurately, and do not misrepresent findings. Final reports should go through a rigorous review process. On submission, the report becomes a public document and may be used by some stakeholders long after the evaluation is over. Members of an evaluation advisory group should review reports. Seek someone who has no knowledge of the evaluation to review the reports, statistical analyses, and narrative analyses. Particular attention should be paid to the interpretations and recommendations of the findings. Do the reports show a clear connection between the findings and the interpretations? There is more discussion of report writing in chapter 6.

Sixth, inform stakeholders if it is felt that certain procedures will produce misleading results. That is, evaluators should inform stakeholders of the limitations of certain methodologies (a subject discussed further in chap. 5). While stakeholders will still be free to employ the methodologies they prefer, at least they will be choosing those methodologies knowledgeably. For example, one evaluator found herself involved in a situation in which the agency had already distributed surveys to staff. Her job was to help compile the results electronically and then report frequencies and percentages of responses. It turned out, however, that the survey method was not reliable and the results not valid and, therefore, that no inferential statistics could be calculated. Still, the evaluator was able to suggest other, more reliable standardized instruments, thus reinforcing this beginning attempt at evaluation.

Finally, disclose to all stakeholders the financial support for the evaluation. State the funding source and the amounts contracted for the different tasks. Staff time is an important resource. Social service workers may be asked to serve on an evaluation advisory board or even to help carry out the evaluation plan. How, if at all, will worker time be compensated? Is the worker expected to participate on his or her own time? Does the employer view evaluation activity as part of the employee's normal work responsibilities? The issue of making time to evaluate and being compensated for that time is an obstacle that many social service workers experience. The topic of budgeting and conducting evaluations feasibly is discussed in chapter 3.

EVALUATION STAKEHOLDER PLAN

A major theme of this chapter is that no evaluation is the work of one person. The collection of the information needed for an evaluation requires a cooperative effort—between direct-service workers and agency administrators and planners, in the case of external and internal evaluations, and between students and both faculty advisers and agency staff, in the case of class projects.

An **evaluation stakeholder plan** delineates the persons responsible for overseeing and completing an evaluation. The plan includes the resources each stakeholder brings to the evaluation, the reports expected from each stakeholder, and the time line on which the evaluation activities will be completed. A brief discussion and case application (Figure 2.8) of each of the general stakeholder categories follows. A list of resources that support agency-university partnerships in carrying out such plans can be found in the "Further Readings" section of this chapter.

Stakeholders Authorizing the Evaluation.   Who is requiring the evaluation? What individual, group, or organization does this person represent? What evaluation questions does the authorizing person want answered? Individuals authorizing evaluations fall into three categories: (1) external funders overseeing grant awards to multiple agencies that have similar goals, programs, and results; (2) internal stakeholders wanting to answer local program evaluation questions; and (3) students and agency workers who want to answer local program evaluation questions.

Case examples of external evaluations initiated by state funders and of an internal evaluation initiated by a private foundation are given in figures 1.3, 1.6, and 1.5. A challenge in all these examples was to evaluate common desired results among programs while at the same time allowing local programs to develop unique interventions and results geared to their target populations. In the evaluation of family violence prevention planning (figs. 1.5 and 2.3), all five funded grantees reached the desired outcome of writing a strategic plan that was based on collaborative community involvement and information demonstrating the need for the proposed interventions. At the same time, the specific plans varied considerably among grantees. One grantee's strategic plan needed to account for the fact that its county was experiencing rapid population growth, which would likely increase the incidence of family violence during the time the prevention plan would be implemented.

The case examples in figures 1.2 and 1.6 of internally initiated evaluations focused on exploratory and descriptive evaluation questions, whereas there was pressure in the externally driven evaluations to answer explanatory evaluation questions if possible. External evaluations in the case examples also had a defined time frame, ranging from one to two years, whereas the internal evaluation case examples had a more flexible time frame.

The student examples covered exploratory, descriptive, and explanatory evaluation questions and also ranged from a ten-week class project to a two-year dissertation study. The challenge for students is to utilize the academic research to further their own education and at the same time contribute to agency interventions. Of the academic examples given in figure 1.7, all were of projects that were conducted in consultation with agency workers and whose results were reported to agency stakeholders.

Evaluation Advisory Board.   Who is overseeing the planning and implementation of the evaluation? Members of an advisory team may be persons in addition to those authorizing the evaluation. An evaluation advisory team existed for most evaluation case examples given in this book.

Figure 2.8.   Case example: Developing the evaluation stakeholder plan.

The decisions that must be made in developing an evaluation stakeholder plan are applied here to the Children's Health Insurance Program (CHIP) outreach evaluation discussed in figure 1.6.

The *authorizing stakeholders* were: *A review team from the state Department of Jobs and Family Services (DJFS) awarded an evaluation grant based on a competitive request for proposal process.*

They agreed to complete the following tasks within the time frame stated: *A representative from DJFS was assigned to the evaluation team. He met with the team to clarify the scope of the evaluation. He corresponded with the team through telephone conference calls monthly during the first six months of the evaluation.*

They agreed to provide the following resources: *The DJFS representative facilitated an information meeting with directors of county programs to receive local support for the evaluation team's county site visits. He sent a letter to the ten participating county agencies authorizing the activities of the evaluation team. He also collected the CHIP enrollment data that were analyzed by the evaluation team.*

The *evaluation advisory board* consisted of: *The DJFS representative communicated with two members of the evaluation team the expectations of the DJFS members who approved the evaluation grant. The DJFS representative reported to other stakeholders at the state agency.*

They agreed to complete the following tasks within the time frame stated: *All tasks of the advisory team were communicated and conducted by the DJFS representative.*

They agreed to provide the following resources: *All resources requested by the evaluation team were delivered by the DJFS representative.*

The members of the *evaluation team* were: *Seven faculty and staff who represented the following disciplines: social work; psychology; and community health.*

They agreed to complete the following tasks within the time frame stated: *(1) Conduct a quantitative analysis of CHIP enrollment data over a specified time period to determine the ten most successful counties across the state in enrolling eligible children. Two members of the evaluation team were primarily responsible for this task. The analysis was conducted in the first six months of the two-year evaluation period. (2) Develop the plan for conducting qualitative site interviews with key stakeholders in the ten most successful counties determined in task 1. Two members of the evaluation team developed the site visit plan. The site visit plan was completed by the end of the first six months. Site visits were actually conducted between the ninth and the twelfth months of the grant. The site visit information was analyzed and reported within the first six months of the second year of the grant. (3) Provide an annotated bibliography of research and evaluations nationwide related to CHIP enrollment. One faculty member and two of her students conducted the literature search to create the bibliography. The bibliography was completed within the first year of the grant and updated for the final report.*

They agreed to provide the following resources: *(1) Purchase the software to analyze the quantitative data. Analyze and report the data to the DJFS representative. (2) Purchase the equipment needed for the site interviews: tape recorders; special microphones to record up to ten focus group participants; laptop computers to record the sessions; software to analyze the qualitative interviews; and poster board to facilitate the focus groups. Purchase grocery store vouchers for each consumer who participated in individual or group site interviews. Cover travel expenses, including overnight lodging for some of the site interviews. (3) Have access to library resources, that is, Web sites and academic research on the topic.*

They agreed to provide the following reports from the evaluation: *Submit six-month progress reports. Submit a final report, including an executive summary. The final report included the procedures followed to carry out the three contracted tasks. The appendixes of the report included the procedures and findings of the three tasks.*

For some external evaluations there was a general advisory board to the state funders. The funder communicated the desires of the advisory board to the other persons in the stakeholder plan. Such an arrangement characterized the statewide evaluation of FSIs and the statewide study of competencies for direct-care mental health workers. The advantage of this advisory arrangement was that the evaluator's time was better spent gathering information than engaging in long discussions of political issues related to program planning, practice, and evaluation.

At the same time, it was beneficial for at least one member of the evaluation team to be aware of how evaluation advisory team concerns affected the scope of the evaluation. In the evaluation of FSIs, the evaluation advisory team required that student performance outcomes be measured. In the study of direct-care mental health workers' competencies, the evaluation advisory team required that certain competencies appear on the survey distributed to mental health workers.

Local programs also had their own advisory boards in the external evaluation examples. The evaluators needed to be aware, not only of the desires of the primary funders, but also of the desires of the local monitors of the funded intervention. In the case of the FSIs, there was much variety in the interventions provided locally to reach the common goal of improving family functioning. In the case of the direct-care mental health workers' competencies, some local behavioral health organizations had special populations, such as youth or older adults, that were not targets of the other behavioral health organizations.

The advisory board to the family violence prevention planning process had more than a purely advisory role. A subcommittee of the board was formed specifically to oversee the evaluation activities. The evaluator was very involved in discussions with the general advisory board and the evaluation advisory board about political issues shaping planning and evaluation. For a description of the roles that the evaluator shared with other stakeholders, see figure 2.3.

Consumer representation was sought for the state and local evaluation advisory teams in all the case examples. Often, one or two consumers were on the boards. In the family violence prevention planning example, an agency stakeholder met separately with the youth consumers of prevention efforts to decipher the adult dialogues that occurred during the advisory board meetings. In the mental health competency example, client advocates rather than clients were on the advisory board—because the competencies being developed were for workers in agencies for persons with long-term mental illness. The stakeholders all agreed that client advocates, not the clients themselves, should be on the advisory board.

Persons initiating internal evaluations and students arranging to conduct evaluations or research for academic reasons sometimes lose sight of the fact that the evaluation still needs an advisory process. Minimally, all evaluations need to follow ethical guidelines. The role of institutional review boards in ensuring that such guidelines are followed is discussed in the next chapter, a discussion that applies to all evaluation and research conducted by university students and faculty. It was recommended earlier in this chapter that agencies have an IRB also.

Students and agency workers also commonly lose sight of the fact that, eventually, other stakeholders' support is needed either to carry out the evaluation or to implement the recommendations that emerge from the evaluation. In the internally driven evaluation of out-of-home placements of African American children, the workers were permitted to use work time to study and discuss the issue. Eventually, they needed administrative support to engage other persons in the case review process and to follow up on the discoveries of the evaluation.

Primary Evaluator and Evaluation Team.   Who are the primary persons responsible for implementing the evaluation activities? It takes a collaborative team to deliver social services to clients. It also takes a collaborative team to complete an evaluation in a timely and reasonable manner.

Even when there is only one evaluator, that person still forms a team with the other stakeholders. In the evaluation of the SCBM program presented in figure 1.2, the evaluator formed a team with the program director and his staff in order to clarify the scope of the evaluation and to receive access to the clients, who became the primary participants in the evaluation.

In all the external evaluation examples in figures 1.3, 1.5, and 1.6, there were several persons involved in implementing the evaluation. In each example, one person was responsible for ensuring that all the evaluation activities were completed and reported in the manner agreed on by the stakeholders. In the larger evaluations, the primary evaluator became the person who met with evaluation advisory board members.

MAJOR POINTS

The following persons have a stake in the process and results of an evaluation and shape how the evaluation activities are negotiated:

funders

social service providers

consumers of social services

community members

evaluators

Evaluations can be internally driven by agency practitioners and administrators, externally driven by funders and policy makers, and driven by research interests. An evaluation advisory board of stakeholders can oversee all evaluation activities. A list of questions to ask potential evaluators was provided. The AEA's seven points related to integrity and honesty of stakeholder negotiation was discussed and applied to a case example.

Social service workers who are responsible for conducting a social service practice evaluation can ask these questions at the very beginning of the evaluation:

What is at stake for each stakeholder?

What does each stakeholder have to gain?

What does each stakeholder have to lose?

What is each stakeholder willing to invest in the program and evaluation?

This chapter concluded with a discussion of an evaluation stakeholder plan that delineates the resources provided and reports expected from key stakeholders within a specified time frame.

FURTHER READINGS

Evaluation Web Sites

American Evaluation Association. The main Web site is http://www.eval.org. Membership in the AEA includes subscriptions to the following two journals: *New Directions for Evaluation* and the *American Journal of Evaluation*. The AEA annual conference provides very practical and hands-on evaluation tools as well as presentations on theory pertaining to social service evaluation.

Campbell Collaboration. The main Web site is http://www.campbellcollaboration .org. It maintains references for evidence-based research related to health and social service settings. For the guidelines according to which research is selected for the database see the Web site.

Family Support America. The Web site is http://www.familysupportamerica.org. The organization supports the implementation and evaluation of community-based family support programs. It publishes a regular newsletter and sponsors a biannual conference. See the resource for agency evaluation called How Are We Doing? A Program Self-Assessment Toolkit.

Harvard Family Research Project. The Web site is http://www.gse.harvard.edu/hfrp. The project is sponsored by the Harvard Graduate School of Education. The Harvard Family Research Project's evaluation periodical, *Evaluation Exchange,* highlights innovative methods and approaches to evaluation, emerging trends in evaluation practice, and practical applications of evaluation theory.

Healthy Communities, Healthy Youth. The Web site is http://www.search-institute .org/research.

Institute for the Advancement of Social Work Research. The Web site is http://www .iaswresearch.org. This weekly Listserv announces conference presentations and funding opportunities that are relevant to social service evaluation. ISWR has a great resource for National Institute of Mental Health–funded social work research development centers, which are currently funded through 2005. Also, ISWR provides links to federal agencies, foundations, and research and information sites.

Society for Social Work Research. The Web site is http://www.sswr.org. Membership includes subscription to the journal *Research on Social Work Practice.* The society's annual conference provides resources and presentations on social service evaluation and research.

University of Western Michigan Checklists Project. The Web site is http://www .wmich.edu/evalctr/checklists. The Checklists Project offers checklists for designing, budgeting, contracting, staffing, managing, and assessing evaluations of programs, personnel, students, and other evaluations; collecting, analyzing, and reporting evaluation information; and determining merit, worth, and significance.

W. K. Kellogg Foundation. The Web site is http://www.wkkf.org. It contains several evaluation handbooks and information about funding for social service evaluation.

American Journal of Evaluation. Journal.

Evaluation Review: A Journal of Applied Social Research. Journal.

Journal of Baccalaureate Social Work. Journal.

Journal of Multidisciplinary Evaluation. Journal.

Journal of Social Work Education. Journal.

Journal of Social Work Research and Evaluation. Journal.

New Directions for Evaluation. Journal.

Research on Social Work Practice. Journal.

Social Work. Journal.

Social Work Abstracts. Journal.

Social Work Research. Journal.

REFLECTIVE JOURNAL ACTIVITIES

For questions 2–5, students may interview social service workers about actual evaluations conducted at the agency. Students may also answer these questions as they apply to a future evaluation.

1. Answer the questions in figure 2.4 related to your comfort level with evaluation skills. How does your comfort level with evaluation affect your negotiation with different evaluation stakeholders?

2. Think of an agency evaluation, and go through the list of stakeholders described at the beginning of this chapter. Did any conflicts exist between these stakeholders? What were the reasons for the conflicts?

3. If the evaluation was internally driven, were there any conflicts among agency staff in clarifying the scope of the evaluation? What were the conflicts?

4. If the evaluation was externally driven, were there any conflicts between agency staff and the external stakeholders in clarifying the scope of the evaluation? What were the conflicts?

5. How might any of the conflicts that you described in response to questions 2–4 be avoided or mitigated in the future?

6. Think about your past evaluation experiences. What made these experiences positive or negative for you? For other stakeholders?

7. Look up some of the Web sites listed in this chapter's "Further Readings" section. How can you integrate some of the information available at these Web sites into your daily practice?

PROCEDURAL JOURNAL ACTIVITY

1. Answer the questions from the Evaluation Decisionmaking Model in figure 2.9 as they pertain to negotiating with stakeholders in a past or proposed evaluation. For an example in which the model is applied see figure 2.8.

Figure 2.9.   Evaluation decisionmaking model: The evaluation stakeholder plan.

The *authorizing stakeholders* are: _____

    They agree to complete the following tasks within the time frame stated: _____

    They agree to provide the following resources: _____

    They agree to provide the following reports: _____

The *evaluation advisory board* consists of: _____

    They agree to complete the following tasks within the time frame stated: _____

    They agree to provide the following resources: _____

    They agree to provide the following reports: _____

The members of the *evaluation team* are: _____

    They agree to complete the following tasks within the time frame stated: _____

    They agree to provide the following resources: _____

    They agree to provide the following reports from the evaluation: _____

CHAPTER 3

VALUE-DRIVEN EVALUATION DECISIONS

The discussion in this chapter can help social service workers prioritize the values that should drive evaluation decisions. The key stakeholders identified through the exercises in chapter 2 should be included when planning the evaluation in order to ensure such a prioritization. The values discussed in this chapter follow the guidelines of the National Association of Social Workers (NASW) Code of Ethics (see app. A) and also emphasize the different client systems, focusing on their strengths. The prioritization of values guiding evaluation decisions will lead to key evaluation activities. The values to consider in this chapter fit under the acronym SCREAM—strengths, culture, resources, ethics, agreement, and multiple systems. The SCREAM values should be applied when answering exploratory, descriptive, and explanatory evaluation questions.

The *learning outcomes* for this chapter are as follows:

1. Prioritize the values for a particular evaluation.

2. Identify how the *strengths* of evaluation participants will be measured.

3. Identify how the *culture* of stakeholders and participants will be respected.

4. Identify the *resources* available for the evaluation and how the evaluation can be conducted within the limits imposed by those resources.

5. Identify how adherence to *ethical* guidelines for evaluation activities will be documented.

6. Identify how stakeholder *agreement* about evaluation decisions will be documented.

7. Identify how stakeholders and participants will be selected to represent *multiple* systems.

Before we turn to the SCREAM values themselves, we must first discuss the distinction between personal values, group values, and professional ethics.

EVALUATION VALUES

Values are preferences, beliefs, cherished ideas, worldviews, assumptions, traditions, and morals that consciously and unconsciously shape and influence decisions of individuals and groups. Values are observed in actions, behaviors, customs, language, and attitudes. Each stakeholder involved in a social service evaluation has a unique set of values concerning evaluation, beginning with whether he or she considers evaluations to be important. Values supported in any given evaluation of necessity reflect the values held by individual stakeholders involved and the agencies, communities, and professions that they represent.

Personal Evaluation Values.   Individual stakeholders have different values when it comes to the purpose of evaluation, the preferred methods for collecting information, and the role of theory in evaluations. Even in the evaluation and research literature one can find different preferred foci for evaluations. To illustrate this point, reflect on how other students, colleagues, professors, social service workers, and clients respond to the value statements listed in figure 3.1. It helps to understand how value preferences can influence evaluation decisions.

Agency Evaluation Values.   Value-based policies influence evaluation decisions. An assumption of evaluation is that agency program implementation and planning decisions are made on the basis of the information collected in the evaluation. Evaluation is not the only process that guides agency practice. Values inherent in policy may influence agency decisions more than information gained during an evaluation. Policies may be internally driven—by an agency's mission, its goals, and procedures set by a local board of directors or administrators. Or they may be externally driven—by state law mandating the mission, goals, and procedures of publicly funded agencies. In some external evaluation case examples given in this book, programs were discontinued because of cuts in state funding regardless of the evaluation results.

When an evaluation involves more than one program, differences in values among staff from the different programs become apparent. As we saw in figure 1.3, while all the family support interventions (FSIs) evaluated had as their state-mandated goal the improvement of family functioning, none employed the same methods to achieve that goal, and some even employed methods that had not yet been proven effective. Here we see the important role that values can play in an intervention.

Consider how each of the following value statements of different FSIs lead to different interventions:

> We prefer to start with helping children because healthy children lead
> to healthy families.

We prefer to start with helping parents because healthy parents lead to healthy families.

We prefer to start with changing the agency environment because accessible services lead to healthy families.

We prefer to start with changing the community environment because healthy communities lead to healthy families.

The statewide evaluation helped the state level planners and the local agency staff clarify, not just their preferred interventions, but the theories guiding those preferences. Theory and logic models guiding program decisions are discussed in the next chapter.

Community and Societal Evaluation Values.   The current U.S. political climate is one that values producing outcomes, implementing programs proven to be effective and, above all, accountability. No publicly funded agency can escape accountability. These values may influence some

Figure 3.1.   Evaluation decisionmaking tip: Understanding stakeholders' personal values related to evaluation.

Values are preferences, in this case about the general activity of evaluation. Persons' values are shaped by experience, socialization, and learning. They tend to be applied to general situations with little regard to specific circumstances, in this case the specific scope of the evaluation at hand.

Consider having all stakeholders at the beginning of an evaluation check whether they agree with the following value statements:

____ I do not see the value of evaluations.

____ Social service workers must be accountable for the services they deliver.

____ All program changes should be based only on results from rigorous evaluations.

____ All program decisions should be based only on evidence-based research.

____ All evaluations should follow quantitative data collection.

____ All evaluations should follow qualitative data collection.

____ Evaluations should always use both quantitative and qualitative data collection.

____ All programs should follow a logic model that guides evaluation.

____ All programs should have clear, measurable outcomes.

____ All evaluations should have input from the following stakeholders: _____.

____ All evaluations should be conducted by an evaluator not connected to the agency.

____ These additional values should be present in all evaluations: _____.

stakeholders, especially those from external funding sources, to prefer specific evaluation activities assumed to "prove" the effectiveness of social service programs. These activities include:

the measurement of client outcomes

the use of standardized instruments

the implementation of only evidence-based interventions

the hiring of external evaluators to assess the effectiveness of the program objectively

For an example of the influence of current public policy on service delivery, consider the national and state policies that school systems be held accountable for the educational outcomes of all students. One of the goals of the school-based FSIs discussed in figure 1.2 was, "All children will be ready to perform academically." All these FSIs were required to demonstrate that they had attained that goal by measuring attendance, graduation, and the percentage of students passing the proficiency tests from the fourth grade on.

The debate about values among participants in this evaluation mirrored the national debate about values. Among concerns raised were the following:

Are proficiency scores a fair way to measure educational performance?

Who is accountable for student performance: students, parents, or teachers?

What noneducational support, if any, should schools be providing students in order to improve their performance?

Professional Values.   **Ethics** are embodied in an organization's written statement of the values, principles, and behaviors expected of all members of that organization. The text of the most recent NASW Code of Ethics pertaining to research and evaluation is reprinted in appendix A because these ethical guidelines apply to all social workers. Professional standards are embodied in a professional organization's written statements of the principles and behaviors expected of all members of that organization. The professional standards most often applied to evaluation are the Guiding Principles for Evaluators of the American Evaluation Association (AEA), which are reprinted in appendix B. For a range of evaluation competencies that adhere to these standards, see King, Stevahn, Ghere, and Minnema (2001). Social service workers must also abide by the standards enforced by their agency, standards that are most often influenced by larger accrediting organizations, such as the Child Welfare League of America or the National Head Start Association, and public overseeing organizations, such as the U.S. Department of Jobs and Family Services.

Evaluation Values.   Evaluation values, then, are found at the inter-section of personal, agency, and community values; professional ethics; and professional standards that influence the decisions made during an evalua-tion. *Evaluation values* is a term more inclusive than the term *evaluation ethics,* for three reasons.

First, as Unrau et al. (2001, p. 270) state: "Evaluation ethics is concerned with the moral practice of evaluation or the 'code of right and wrong' for de-ciding how to handle data, how to interact with clients, and, in a general sense, how to proceed in politically charged situations." Framing the discus-sion in terms of evaluation values instead of evaluation ethics allows room for the consideration of values beyond those of one's profession or organization.

Second, the term *ethics* usually implies coercion. That is, discussions framed in terms of ethics tend to focus on the negative consequences of not adhering to professional codes, whereas discussions framed in terms of val-ues tend to focus on the positive rewards of acting in accord with personal value systems.

Third, a focus on ethical behavior tends to obscure the underlying values motivating that behavior. For example, social service workers conducting evaluations may focus on the amount of time it takes to develop procedures to protect participants' confidentiality and lose sight of the underlying value motivating the development of such procedures, the protection of human dig-nity and privacy. Values are applied throughout the evaluation process.

Decisions as to what is right and what is wrong involve practitioners, agency management, and community representatives, including funders or public administrators. Social service workers follow personal values and standards. They also work for agencies and belong to organizations that es-tablish standards. Every evaluation brings together individuals with different personal values and professional standards, all of which must somehow be made to work together. When values and standards clash, it is important to remember that there is no one, right evaluation code.

Value decisions are all about preferences and making choices. What compromises, if any, are made when stakeholders disagree on a list of pre-ferred behaviors or values? Social service workers can approach value preferences optimistically, as a set of positive choices that they themselves can make, or pessimistically as a set of negative requirements that some-one else forces on them. Be clear about the values and behaviors that you prefer in an evaluation, and communicate those preferences to other stake-holders.

Clarifying Evaluation Values.   Sometimes stakeholders simply list expected values without clearly stating the reason for their inclusion. But the reason makes a difference and must, therefore, be made explicit. Consider the expected value "involve stakeholders from different cultures." Cultural inclusion could be a purely methodological consideration (ensuring that the distribution of cultures among those involved in the evaluation matches the distribution of cultures in the general population) or simply a matter of fairness (ensuring that persons from all cultures have a say in the evaluation process regardless of the distribution of cultures in the general population). It is also important that enforcement mechanisms, or the consequences of not operationalizing an expected value, be made explicit. For example, continued funding could be made contingent on the involvement of persons from different cultures in the evaluation. Finally, what it is that constitutes evidence of compliance must be established as well. For a schematization of the clarification process, see figure 3.2.

Standard ethical procedures as dictated by a university institutional review board (IRB) were the ethical values guiding most of the evaluation examples in this book. The reinforcement for meeting IRB standards was the authority to conduct the evaluations. The consequences for not following these procedures would have been reprimands, resulting in possible discontinuation of academic studies and employment and loss of funding for the current and future projects.

Clarify with stakeholders which values and behaviors are legally binding and which stakeholders are legally bound to follow them. Any evaluator working for a university will be required to have the information-gathering procedures approved by an IRB to ensure ethical conduct.

Neuman and Kreuger (2003, p. 99) provide a helpful discussion of personal, ethical, and legal behaviors. They make the point that a behavior may be "unethical but not break the law." For example, while social workers are trained to respect client confidentiality, others involved in the evaluation may not be. Stakeholders should openly discuss the ethical values and

Figure 3.2.   Evaluation decisionmaking tip and example: Clarifying evaluation values.

Apply these three steps to an evaluation in your agency or practicum setting. Use the example as a model.

Steps	*Example*
1. Identify the preferred and acceptable values underlying the evaluation.	Ensure evaluation planning and participation involves key community stakeholders.
2. Define the behaviors that exemplify the acceptable values.	Invite key community stakeholders to participate in the evaluation advisory board.
3. State how values and behaviors will be reinforced or the consequences, if any, if the values are not held.	Funding will not be extended if stakeholder participation is not demonstrated.

Figure 3.3.   Evaluation decisionmaking tip: Identifying stakeholder evaluation values.

Complete this form as it applies to an evaluation in your agency or practicum setting. The following preferred or valued activities are expected by stakeholders to be present in the evaluation:

Value: _____.
Requested or required by the following stakeholder: _____.
Reinforcement for meeting the value: _____.
Consequence for not meeting the value: _____.

Value: _____.
Requested or required by the following stakeholder: _____.
Reinforcement for meeting the value: _____.
Consequence for not meeting the value: _____.

Value: _____.
Requested or required by the following stakeholder: _____.
Reinforcement for meeting the value: _____.
Consequence for not meeting the value: _____.

---

behaviors described in this chapter even if for them they are not legally binding. The discussion itself may lead to more humane interaction among all persons involved in an evaluation.

Figure 3.3 offers a form that will help the reader identify the general values expected of any evaluation. The remainder of this chapter is devoted to the common evaluation values summarized by the acronym SCREAM:

Measure *strengths*.

Respect *culture*.

Conduct evaluations within the capacity of your *resources*.

Follow professional codes of *ethics*.

Reach a written *agreement* about evaluation decisions with evaluation stakeholders.

Measure changes across *multiple* systems.

Reaching stakeholder agreement was covered in chapter 2. Discussion of the remaining SCREAM values follows.

STRENGTHS

Acknowledging the strengths of individuals, agencies, and communities participating in program planning, practice, and evaluation is a common expectation of many agency grants. Yet the desired results more often identified by stakeholders are a decrease in deficits or negative behavior (e.g., clients will no longer rely on public assistance) or the prevention of a negative behavior (e.g., there will not be an increase in family violence). Individuals such as youth and older adults can be viewed as gifts to a community rather than as delinquent, poor, or dependent (see Kretzmann & McKnight, 1993; McKnight & Kretzmann, 1997).

Strengths are behaviors and beliefs that help individuals, families, and communities reach their optimal level of social functioning. There is a wide social work and social service literature base dealing with the integration of strengths into practice and evaluation (Benson, 1997; Glicken, 2004; Kretzmann & McKnight, 1993; McKnight & Kretzmann, 1997; Saleebey 1992, 1997, 2002). The strengths perspective arises from the profession of social work's commitment to social justice and the dignity of every human being. "When we talk of building on client strengths, of respecting people's accounts of their lives, of revering a people's culture, of hearing out an individual's stories, we are, in a sense, giving testimony that, in spite of injustice and inequity, people do have prospects" (Saleebey, 1997, p. 233).

Strengths can be measured for all systems: healthy individuals; healthy families; healthy communities; healthy societies. Strengths lead to emotional and physical health. Strength behaviors of agencies are evinced when systems function well or function beyond minimally expected levels. Systems rely on strengths to cope with normal challenges and stressful situations. Strengths are behaviors and beliefs that systems want to increase and promote.

Strengths are measurable and can be incorporated into all evaluations (Dunst, Trivette, & Deal, 1994; Glicken, 2004; Saleeby, 1992, 1997, 2002). For the ways in which the strengths perspective was applied in the case examples described in this book, see figure 3.4.

Tips to consider when valuing strengths in an evaluation are as follows:

Build strengths assessment into the evaluation from the beginning, not as an afterthought. If describing the needs of the community, also describe its resources, assets, and strengths.

Build strengths into the program theory that describes the agency goals, activities, and results.

Measure strengths of individuals, families, groups, and communities.

Utilize the assets of stakeholders by valuing their feedback.

Utilize consumers' motivation to assist with evaluation planning.

CULTURE

Culture is the values, beliefs, customs, language, and behaviors passed on among individuals, families, communities, and societies. Cultural groups are composed of persons who are connected by a similar heritage, purpose, or

Figure 3.4.   Case examples: Valuing a strengths perspective in evaluations.

The intervention evaluated in figure 1.2 was a Strengths-Based Case Management approach with persons discharged from a substance abuse rehabilitation program.

A desired result across all the thirty-eight evaluated family support interventions described in figure 1.3 was increased family functioning. Several of the evaluated programs implemented a strengths-based intervention with children, families, and community groups.

The family violence prevention planning group described in figure 1.5 worked collaboratively with a similar community grant activity that measured youth assets rather than youth deficits. The evaluation process in this same example utilized evaluation advisory board members' motivation and knowledge to carry out some of the information-gathering activities.

The evaluation advisory boards described in several case examples in this book began with the assumption that they would rely on community members' assets in planning and implementing the evaluation.

The qualitative focus group approach to collecting information in several of the case examples allowed participants to focus on their own strengths and the strengths of others.

The consumer of a behavioral parenting intervention described in figure 1.7 reported to the agency staff the increase in the amount of time that her two boys were able to interact positively.

The exploratory, naturalistic dissertation study described in figure 1.7 built on the academic literature that demonstrated the strengths that African American families utilize to raise their children.

---

identity that includes a set of values, beliefs, customs, and behaviors and a common language. Cultural groups can be based on race, ethnicity, age, gender, religious belief, income, geographic location, political belief, and group membership. Each person is unique because behaviors and values are shaped by the interaction of the individual with the group culture. Social service workers need to question generalizations that are made about an entire cultural group.

Culture, and how it affects program planning, implementation, and evaluation, needs to be clarified in every evaluation. Treating culture as a component of an evaluation may be expected by stakeholders—even though that expectation may remain unstated. One reason that culture is often ignored is that persons tend to equate culture with race. In communities where there is minimal racial diversity, some stakeholders may claim that culture was not measured because there was no racial diversity among clients. Stakeholders can expand their definition of *culture* to include other expressions, such as income, status, and personal values.

Stakeholders should make a point of identifying diversity within targeted cultural groups. In the evaluation of the family violence prevention planning grant, one advisory board member questioned the need to target the faith-based community for educational workshops on violence prevention. The assumption was that the workshops would literally be preaching to the choir, that churchgoers were less likely to be violent toward family members than were nonchurchgoers. A minister on the advisory board quickly gave national and local statistics demonstrating that family violence occurs among persons who attend church at rates higher than the public perception.

How considerations of culture should affect an evaluation is the subject of much theoretical debate. Some authors argue that dominant evaluation designs and approaches inherently favor white-male worldviews and, thus, are simply yet another way in which the oppression of women and people of color is institutionalized (Hood, 2004; Mertens, 2003; Netting & Rodwell, 1998; Stanfield, 1999). For more discussion of ways to reduce the cultural biases that are ingrained in evaluation, see this chapter's "Further Readings" section.

Culturally competent evaluation is a process of social service workers becoming aware of their own cultural values and beliefs and of how those beliefs differ from those of the participants in and stakeholders of an evaluation and becoming knowledgeable of the research and evaluation reported in the literature related to cultural groups represented in the evaluation. Culturally competent evaluation is a multiple systems approach that acknowledges that macro level racism and oppression affects social service implementation and evaluation (Fong & Furuto, 2001).

Social service workers can apply the following principles of culturally competent evaluation:

Become aware of your own cultural limitations in understanding the culture of stakeholders.

Become aware of the cultural values, knowledge, and skills of stakeholders.

Identify the best interventions and evaluations available within the mainstream and clients' cultural groups, that is, those that support clients' growth, values, knowledge, and skills (see Fong & Furuto, 2001).

Construct an evaluation advisory team that has representatives from different cultural groups to review all aspects of the evaluation, including the interpretation of findings (see Patton, 1997; Royse et al., 2001).

Try to locate instruments that display a sensitivity to the cultural groups participating in the evaluation; norm instruments with the cultural group in a current evaluation (see Royse et al., 2001).

Reexamine your own definitions and perceptions of cultural groups that will negatively influence the evaluation process (see Ginsberg, 2001; Royse et al., 2001).

Figure 3.5.   Case examples of culturally competent evaluations.

Villa (2001, p. 370) developed a two-factor model called *la fe de la gente* that addresses "issues of culture, traditions, values, religion, and spirituality among Mexican Americans." The first factor, the vertical dimension of spirituality, contained eleven variables, including belief in God and "feelings of faith, hope, and love as critical aspects of coping" (p. 374). The second factor, the horizontal dimension of spirituality, focused on the importance of caring for others and the impact of social conditions, such as poverty, on one's spirituality.

Gilbert and Franklin (2001) described a seven-step evaluation process that emphasizes the trusting working relationship between the social worker and the Native American client during intervention and evaluation. The authors provided a case example that utilized a single system and qualitative design with an eighteen-year-old Native American girl. Qualitative, open-ended interviews and journaling were used to identify in the girl's own words her target behavior and goals. The charting of behaviors following the AB single system design showed a decrease in flashbacks about a car accident that took her boyfriend's life and an increase in completed assignments at school.

Lewis (2001) discussed the importance of Patton's utilization-focused evaluation and provided clear, practical guidelines to follow when conducting evaluations with Native American groups, including (1) knowing the specific evaluation protocol, (2) actively involving Native American leaders in the process, (3) determining outcome indicators, and (4) writing final reports. She advised persons to measure outcomes among those who participated in the intervention rather than using communitywide outcome measures. She advised analyzing the relevance of a standardized instrument for Native Americans, searching the literature for evidence of use with Native Americans, and utilizing statistical factor analysis to determine whether the concepts apply to the current population. Lewis discussed writing two reports: one addressing the community's questions, needs, and cultural values; and a second, technical one focusing more on specific questions asked by a source outside the community, usually the funder.

Matsuoka (2001) emphasized the implementation of qualitative data collection through participatory action research methods and the use of quantitative indicators of different systems levels, including a person's spirituality and the role of the family, community, and social influences. He provided a case example using Geographic Information System mapping in order visually to display statistical information. His example displayed residential, farming, and fishing communities as areas on a specific Hawaiian island that should remain protected from land development. Matsuoka provided a case example of using a logic model to assist a Hawaiian community's evaluation of its economic plan.

From Fong, R., & Furuto, S. (Eds.). (2001). *Culturally Competent Practice: Skills, Interventions, and Evaluations.* Boston: Allyn & Bacon.

Figure 3.6. Evaluation decisionmaking tip: Conducting culturally inclusive evaluations.

Mertens (2003) stated that all stakeholders of all evaluations should answer the following questions to ensure culturally inclusive activities (pp. 104–5):

> What are the influences of personal characteristics or circumstances, such as social class, gender, race and ethnicity, language, disability, or sexual orientation, in shaping interpersonal interactions, including interactions between evaluators, clients, program providers, consumers, and other stakeholders?
>
> What evidence is there that the evaluation was conceptualized as a catalyst for change (e.g., [meant to] shift the power relationships among cultural groups or subgroups)?
>
> Were the time and budget allocated to the evaluation sufficient to allow a culturally sensitive perspective to emerge?
>
> Did the evaluator demonstrate cultural sophistication on the cognitive, affective, and skill dimensions?
>
> Was the evaluator able to have positive interpersonal connections, conceptualize and facilitate culturally congruent change, and make appropriate cultural assumptions in the design and implementation of the evaluation?

Selected examples of culturally competent evaluation taken from Fong and Furuto (2001) are contained in figure 3.5. These examples emphasize a commitment among stakeholders to value culturally competent evaluation by accepting the range of choices available in evaluations. This means choosing qualitative as well as quantitative measures and individual, group, and community measures, as well as measuring both strengths and weaknesses.

Mertens (2003) recommended ways in which all evaluations could be made inclusive of multiple cultures. "An inclusive approach has implications for every step of the evaluation process: the design of the study, definition of the problem, selection of indicators of success, sampling and data collection decisions, development of intervention strategies, addressing power differentials in the study, and setting standards for good evaluation" (p. 96). She concluded by providing a list of questions that, when added to an evaluation, can ensure cultural inclusiveness, a list that is reprinted in figure 3.6.

RESOURCES

Resources are the time, materials, and training needed to complete evaluation tasks. Some agencies set aside absolutely no time or budget for evaluation. Some grants may require evaluations but provide a very minimal budget for them, often as little as less than 10% of the entire program budget. Evaluations should be conducted within the budgeted resources. Listed below are the Joint Committee on Standards for Educational Evaluation (1994a;

1994b) standards of feasibility, which are intended to ensure that an evaluation will be realistic, prudent, diplomatic, and frugal:

> Feasibility Standard 1 (F1)—Practical Procedures. The evaluation procedures should be practical, to keep disruption to a minimum while needed information is obtained.
>
> Feasibility Standard 2—Political Viability (F2). The evaluation should be planned and conducted with anticipation of the different positions of various interest groups, so that their cooperation may be obtained and so that possible attempts by any of these groups to curtail evaluation operations or to bias or misapply the results can be averted or counteracted.
>
> Feasibility Standard 3—Cost Effectiveness (F3). The evaluation should be efficient and produce information of sufficient value, so that the resources expended can be justified.

These feasibility standards and the other educational evaluation standards are available at the Joint Committee's Web site, which is www.wmich.edu/evalctr/joc. For more discussion of the standards, see Stufflebeam (2000).

Time is the most valuable resource for conducting a thorough and accurate evaluation. Time is related to all three feasibility standards listed above. It is needed to plan an evaluation well before information is collected from participants. It is needed to ensure that the ethical guidelines discussed in the next section of this chapter are followed, thus ensuring minimal disruption to services provided to clients (F1). It is needed to explore possible political implications and conflicts of interest and to obtain input from all key stakeholders (F2). It is needed to clarify the purpose of the evaluation, the appropriate data-collection methods, and how the evaluation will be utilized (Patton, 1997). Producing processes, results, and reports that were not intended by the key stakeholders wastes valuable time (F3).

Time costs money. Some of the many time-consuming tasks involved in evaluation are listed below (chapters in which topics are discussed in more detail are listed in parentheses):

1. Conducting a thorough literature search for research and evaluations similar to the task at hand (chap. 4)
2. Negotiating the evaluation purposes as agreed on by the funders, evaluators, service providers, and clients (chap. 2)
3. Convening an evaluation advisory committee (chap. 2)
4. Developing the evaluation plan (all chapters)
5. Writing an evaluation progress report every three to six months (chap. 6)
6. Having conference telephone or face-to-face sessions with the evaluation team (chap. 2)

7. Completing the human subjects review material to be approved before data collection begins (under "Ethics" in this chapter)

8. Implementing the data-collection procedures (chap. 5)

   a. Securing copyright permissions and purchasing standardized instruments

   b. Developing the questions for individual or focus group interviews

   c. Writing the instructions for informed consent

   d. Selecting and inviting the persons to participate

   e. Collecting and entering quantitative data into statistical software programs

   f. Taking notes during interviews and transcribing interviews (set aside five to seven hours to transcribe verbatim a one-hour interview, longer if there is more than one respondent)

   g. Running the appropriate statistical analysis

   h. Conducting the theme analysis of the narrative data (set aside at least three hours to code a transcript of a verbatim, one-hour interview, which is usually at least fifteen pages long)

   i. Analyzing all the data together and writing the final report, which chronicles the connection between each step of the evaluation

   j. Conducting a formal presentation for stakeholders of the results and implications of the evaluation

Some persons' time is much more expensive than others. Assess how the tasks listed above can be completed in the most efficient way (e.g., perhaps some of the staff, rather than an outside consultant, can conduct some of the literature review). Have a written contract that specifies whether persons will be compensated on the basis of the final product or the time spent on the evaluation. Most consultants charge by the hour rather than by the task. Be clear about the total budget for an evaluator's time and ask him or her for a reasonable prediction of the amount of time that it will take to complete the tasks listed above.

When contracting with a consultant from a university, be aware of indirect costs (e.g., phone use, office equipment, and minimal administrative support) that may be assessed automatically. Usually, these administrative costs are calculated as a percentage established by the university research office that is based on typical government-funded grant rates. For some federal grants, the indirect costs can be 25% or higher. Ask an evaluator to provide a beginning budget at no cost before agreeing to enlist his or her services. All contracts should be reviewed at regular intervals, usually every three to six months.

Many stakeholders will be participating in the evaluation voluntarily, especially during the planning and negotiation stages. Count this time as leveraging when writing evaluation reports. **Leveraging** is the allocation of funds and other resources by organizations other than the primary funder. Many funders expect that the percentage of leveraged funds will increase each year until the point at which the funder is no longer supporting the activities financially. Many agencies allow social service workers to use agency time to participate in evaluation planning. Turn that time into a financial figure based on the person's hourly wage.

The best conservation of time and money is to clarify what you need from the evaluation. Consider all the options that are generated as you read this book. In one evaluation, the logic model (discussed in chap. 4) might already be established, saving you much time in terms of meetings with stakeholders. In another evaluation, implementing a standardized instrument may be the best methodological option, saving you much time in terms of transcribing and analyzing open-ended interviews. This entire book is about making evaluation choices. Get in the habit of putting a price tag on each choice. Also get in the habit of establishing a time limit for each task. Think efficiently, and conducting evaluations may become easier.

Robson (2000, p. 3) outlined some very practical suggestions for conducting "small-scale evaluations." Small-scale evaluations

are local (rather than regional or national);

involve a single evaluator (or possibly a small team of two or three);

occupy a short time scale (perhaps completed in something between one and six months);

have to be run on limited resources;

take place at a single site (or possibly a small number of related sites).

Robson (2000) devoted one chapter to "practicalities," including the idea of "time budgeting," which addresses issues similar to those discussed above. He included a diagram for predicting the months that certain tasks will be completed, breaking the tasks into the three general categories "preparatory," "data gathering," and "analysis and reporting" (Robson, 2000, p. 107). Allot at least 30% of your total time to each of these three stages.

Just as social service workers involve clients in the assignment of tasks while compiling an intervention plan, social service workers can also clarify who will complete each activity of the evaluation plan within the allotted time line. If the evaluation activities are being completed by a team, one person should be the director of the overall project, making sure that all tasks are completed and coordinated. If practitioners contract with a university evaluation team, the director of the project is often called the *primary investigator*. This person is the main liaison between the evaluation team and other stakeholders.

ETHICS

Professional ethics are the values, principles, and behaviors expected of all members of an organization. In a survey and interview study with thirty-one evaluators, "there was nearly unanimous agreement" that ethical conduct was a competency expected from all evaluators (King et al., 2001, p. 239). Know your agency's ethical standards for evaluation. Apply the agency's practice standards to evaluation if there is not a separate policy for evaluation.

Bisman and Hardcastle (1999) demonstrate the following shared values between practice and research/evaluation:

informed consent by consumers to participate in the intervention and evaluation

confidentiality of the participants

the social service worker's responsibility to cause no harm to the consumers and other stakeholders

The key to ethical evaluations is to prevent the violation of a participant's or stakeholder's rights, whether intentional or unintentional. Figure 3.7 contains a positively focused list of ten "thou shalls" of evaluation ethics. The first ethical value, "Thou shall evaluate . . . ," is a theme of this entire book and is supported by the NASW Code of Ethics and the AEA Guiding Principles for Evaluators. Discussion of the remaining ethical points in figure 3.7 follows.

Establish an Ethical Review Process.   There was a discussion at the end of chapter 2 about the role of an agency evaluation committee in coordinating evaluation activities that overlap existing goals, such as strategic planning or maintaining a management information system. Once an evaluation project is planned, assurances need to be given that the evaluation procedures will follow ethical guidelines, procedures, or protocols regulating human interaction. Settings that receive federal funding are required to have a formal structure to approve the evaluation protocol. This structure is often called the human subjects review (HSR) or the IRB.

The primary purpose of an IRB is to ensure that people participating in evaluations are not harmed, physically or emotionally. The need for such safeguards arose from the well-publicized Tuskegee syphilis studies, which cost the lives of many African American men. The role of an IRB is primarily to answer the question, Are the procedures ethical? In order to make sure that this question is answered positively, accurate and competent evaluation methods must be implemented and humane interaction between evaluators and participants must be ensured.

Figure 3.7.   Evaluation decisionmaking tip: Ten "thou shalls" of ethical evaluation.

Check each item below that has been followed for an evaluation in your agency or practicum setting.

_____ Evaluate social service interventions.

_____ Establish an ethical review process.

_____ Do no harm.

_____ Do not coerce.

_____ Do not use a participant's name in vain.

_____ Be honest.

_____ Be respectful of participants' culture.

_____ Evaluate the evaluation.

_____ Explore your own values and conflicts.

_____ Leave the setting better than when you entered.

Evaluators must demonstrate to the IRB the following:

No physical harm will befall participants.

Participation is voluntary.

Participants will be informed of the purpose of the evaluation, the type of information being gathered, the activities expected of them, and that they will have access to the results.

Participants will given written informed consent before participating.

Participants' names and identifying information will remain confidential.

These points are discussed in detail in what follows.

Be patient when undergoing the peer review process and allow sufficient time to collect the information required by the IRB. Also be aware that most proposals submitted to IRBs are not approved the first time but must be resubmitted after incorporating or otherwise addressing suggested amendments. For an example of a protocol approved by a university IRB, see figure 3.8.

Do No Harm.   The infliction of physical harm during the course of a social service evaluation is never warranted, even if the benefits seem to outweigh physical discomfort or pain. Among evaluation situations that will likely result in physical harm to participants are the following:

withholding an intervention

implementing an intervention that is not warranted and/or monitored by a social service agency forcing an intervention that has been refused

participating in an evaluation that exposes participants to the danger of retaliation by, for example, an abusive partner

participating in an evaluation that you know will result in participants losing political power, status, or financial security

Social service workers have a responsibility to be sensitive to the emotional nature of evaluation. Some evaluations collect very sensitive information: whether consumers of services were victims of child abuse; whether they have ever been victims of partner abuse; their beliefs about the role of sex education in the prevention of teen pregnancy; whether they have a history of mental illness; whether they have a criminal record; whether they have a history of substance abuse; and so on.

Train all persons collecting information to interact empathetically. In one evaluation involving a telephone survey, stakeholders were appropriately concerned about questions dealing with partner abuse asked of all women participants. A videotape presentation explaining the dynamics of power and control used by abusive partners was produced and shown to the interviewers to help them recognize indications that participants were victims of partner abuse. The interviewers were instructed not to intervene should they recognize such indication but instead to make it a point of explaining at the end of *all* interviews how to get more information about the services available to victims of domestic violence.

Provide evaluation participants with a list of support services. Have agency staff help compile a resource packet to give participants after the information is collected. Leave contact information in case participants become distressed during or after the evaluation. Debrief participants on the purpose and results of the evaluation at the time the evaluation report is made public.

Also debrief those who helped collect the information. The data collectors, often students, hear many heart-wrenching stories. In one evaluation, three telephone interviews were conducted with parents at six-month intervals. At the two follow-up times, the student telephone interviewers asked the parents whether a specific child was still residing in the home. And it turned out that, in two cases, the child had died in the preceding six months. The student interviewers were, naturally, shaken and not sure how to respond. Project supervisors provided emotional support for the interviewers and counseled that, in such situation, the best response was to listen attentively and direct the participants to agencies that provide assistance in the grieving process.

Do Not Coerce.   The fact that evaluators must think about evaluation every day means that clients must think about evaluation every day also. The easiest way to reinforce that evaluation may be part of receiving services is to

Figure 3.8.   Case example: Institutional review board compliance.

Reproduced below is an actual petition form submitted to the university IRB, adapted by removing some questions related to medical studies that do not apply to most social service settings. This petition was submitted for the evaluation of outreach efforts to enroll children in the Children's Health Insurance Program (CHIP).

Petition for Approval of Research Involving Human Subjects

PLEASE ANSWER ALL QUESTIONS—If a question does not apply to your specific protocol, so indicate (e.g., with "Not Applicable" or "N/A"). If additional space is required, additional pages may be used.

1. Attach a concise (1–2 pages) description summarizing the background, objectives, and procedures to be used in the research (specifically address the subject's role in the research).
   In addition, provide the following information:
   a. Does the nature of the research require deception? (*Note:* The use of placebos is *not* deception provided the subjects are informed that they may receive them.)

      Yes ☐   No ☒

      If *yes,* then explain fully.

   b. If more than a "minimal risk" protocol, identify alternative procedures, if any, not proposed for this activity that might be advantageous to the subject.

      N/A

   c. Do the Investigator or Coinvestigator(s) have a vested interest in any actual or potential commercial enterprise/business associated with any aspect of this protocol?

      Yes ☐   No ☒

      If *yes,* explain fully and identify the safeguards taken to prevent investigator bias in subject recruitment and/or the consent process:

2. Does the research involve:
   a. An investigational new drug (IND)?

      Yes ☐   No ☒

      If *yes,* give IND# and provide regulatory review status:

      Attach *all* relevant documentation.

b. An investigational device (ID)?

Yes ☐   No **X**   If *yes,* does this ID pose:

Significant risk: ☐   Nonsignificant risk: ☐

(*Note:* The IRB will make the final determination.)

If *yes,* provide regulatory review status:

Attach *all* relevant documentation.

3. Concisely summarize the risks/discomforts for the subjects of their participation in the research and indicate how these risks/discomforts for subjects are reasonable in relation to anticipated benefits, if any.

> **The subjects will be asked to participate in interviews. These interviews are voluntary and confidential, thus minimizing any potential risks of answering the questions.**

Are there extraordinary expenses (e.g., tests, drug purchases, hospitalization) to the subject related to this protocol?

Yes ☐   No **X**

If *yes,* then explain fully, and clarify who will be responsible for their payment.

4. Does this study involve an interview, survey, or questionnaire?

Yes **X**   No ☐

If *yes,* check all that apply, and attach the appropriate number of copies of each (see Instructions):

a. **X** In-person interview

b. ☐ Telephone interview

c. ☐ Self-administered questionnaire

d. ☐ Other survey instrument (briefly describe):

e. ☐ Retrospective study (where data have *already* been collected); provide data-collection instrument

5. Confidentiality/anonymity.

a. Indicate the procedure for ensuring *confidentiality* of the data (e.g., responses kept in locked safe, restricted access to information, etc.) or for ensuring the *anonymity* of the subjects (e.g., no names on instrument(s), no personal identifiers linked to instrument(s), no in-person interviews/videos, etc.):

> **Confidentiality will be protected by keeping all audiotapes, videotapes, diskettes containing transcriptions, and interview notes in a locked filing cabinet in the PIs' offices.**

(figure continues)

b. Describe the safeguards taken to protect against identifying, directly or indirectly, any individual subject in any report of the research project.

No person's name will be contained in the final report.

If *identifiable medical information is collected or accessed,* I agree to follow the HIPAA requirements.

6. Research subjects:

a. What are the approximate number and ages of the following?

	Number of Subjects (estimate for all sites if multisite study)		Age Range of Subjects (estimate for all sites if multisite study)	
	Local Site	All Sites	Local Site	All Sites
Subjects	**150**	**150**	**Over 18**	**Over 18**
Controls				

b. Summarize the criteria for selection and exclusion of subjects:

Ten counties that have submitted a Medicaid Expansion Outreach plan will be selected for the interviews. These ten counties were selected because their outreach plans increased the number of eligible persons who became aware of the Medicaid Expansion program. Within each county, five recipients of the program will be interviewed together in a focus group, five administrative staff who implemented the program will be interviewed in a separate focus group, and five direct-service staff of the program will be interviewed in another, separate focus group. Persons can request personal interviews if they feel more comfortable than answering questions in a focus group.

If the subject population is *not* representative of *the population base from which subjects could be selected* with respect to *gender representation* (see NIH guidelines at http://grants.nih.gov/grants/funding/women_min/guidelines_amended_10_2001.htm), please explain:

If the subject population is *not* representative of *the population base from which subjects could be selected* with respect to *minority representation* (see NIH guidelines at http://grants.nih.gov/grants/funding/women_min/guidelines_amended_10_2001.htm), please explain:

c. What is the source of subjects (including patients)? (If subjects are being recruited at a non-WSU site, provide a copy of the permission to use that site signed by an institutional official or, equivalently, approval from their IRB.)

> **Recipients and program staff of the selected ten counties.**

d. How will potential subjects be approached and by whom?

> **For the staff interviews, the PIs will contact the Medicaid con-
> tact person for each selected county to acquire the names of
> administrators and direct-service staff of the programs. For the
> potential recipient participants, the Department of Jobs and
> Family Services (DJFS) contact person will provide a list of all
> new CHIP enrollees to the PIs. The PIs will then send a letter of
> participation to a randomly selected sample. The ODHS contact
> person states that enrollees give consent to release address
> information on the application. The application is enclosed.**

e. Will subjects be paid or otherwise compensated?

Yes [X]   No [ ]

If *yes,* please respond to the following questions:

i. What is the amount of compensation?	**$15.00**
ii. If not monetary, what will be used for compensation?	**Gift certificate to a local grocery store**
iii. What is the reason for compensation?	**Incentive to participate**

iv. If subjects are to be remunerated, indicate how this remuneration will be prorated over the course of their participation.

> **Gift certificates will be given only one time—after the focus
> group participation.**

f. Will subjects be recruited by an advertisement   Yes [ ]   No [X]
(e.g., newspaper, radio announcement)?
(*Note:* If an advertisement is to be used, WSU policy requires prior written approval from your departmental chair and dean. A copy of the
advertisement, with approval of your chair and dean, must be submitted
with this application for IRB review.)

g. Where will the procedures be carried out?

> **The interviews will occur in an office or conference room ar-
> ranged by the Medicaid Outreach agencies selected for the study.**

h. Check if this protocol involves:

[ ] Children under 18

[ ] Pregnant women, fetuses, or neonates (i.e., newborns up to 28 days)

(figure continues)

☐ Prisoners

☐ Other vulnerable subjects (e.g., handicapped, economically/
educationally disadvantaged, or mentally disabled)

If any box is checked, describe both (1) the reason for their involvement
and (2) additional safeguards used to protect their rights and welfare:

8. Will this protocol be reviewed by any other human subject review committee?

Yes ☐   No ☒

If *yes,* please specify below and provide a copy of the IRB approval when
available.

(*Note:* If these activities are being reviewed by other IRBs, you must wait for
approval from *all* applicable IRBs prior to initiating the study(ies). Send
copies of the other IRB approvals to RSP as soon as available.)

9. Provision for informed consent. Indicate the type of form to be used. Include
copies of the informed consent document(s) with the petition. Also include any
written narrative to be presented to the subjects (e.g., cover letter, debriefing
information, etc.). You may check more than one response.

   a. ☒ Cover letter(s) attached

   b. ☒ Consent form(s) attached

   c. ☐ Debriefing information attached

   d. ☐ If none attached, please explain:

10. ☒ I agree that subjects may withdraw from the project at any time without consequences or loss of benefits.

If *you do not agree,* please explain:

11. Does the consent form or cover letter inform subjects how and when they will
be able to obtain, should they so choose, an abstract or summary of the completed study results when they (the results) become available?

Yes ☒   No ☐

If *no,* please explain:

☒ I agree that individual results from other subjects will not be made
available to any subjects, nor will any individual results be interpreted in reference to the study objectives.

If *you do not agree,* please explain:

12. Check whether the protocol involves the intentional use of or introduction into
subjects of:

Biohazards (e.g., rDNA, microorganisms, biological toxins)   ☐

Radioisotopes, radiation, or x-rays   ☐

Hazardous chemicals (not covered elsewhere in this petition)   ☐

If *yes,* identify and briefly describe here any and all that are applicable. In addition, complete details (e.g., nature of the hazard, scientific justification for its use, route and form of administration, safety precautions, risks to subject, etc.) must be given in the protocol, *and* the investigator must provide evidence that licenses and pertinent review committee approval has been granted.

N.B.: Sufficient procedural, risk, & and safety precaution information must be presented to the subjects so that he/she can assess the degree of individual risk. Indicate relative amounts, e.g., equivalent to a chest x-ray, etc.

☐ Check if this protocol includes proprietary/confidential information. Provide a statement and any relevant documentation. (*Note:* The IRB *cannot act* on a request for consideration of confidentiality *without* appropriate justification and relevant documentation.

Principal Investigator's Statement:

As principal investigator, I acknowledge that:

I am responsible for reporting any emergent problems or serious adverse effects or reactions.

I will submit any proposed procedural modifications to the IRB for its review and approval, and, except where necessary to eliminate apparent immediate hazards, no such modifications will be put into effect without prior IRB approval.

Unless otherwise directed by the IRB chairperson, I will renew this application with the IRB no less than annually.

The research project is being conducted in compliance with the IRB's understanding and recommendations.

The IRB is provided all the information on the research project necessary for its complete review.

This research project will not be put into effect until final IRB approval is received.

If this protocol involves more than minimal risk *and* the research is or is proposed to be funded by an external grant/contract, you must include two (2) copies of the external grant/contract proposal. (*Note:* Grant/contract proposals for external funding that is to be administered by Wright State University must be processed through Research and Sponsored Programs.)

(figure continues)

More than minimal risk
and externally funded; I have
included 2 copies of the proposal.

☐   N/A [X] [One box *must* be
                 checked.]

_____

Signature of principal investigator

All other investigators and/or faculty adviser listed on the cover of this petition (if any) must sign to acknowledge their participation in this project:

_____

Signature of faculty advisor

_____   _____

Signature of coinvestigator   Signature of coinvestigator

_____   _____

Signature of coinvestigator   Signature of coinvestigator

---

include a statement about evaluation on the agency release of information or consent form. Agencies have consent forms because providing services entails consulting with persons who have information that is needed to complete the current assessment and service plan. The same is true for evaluation. Evaluating practice is just as important as the assessment and service plan.

Some social service practitioners express a concern that evaluations burden clients by taking up their valuable time. But this is not necessarily the case. Clients often enjoy being involved in an evaluation, especially when information is gathered through open-ended interviews, in which they can express their views in their own words. Contrary to concerns that they will give only positive feedback about evaluated programs, clients can be very open in providing negative feedback about services.

Including on the normal agency consent form a statement that any information collected can be used, and follow-up calls made, for evaluation purposes ensures that a potentially useful data source is not lost. If permission to release names and locating information to an evaluator has not previously been secured, agency workers must first recontact all clients requesting permission and only then, after permission has been obtained, send a letter describing the evaluation along with a consent form. By the time the process has been completed, many participants are no longer available.

Most clients participating in program evaluations have limited resources. Therefore, many agencies offer the incentive of compensation in return for participation. Compensation can take many forms: cash, grocery store coupons, gas station vouchers, baskets of household supplies, and so on. A common argument against compensation is that it renders participation involuntary, making clients an offer they can't refuse. A counterargument is that compensating clients for their time is only fair. Besides, the practice is commonplace in marketing evaluation, where the targeted population is usually the middle and upper classes. Why should the poor be treated any differently?

When compiling consent forms for client participants, it is necessary to include a statement that the agency will continue providing services whether or not the client chooses to participate in evaluation. An outside evaluator needs assurances from the agency that it will comply with this stipulation. The same openness and trust could be extended to social service worker participants. That is, funders could agree that information provided by the agency workers would not result in discontinuing funding for the service. This expectation is not always feasible, however, one of the reasons for conducting the evaluation often being to make decisions about continuing, changing, or stopping the evaluated program.

Participants should be told how they can obtain results of an evaluation. If feasible, establish a toll-free number. Alternatively, develop a Web site. Minimally, leave participants with a telephone number, an e-mail address, and/or a mailing address to contact. Be prepared to be asked for the results, especially by agency representatives.

Do Not Use a Participant's Name in Vain. The necessity of protecting the confidentiality of individuals (e.g., clients, workers, and community representatives) participating in an evaluation is often understood, but it is not always clear whether it is necessary to protect the confidentiality of agencies as well. In figure 1.3, the evaluators reported the interview data collected from clients, direct-care staff, and administrators collectively for the entire state. Some stakeholders asked that findings be reported separately by county. The IRB decided that only the confidentiality of individuals, not that of agencies, was protected. Also, state "sunshine" laws permitted stakeholders to access the data summaries since they were public documents. Ultimately agency-specific reports were provided to each county and the state funders. The lesson learned was to discuss at the *beginning* of an evaluation the confidentiality of all systems, not just individuals.

Participatory and empowerment evaluations pose special confidentiality concerns since service users may be involved in collecting data from other service users (Fetterman, 2001). Evans and Fisher (1999) discuss steps that can be taken to ensure that service users consent to the analysis of agency documents pertaining to them. Ristock and Pennell (1996) provide examples of consent forms to be used with youth that specify that confidentiality can be broken if information about abuse is disclosed. They also provide guidelines for evaluations that analyze the power relationships between the deliverers and the consumers of the service.

Be Honest. The lead-in sentence of section C of the AEA Guiding Principles for Evaluators (see app. B) states: "Evaluators ensure the honesty and integrity of the entire evaluating process." The "entire evaluating process" begins with the first discussion of the evaluation with stakeholders and continues through the evaluator's final contracted task and any further uses of the evaluation results long after the evaluation itself has ended. For further discussions of engaging in open conversations with stakeholders about potential conflicts of interests, see Patton (1997), Posavac and Carey (2003), Unrau et al. (2001), and Weiss (1998). The application of the AEA guideline for integrity and honesty was provided in figure 2.7.

Be Respectful of Participants' Culture.   The value of cultural respect was discussed earlier in this chapter. State very clearly at the beginning of an evaluation the expectations for including persons from different cultural backgrounds as evaluation stakeholders and participants. Consider the following when clarifying culturally competent evaluation activities:

Define *culture* for this evaluation. Is it defined by race, ethnicity, gender, sexual preference, age, income, religion, political views, or some other characteristic? Should there be representation by some stakeholder constituency (e.g., consumer, direct-care worker, administrator, or community resident)? What other cultural groups do stakeholders want represented in the evaluation?

Define *cultural group inclusion*. Once the cultural groups involved are identified, how should representatives from the different groups be included in the evaluation process? Should each group have one representative on the evaluation advisory board? Or should representation be proportional?

Define *culturally sensitive methods of collecting information*. How will the values, attitudes, and beliefs of different cultural groups be respected during the information-gathering process (discussed in chap. 5)? Is the wording of consent forms changed as necessary to ensure that it is understood by the targeted cultural group? Are evaluation materials translated into the primary languages of all cultural groups involved in the evaluation? Should information be collected by persons of the same cultural group as the participants? Are standardized instruments normed to different cultural groups?

Define *culturally sensitive methods of reporting results*. How will the final reports reflect the cultural representation of the evaluation? Will the art used on the report cover reflect the cultural diversity involved? Are discussions of persons from different cultural groups conducted in a respectful manner, one that does not reinforce negative stereotypes? How will the confidentiality of cultural groups with only a small representation be protected?

Define *culturally sensitive integration of knowledge learned from the evaluation*. Will the manner in which the results are shared with persons from different cultural groups respect those groups' values, attitudes, and beliefs? How will changes made on the basis of the evaluation be shared with persons from different cultural groups? How will different groups be able to respond to the findings of the evaluation?

Evaluate the Evaluation. How will you determine whether the evaluation is successful? This question guides practice and planning activities in an agency, so it makes sense that social service workers identify the criteria for a successful evaluation. The Evaluation Decisionmaking Model applied in the procedural journal activities at the end of each chapter can become the basis for evaluating the evaluator and the evaluation process. Stakeholders should agree on the evaluators' tasks for each step of the evaluation and agree on how successful completion of these tasks will be measured. At specified times, measure whether the evaluator successfully completed the tasks.

Explore Your Own Values and Conflicts. Some conflicts of interest between stakeholders deal with differences in personal values and worldviews. Wrestle with these issues in your reflective journal. If you do differ philosophically with other evaluation stakeholders, respect their views just as you would the views of clients. Evaluators may overempathize, consciously or unconsciously, with some stakeholders. Reflecting back on the statewide evaluation of FSIs referenced throughout this book, I found myself being more understanding of direct-line social service workers than I did of administrative staff who countered the direct-line workers' views. I needed to put this bias in check.

Be open and honest about value conflicts with other stakeholders. Be genuine and respectful of all stakeholders in evaluation situations just as you would in clinical situations. Confront persons when you are adamant about the methodology or protocol. Stick to your position when you feel that it is warranted. Although your views may create a conflict between your goals and those of other stakeholders, be explicit about those views, and do not conceal the conflicts. Conflicts can be resolved and negotiated much more quickly when people work through the differences openly and honestly.

Leave the Setting Better Than When You Entered. Evaluated practice should be a better setting than unevaluated practice. Many practitioner changes begin soon after the planning and implementing of an evaluation starts. A theme of this book is that evaluation is in itself an intervention. People change when they are involved in evaluation. That's intervention. At the same time, this does not mean that all evaluations are credible and systematic. A poorly conducted evaluation can actually lead to agency decisions that are more harmful than those made by an agency that has not been evaluated. Evaluators can leave helpful reports behind. Reports that can be left with stakeholders and used long after the evaluation include evaluation training manuals, critiques of standardized instruments measuring results pertinent to the evaluation, annotated bibliographies, final reports, and

Figure 3.9.   Evaluation decisionmaking tips: Ethical guidelines to consider.

Check all items that have been completed for a current evaluation in your agency or practicum setting.

_____ Establish an ethical review board or committee that will approve evaluation activities prior to information being collected from participants. The primary role of this committee is to ensure that ethical guidelines are followed during the evaluation process.

_____ Train all persons collecting information on ways to interact with participants empathetically.

_____ Provide all evaluation participants with a list of supportive services.

_____ Debrief persons who help collect the information.

_____ Include consent to participate in evaluation as part of the normal agency consent form.

_____ Provide client participants with a token of appreciation for their time, such as a voucher to purchase groceries or gas.

_____ Include a statement on consent forms that no discontinuation of social services will occur if persons participate or do not participate in the evaluation.

_____ Develop a Web site where participants can find the results of the evaluation.

_____ Do not state the names of individual participants in any of the evaluation reports.

_____ Discuss with stakeholders at the beginning of the evaluation whether the names of participating agencies or organizations will be kept confidential in final reports.

_____ Report results collectively rather than for individual participants.

_____ Develop a written evaluation contract signed by key stakeholders outlining the scope of the evaluation and stating that no conflicts of interest exist among stakeholders and that results will be reported accurately and in a timely fashion.

_____ Clarify at the beginning of the evaluation how different cultural groups will be involved as stakeholders and participants.

_____ Involve stakeholders, including clients, in agency or conference presentations related to the evaluation.

_____ Set the criteria by which you will evaluate the success of the evaluation.

---

published articles related to the evaluation. For a list of possible evaluation reports, see figure 2.6.

Evaluation stakeholders can also be encouraged to share their positive experiences. Clients and social service workers can participate in presentations at agency staff meetings. For example, one client, the mother of two boys, ages six and seven, reported the positive results of an intervention to a staff of psychologists and social workers. Before the intervention, the boys had behaved so aggressively toward each other that the older of the two had pushed the younger out a second-story window. Thanks to the intervention, however, the mother was able successfully to implement reinforcement and time-out procedures, in the process monitoring the decrease in the boys' hitting behaviors. While making her report, she proudly shared the behavior modification charts that showed a change in both her behavior and the boys'.

Evaluation findings can also be reported at local, state, and national conferences. Some annual conferences that actively encourage presentations by both clients and social workers are those of National Head Start, the Family Violence Prevention Project, Family Support America, the Family Strengths Project, and the Child Welfare League of America.

For tips that can help in following ethical guidelines, see figure 3.9. For an example of an evaluation agreement that adheres to ethical guidelines, see figure 3.10.

AGREEMENT

Agreement is the verbal and written plan between stakeholders clarifying all steps of the Evaluation Decisionmaking Model. Negotiating stakeholder agreement about evaluation decisions has already been discussed in chapter 2. Figure 2.9 in particular provided a structure that the key stakeholders—authorizing stakeholders, the evaluation advisory board, and the evaluation team—could utilize to facilitate the documentation of an evaluation plan. For a breakdown of all decisions to be made, see appendix C, which outlines the Evaluation Decisionmaking Model. It cannot be stressed enough that all stakeholders should be in agreement about all decisions.

MEASURING MULTIPLE SYSTEMS

Multiple systems are the individuals, families, groups, organizations, and communities that are the targets for change and the sources for creating change. Social service workers often implement a systems approach, meaning that a change in one system will affect all other systems. For example, McKnight and Kretzmann's (1997) community asset mapping can be used to identify individuals and community resources that can be tapped to influence positive community change. A premise of community asset mapping is that local organizations (e.g., churches, neighborhood groups, and cultural organizations) and institutions (e.g., parks, libraries, schools, colleges, police, and hospitals) can make communities economically stronger. Economic assets can be measured through investment by local companies in the local economy, community development credit unions, and improved physical assets (e.g., acquiring and utilizing abandoned buildings, conserving energy sources, and improving parks).

A systems approach applies to evaluations also. In the evaluation of thirty-eight different FSIs statewide, one of the evaluation questions for the first year was, "What are the common desired results across all of these multiple service programs?" Figure 3.11 contains a diagram of the findings based on

Figure 3.10.   Case example: Evaluation agreement and adherence to ethical guidelines.

The agreement reproduced below relates to the case example of the evaluation of out-of-home placements for African Americans in a public child welfare agency:

PROPOSED ASSESSMENT PLAN BETWEEN CARL BRUN AND THE AGENCY DIVERSITY COMMITTEE

Carl Brun will be working with the committee to carry out the diversity plan for FY 2001–2. The proposed assessment activities for February 1–June 30, 2002, are:

1. Analyze composite group data of a sample of children placed in out-of-home care for the time period 1996–2001. Look specifically at the relationship between race of children (African American or white) and characteristics such as type of maltreatment, length of time in care, and types of services received.

Procedures. Carl will be looking only at group data that have already been collected by the agency. He will not be analyzing individual case records. His contact person at the agency will be ____. Requests for data will be made only to this person. Carl will enter the data into an SPSS software on his laptop computer. This computer will be kept in a locked office. The computer file can be opened only with his password.

Adherence to Confidentiality and Voluntary Participation. Carl will have no contact with individual clients. He will not have access to individual case folders. He will keep all statistical files confidential. Analysis of the data contained in a final report will be presented to the Diversity Awareness Committee.

2. Analyze the results from the recent staff surveys distributed by the Diversity Awareness Committee.

Procedures. A staff person from the agency will enter the results of each survey into an SPSS file according to the code book developed by Carl. An identifying number will be assigned to each survey so that Carl will not know the name of the survey respondent. Carl will copy the SPSS file and perform frequency distributions and cross-tabulations of the group results.

Adherence to Confidentiality and Voluntary Participation. Carl will not have access to anyone's actual survey. He will have only the responses to each survey as coded by the designated staff member. He will keep all statistical files confidential. Analysis of the data will be presented to the Diversity Awareness Committee.

3. Facilitate the Diversity Awareness Committee retreat on February 22. The goal of the retreat is to arrive at further assessment activities between March and June 2002 related to the mission of the Diversity Awareness Committee. It is preferable that at least two parent consumers attend this retreat and serve on the Diversity Awareness Committee.

Procedures. Carl will prepare the agenda for the retreat with the committee cochairs. Carl will facilitate the retreat activities.

Adherence to Confidentiality and Voluntary Participation. All participants in the retreat will be asked to sign an informed consent form. The form will state that participation in the retreat is voluntary and confidential and that no negative consequences will occur to staff or clients for their comments or actions at this retreat. No deliberate verbal or physical harm to any participant will be tolerated.

4. Develop outcome measurements of the activities carried out by the Diversity Awareness Committee between March and June 2002. Provide a report of the results with recommendations.

Procedures. A more specific assessment plan will be developed on the basis of the discussions at the committee retreat. This assessment plan will be presented to the agency Administrative Council before any further action is taken.

Adherence to Confidentiality and Voluntary Participation. The plan will be developed by the retreat participants. Participation is voluntary and confidential. The final report of the year's activities will be presented to the Diversity Awareness Committee.

Figure 3.11. Case example: Illustration of desired results across multiple systems.

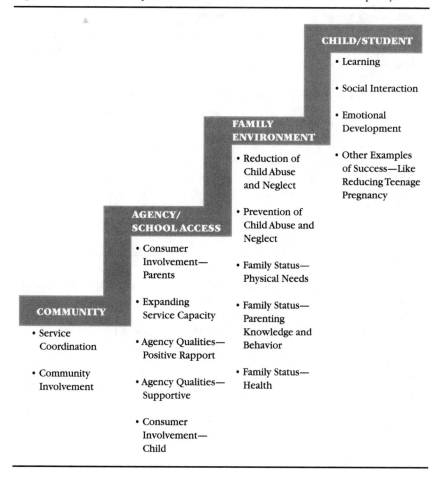

Figure 3.12.   Case example: Description of desired results across multiple systems.

In the evaluation of family support intervention, the most often mentioned measurements of *positive community change* discussed across all sites were:

1. *Increased service coordination:* (a) increase in the number of referrals between agencies; (b) updated information and referral database available to members of the community; (c) implementation of cross-agency client consent for information form; (d) number of agencies participating in a specific program).

2. *Increased community involvement:* (a) increased sense of community (based on narrative interviews); (b) increase in community assets; (c) increase in the number of volunteers; (d) increased economic investment by local businesses; (e) increased funding from local services.

Measurements of *positive agency change* were:

1. *Increased parent involvement:* (a) number of parents attending a program; (b) number of times an individual parent attended an activity; (c) the number of parents who volunteer or work at the agency.

2. *Expanded service capacity:* (a) increased number of services provided; (b) increased number of persons participating in program activities.

3. *Agency quality, positive rapport with consumers:* positive responses on satisfaction surveys.

4. *Agency quality, increase in supportive services:* providing transportation, child care, financial assistance, free services, and so on.

5. *Increased child involvement:* (a) number of children attending a program; (b) number of times an individual child attends a program; (c) child satisfaction with the program.

Measurements of *positive family change* were:

1. *Reduction of child abuse and neglect:* (a) decrease in child abuse and neglect reports; (b) decrease in out-of-home placements.

2. *Prevention of child abuse and neglect:* (a) participating in prevention programs; (b) desired emotional and behavioral changes in family; (c) achievement of service goals for family.

3. *Family status, physical needs are met:* (a) parent(s) acquired employment; (b) parent(s) acquired further education; (c) family received food, clothing, financial assistance, or housing.

4. *Family status, increased knowledge and behavior related to appropriate parenting:* measured on pre- and poststandardized instruments.

5. *Family status, health:* (a) improved health among members; (b) health concerns treated; (c) children received immunizations; (d) family members were referred to health care.

Measurements of *positive changes in an individual* child were:

1. *Increased learning:* (a) increased attendance at school; (b) passed the proficiency test; (c) improved grades; (d) progressed along normal developmental milestones.

2. *Positive social interaction:* (a) positive peer interaction; (b) positive child-adult interactions; (c) not being suspended for conduct.

3. *Positive emotional development:* (a) self-reported or observed positive self-esteem; (b) referred for emotional health services; (c) desired emotional changes in the child; (d) progress toward child service goals.

4. *Other problem-specific changes in child:* (a) not becoming pregnant; (b) not using substances or alcohol.

---

open-ended interviews with consumers, direct-care staff, administrative staff, principals, and other community service providers at each of the thirty-eight sites. In figure 3.12 a written description of each of the desired results is provided.

Before using multiple systems measurements, a participating agency needs to take the following four steps:

1. Agree on the *logical connection* between changes at each level. In figures 3.11 and 3.12, some programs targeted community change first, theorizing that positive changes in the community and agencies were related to positive changes in families and children, whereas some stakeholders assumed programs would target child and family change first.

2. Clarify the following terms: *results, process,* and *outcomes.* Results are changes to participants that can be attributed to the intervention. Results can be outcomes (e.g., an increase in referrals) or processes (e.g., interagency collaboration). Some stakeholders may have different definitions of these terms. Some stakeholders may define agency results (e.g., the provision of day care) as processes only, whereas others may conceptualize agency changes as outcomes.

3. Agree on the *methods* for measuring the agreed-on results, for example, through observation, surveys, or secondary documents (e.g., agency records or county abuse and neglect reports). Methods for collecting information are discussed in chapter 5.

4. Remember that this chapter is all about *values.* Stakeholders may prefer targeting different systems than the funding source. Persons need to be able to justify those preferences.

MAJOR POINTS

Evaluation values reflect personal, agency, and community values. Evaluation stakeholders follow professional ethics such as the NASW Code of Ethics and professional standards such as the AEA Guiding Principles for Evaluators. Actual activities and stakeholder behaviors can be clarified to demonstrate that agreed-on values are followed in an evaluation.

Examples and tips were given for adhering to the SCREAM values described in this chapter: measure *strengths,* respect *culture,* conduct eval-

Figure 3.13. Evaluation decisionmaking tip: Reaching agreement on activities related to evaluation values.

Check all items that apply to a current evaluation at your agency or practicum setting.

These values and ethics will be followed for this evaluation:

_____ Ensure written informed consent of all participants.

_____ Ensure confidentiality of all participants.

_____ Ensure anonymity of all participants.

_____ Ensure that no physical harm will occur to any participant.

_____ Ensure that no emotional harm will occur to any participant.

_____ Ensure that all participation is voluntary.

_____ Ensure that a participant is not denied services because of his/her participation or lack of participation in the evaluation.

_____ Ensure that the results of the evaluation will be made available to all participants.

_____ Ensure involvement from persons of all cultural backgrounds in the design, implementation, and participation in the evaluation.

_____ Ensure involvement from all stakeholders in the design and implementation of the evaluation.

_____ Ensure that the results of the evaluation will be made available to all stakeholders of the evaluation.

_____ Assure the participants and stakeholders that the results will be accurate.

_____ The evaluation will be evaluated by another person/other persons.

_____ Allow the participants to give feedback about the interpretation of their data.

_____ Allow the stakeholders to give feedback about the interpretation of the evaluation data.

_____ Allow the participants to help write the evaluation report.

_____ Allow the stakeholders to help write the evaluation report.

_____ Decide not to conduct the evaluation if a stakeholder deems the evaluation question and/or purpose unethical.

_____ Decide not to conduct the evaluation if the stakeholders will not supply in writing a statement of how the evaluation will be utilized.

_____ Decide not to conduct the evaluation if it is not feasible to answer the evaluation questions using the allotted resources.

_____ Decide not to conduct the evaluation if there is no agreement among stakeholders on the evaluation question or purpose.

_____ Apply the following ethical guideline(s) not listed above:

_____

_____

_____

uations within the capacity of your *resources,* follow professional codes of *ethics,* reach a written *agreement* about evaluation decisions with evaluation stakeholders, and measure changes across *multiple* systems. For a list of possible evaluation values to discuss with stakeholders, see figure 3.13.

FURTHER READINGS
Strengths-Based Evaluation

Asset-Based Community Development Institute (ABCD), Institute for Policy Research, Northwestern University. Web site: www.northwestern.edu/ipr/abcd. ABCD is directed by John McKnight and John Kretzmann. It offers literature review and workbooks to help organizations develop assets mapping and assess economic capacities.

Family Support America (FSA), Chicago. Web site: www.familysupportamerica.org. FSA provides journals, newsletters, evaluation tools, and published research on family support interventions. It emphasizes the collaborative efforts of families and social services to increase family functioning.

Glicken, M. (2004). *Using the strengths perspective in social work practice.* Boston: Allyn & Bacon.

Kretzmann, J., & McKnight, J. (1993). *Building communities from the inside out: A path toward finding and mobilizing a community's assets.* Evanston, IL: Asset-Based Community Development Institute, Northwestern University.

McKnight, J., & Kretzmann, J. (1997). Mapping community capacity. In M. Minkler (Ed.), *Community organizing and community building for health* (pp. 157–72). New Brunswick, NJ: Rutgers University Press.

Search Institute (SI), Minneapolis. Web site: http://www.search-institute.org. Directed by Dr. Peter Benson, this organization has developed a tool to measure forty developmental assets divided into two categories: (1) internal assets (support, empowerment, boundaries and expectations, and constructive use of time) and (2) external assets (commitment to learning, positive values, social competencies, and positive identity). The assessment tools can be used with youth and adults as well as with entire communities.

Culturally Competent Evaluations

Affilia. Journal.

African American Research Perspectives. Journal.

Figueira-McDonough, J., Netting, F., & Nichols-Casebolt, A. (Eds.). (1998). *The role of gender in practice knowledge: Claiming half the human experience.* New York: Garland.

Fong, R., & Furuto, S. (Eds.). (2001). *Culturally competent practice: Skills, interventions, and evaluations.* Boston: Allyn & Bacon.

Grinnell, R. (1997). *Social work research and evaluation: Quantitative and qualitative approaches* (5th ed.). Itasca, IL: F. E. Peacock. See esp. the appendix, "Cultural Factors Related to Research" (pp. 605–630).

Guzman, B. (2003). Examining the role of cultural competency in program evaluation: Visions for new millennium evaluators. In S. Donaldson & M. Scriven (Eds.), *Evaluating social programs and problems: Visions for the new millennium* (pp. 167–181). Mahwah, NJ: Erlbaum.

Hernandez, M., & Isaacs, M. (Eds.). (1998). *Promoting cultural competence in children's mental health services.* Baltimore: Paul H. Brookes.

Hood, S. (1999). Assessment in the context of culture and pedagogy: A collaborative effort, a meaningful goal: Introduction and overview. *Journal of Negro Education, 67*(3), 184–186.

Hood, S. (2004). A journey to understand the role of culture in program evaluation: Snapshots and personal reflections of one African American evaluator. *New Directions for Evaluation, 102,* 21–38.

Lum, D. (2003). *Culturally competent practice: A framework for understanding diverse groups and justice issues* (2nd ed.). Pacific Grove, CA: Brooks/Cole.

Mertens, D. (2003). The inclusive view of evaluation: Visions for the new millennium. In S. Donaldson & M. Scriven (Eds.), *Evaluating social programs and problems: Visions for the new millennium* (pp. 91–108). Mahwah, NJ: Erlbaum.

Seigart, D., & Brisdara, S. (Eds.). (2002). *Feminist evaluation: Explorations and experiences* (New Directions for Evaluation, no. 96). New York: Jossey-Bass.

Thompson-Robinson, M., Hopson, R., & SenGupta, S. (Eds.). (2004). *In search of cultural competence: Toward principles and practices* (New Directions for Evaluation, no. 102). New York: Jossey-Bass.

Tripodi, T., & Potocky-Tripodi, M. (2003). Research on advancement and empowerment of women. *Journal of Social Work Research and Evaluation, 4*(1), 3. Part of a special issue devoted to research and the advancement of knowledge related to women.

Resources and Feasible Evaluations

Bamberger, M., Rugh, J., Church, M., & Fort, L. (2004). Shoestring evaluation: Designing impact evaluations under budget, time and data constraints. *American Journal of Evaluation, 25*(1), 5–37.

Robson, C. (2000). *Small-scale evaluation.* London: Sage.

Ethical Guidelines for Evaluation

Ginsberg, L. (2001). *Social work evaluation: Principles and methods.* Boston: Allyn & Bacon.

Patton, M. Q. (1997). *Utilization-focused evaluation: The new century text* (3rd ed.). Thousand Oaks, CA: Sage.

Posavac, E., & Carey, R. (2003). *Program evaluation: Methods and case studies* (6th ed.). Upper Saddle River, NJ: Prentice Hall.

Reamer, F. (1998). *Social work research and evaluation skills: A case-based, user-friendly approach.* New York: Columbia University Press.

Reamer, F. (2001). *The social work ethics audit: A risk management tool.* Washington, DC: NASW Press.

Royse, D., Thyer, B., Padgett, D., & Logan, T. (2001). *Program evaluation: An introduction* (3rd ed.). Belmont, CA: Brooks/Cole.

Unrau, Y., Gabor, P., & Grinnell, R. (2001). *Evaluation in the human services.* Belmont, CA: Brooks/Cole.

Weiss, C. (1998). *Evaluation: Methods for studying programs and policies* (2nd ed.). Upper Saddle River, NJ: Prentice Hall.

Multiple Systems Measurements

Annie E. Casey Foundation. Web site: http://www.aecf.org. See *Evaluating comprehensive community change* (1997), a report from the Annie E. Casey Foundation's March 1997 Research and Evaluation Conference.

Center for Community Change. Web site: www.communitychange.org.

Day, P., Robinson, S., & Sheikh, L. (1998). *Ours to keep: A guide for building a community assessment strategy for child protection.* Washington, DC: Child Welfare League of America.

National Congress for Community Economic Development. Web site: www.ncced.org.

Neighborhood Reinvestment Corp (Neighbor Works). Web site: www.nw.org/network/home.asp.

REFLECTIVE JOURNAL ACTIVITIES

1. Do you agree with the SCREAM values described in this chapter? Are there some of the SCREAM values that you feel are not necessary for every evaluation? Are there additional values that should be included in every evaluation?

2. Do you agree with the discussions of how to include the SCREAM values? Are there other ways you would incorporate some of these values into evaluation?

3. Do you agree that this chapter on values should be given the same weight as the later chapters on theory and data gathering?

PROCEDURAL JOURNAL ACTIVITIES

Answer the Evaluation Decisionmaking Model questions in figure 3.14 as they pertain to an evaluation in your agency or practicum setting.

Figure 3.14. Evaluation decisionmaking model: Evaluation values and ethical guidelines.

Check all items that pertain to a current evaluation at your agency or practicum setting.

The following values are expected by stakeholders (list as many as apply):

Value: _____

Requested or required by the following stakeholders: _____

Reinforcement for meeting the value: _____

Consequence for not meeting the value: _____

SCREAM values for this evaluation:

__ Strengths
Strengths of evaluation participants will be assessed in the following ways: _____

__ Culture
The culture of evaluation stakeholders and participants will be respected in the following ways: _____

__ Resources
The following resources are available for this evaluation (list as many as apply):

$____ from _____ with the following stipulations:

__ hours of consultation and training from _____ with the following stipulations:

__ Ethics
Voluntary, confidential, and nonharmful participation in the evaluation is ensured through the following procedures:

__ Agreement
The following persons agree to the conditions of this evaluation:

__ Multiple Systems Results
Desired results will be measured for:

The following individuals: _____

The following groups: _____

The following organizations: _____

The following communities: _____

CHAPTER 4

THEORY-DRIVEN EVALUATION DECISIONS

> Researchers complain that practitioners do not use the
> knowledge they generate, and practitioners complain that
> knowledge tastes like cardboard. Clearly, we need to
> better understand the process of knowledge utilization.
> (Marsh, 2003b, p. 293)

> Let us relegate theory to its proper role. It is neither
> essential nor necessarily desirable for research on social
> work practice to be theoretically driven. There are many
> negative consequences for our field's current insistence
> that dissertations be exercises in theory building. Rather
> than mandating that, by definition, a social work disserta-
> tion must be either theoretically based or contribute to
> theory, let us recognize the value of nontheoretical
> research contributions and not accord them secondary
> status. (Thyer, 2001b, p. 22)

The discussion in this chapter can help social service workers prioritize how
theory drives evaluation decisions. **Theory** in social services is a description or explanation of the relationship between an intervention or program
and desired results for clients, and can help workers answer the question,
"Why do you plan to use or why are you using that intervention?" frequently
asked by stakeholders.

The key stakeholders identified through the exercises in chapter 2
should be included when deciding the role that theory plays before, during,
and after the evaluation is conducted. Given the decisions agreed on in the
previous chapter, the application of some general theories, models, or perspectives may be expected by stakeholders throughout the entire evaluation. General theoretical models such as the strengths perspective, cultural
competency, and systems theory guide the evaluation team to include certain processes and outcomes in the evaluation, as described in chapter 3.
Specific theories that apply to the intervention or program being implemented or planned also influence evaluation decisions.

A literature review and a logic model are two tools that help social service workers connect theory to program planning, practice, and evaluation.
The literature review helps social service workers learn how other programs
similar to their own applied theory to practice. The logic model helps social

service stakeholders clarify their own program theory, which is the connection between the goals, the activities, and the desired results of their evaluated programs.

The *learning outcomes* for chapter 4 are as follows:

1. Understand how social service workers use theory.
2. Understand the complementary benefits of theory building and theory testing.
3. Understand the role of theory in the constant interchange between planning, practice, and evaluation.
4. Conduct a literature review using the procedures agreed on by key evaluation stakeholders.
5. Understand the role of theory for planning and implementing evidence-based practice.
6. Understand how theory is utilized differently in exploratory, descriptive, and explanatory evaluations and research reported in the literature.
7. Understand how qualitative and quantitative data-collection approaches are reported differently in the literature.
8. Reach stakeholder agreement on the sources of literature to review.
9. Reach stakeholder agreement on the key word search procedure and decisions for including and excluding literature located through the search.
10. Construct a logic model.
11. Understand the role of evidence-based theory in constructing a logic model.
12. Understand the role of a logic model in answering descriptive and explanatory evaluation questions.
13. Understand how qualitative and quantitative data-collection approaches are used to construct logic models.
14. Reach stakeholder agreement on how to construct the logic model for planning, practice, and evaluation purposes.

THEORY IN SOCIAL SERVICES

Theory connects research to practice, a connection that was described in chapter 1. Theories, as we have seen, help social service workers answer the question, "Why do you plan to use or why are you using that intervention?" The **literature review** is a summarization and analysis of other evaluations or research studies relevant to the current planning, implementation, or evaluation activities. It provides a partial answer to this "why" question by helping the social service worker learn from written accounts of successful interventions and be able to provide the answer: "Because findings in the literature support the relevance of this intervention with programs and clients similar to our setting." The **logic model** is a clarification of the connection between intervention or program goals, strategies, and desired results. It helps workers answer this "why" question by providing the answer: "Because this is the best intervention to meet our goals and desired results." Both tools will be described separately in this chapter.

The previous chapter focused on how values drive evaluation decisions. This chapter focuses on how theories drive evaluation decisions. The difference is that values are what persons prefer or believe should be present, whereas theories are what they think should be present. Value priorities help evaluation stakeholders resolve ethical dilemmas by guiding them in choosing among a range of preferred ways to interact with others. Theories help evaluation stakeholders resolve theoretical dilemmas by guiding them in choosing among a range of approaches that make sense for evaluation stakeholders.

Ethical decisions are supported by documenting that specified value preferences were honored. For example, one would demonstrate that participants' and stakeholders' rights were respected and persons not harmed by documenting compliance with the mandates of an institutional review board. Theoretical decisions are supported by documenting the theories that guided practice, planning, and evaluation decisions. For example, one would reference and describe the theories that were applied to answer the evaluation questions, guide the methods used to answer the questions, and interpret the findings.

Program planning, practice, and evaluation of necessity involve values and theories. Stakeholders external to the program (e.g., funding sources) may establish value preferences about the program in the request for proposals (RFP) and in the required annual and semiannual reports. For example, a funding source may require that an evaluation carry out the following two values with or without documentation that theoretically connects these activities to client change: (1) collaborate on evaluation planning and implementation with multiple program stakeholders (e.g., clients, direct-care staff, administrators, and community representatives); and (2) include measurements of client strengths in the evaluation.

It is important to acknowledge the opposing views concerning the place of theory in social services as captured in the epigraphs to this chapter. Patton (1997) argues that, in the past, too many evaluations have been conducted without the results having been utilized to improve social service interventions. He states that no evaluation should be initiated until it has been determined how the evaluation will be utilized by key stakeholders. A July 2002 issue of *Social Work* contains multiple examples of responses to Marsh's (2002) challenge to demonstrate the knowledge utility of social service research. There are other examples of social service workers utilizing evaluation and research results contained in the "Further Readings" section at the end of this chapter.

Theory can help social service workers solve client problems. Knowledge gained from evaluation is important, but helping clients achieve desired change is the priority. Social service workers apply theories every day. Not all social workers are in the habit of consciously questioning whether those theories reduce client concerns or improve desired client or program results. Just because a social service worker's applied theories do not appear in a journal does not mean that important knowledge was not gained from an intervention.

Theory can be used to promote the value of strengths. Instead of asking, "How can this intervention reduce negative outcomes?" practitioners can ask, "How can this intervention promote positive results?" Instead of asking, "What went wrong?" practitioners can ask, "What went right?" Social service workers are trained to be rational, logical, problem-solving professionals. To assume that theory is not part of social service intervention is to ignore and devalue the way social service workers make decisions.

Theory building is the process of exploring or describing what one learns while gathering information. **Theory testing** is the process of gathering information to describe or explain the relationship between interventions and client change. The discussion of qualitative and quantitative approaches to gathering information is very much connected to theory building and theory testing. Data-collection methods are the focus of discussion in chapter 5, but they are mentioned here because of the mutual interaction between theory and data collection, which will become obvious during the discussion of literature reviews and logic models.

For now, it is enough to know that a **qualitative approach** is an open-ended gathering of information to *build* theory to answer exploratory and descriptive evaluation questions and that a **quantitative approach** is a closed-ended gathering of information to *test* theory to answer descriptive and explanatory evaluation questions and statements. The relationship between theory, types of evaluation questions, and approaches to gathering information are illustrated in figure 4.1.

Figure 4.1. Evaluation decisionmaking tip: The relationship between theory, evaluation questions, and data collection.

Use this chart to match evaluation questions, data collection, and theory for an evaluation in your agency or practicum setting.

Type of Question	Data-Collection Approach	Role of Theory
Exploratory evaluation questions	Qualitative data collection	Theory building
Descriptive evaluation questions	Qualitative data collection and/or quantitative data collection	Theory building and/or theory testing
Explanatory evaluation questions	Quantitative data collection	Theory testing

Figure 4.2.   Evaluation decisionmaking tip: Plan, implement, evaluate, change cycle of evaluation.

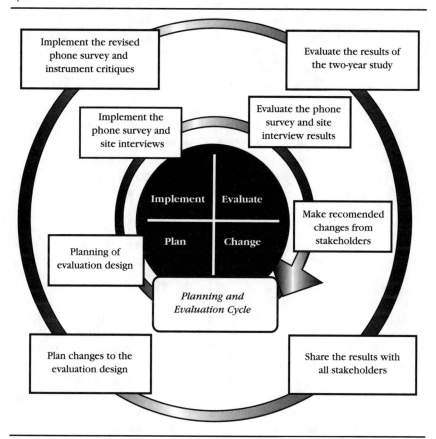

Even though I advocate that stakeholders agree on scope, values, theory, and data-collection methods—in that order—the mutual impact of each of the components discussed in separate chapters is constant. Figure 4.2 provides an illustration of how just one data-collection method employed in evaluation of family support interventions (FSIs) was in a constant cycle of planning, implementing, evaluating, and changing. The evaluators *planned* the telephone survey to answer the explanatory statement, "Consumers of FSIs will significantly improve family functioning." The evaluators then *implemented* the telephone survey. The evaluators and stakeholders agreed to *evaluate* the results of the telephone survey and make *changes* to the telephone survey on the basis of the findings. This planning, implementing, evaluating, and changing cycle was applied to all evaluation decisions.

LOCATING THEORY THROUGH LITERATURE REVIEWS

The main reason for completing a literature review is to learn from relevant evaluations and research conducted by others. The sources and methods for finding the right literature to review for a given evaluation are discussed a little later. First I will cover what to look for in the literature and how the literature can be helpful in making evaluation decisions.

Social service workers utilize the literature in the following ways:

Evidence-based theory and practice reported in the literature can help workers in the planning stage select interventions shown to be the most effective under rigorous data-collection designs.

Exploratory, descriptive, and explanatory evaluation and research reported in the literature can help social service workers make evaluation decisions appropriate to the questions they are posing in the current evaluation.

Qualitative and quantitative data-collection approaches reported in the literature can help social service workers learn the best data-collection methods to use in their current evaluation.

Additionally, social service workers can locate literature that reports statistical or case study evidence of problems or issues that require social service intervention (e.g., the incidence of family violence reported in a given region or nationwide). They can locate articles offering critiques of the literature. And they can locate editorials discussing experience, conceptual applications, or other criteria.

It is no wonder, then, that students and social service workers alike go in different directions in their evaluation decisionmaking, depending on what they read before, during, and after the evaluation. Some literature will lead workers to certain data-collection decisions. Some literature will lead them to reconceptualize the problem or intervention. Findings can, of course, be contradictory, depending on the problems addressed, the interventions attempted, the data-collection methods employed, and the results obtained.

Even if specific findings are not adopted, the literature review will still have affected the evaluation decisionmaking process. Social service workers are expected to be critical readers of reported evaluation and research; this is clearly stated in the Code of Ethics of the National Association of Social Workers (NASW) and the Educational Policy Accreditation Standards of the Council on Social Work Education (CSWE). Critical social service workers are those who question the place of information in the decisionmaking process and are able to recognize what among the literature will be useful to that process.

A brief discussion will now focus on evidence-based practice and how theory is utilized at different stages to answer exploratory, descriptive, and explanatory questions. References will be made to qualitative and quantitative data-collection approaches, methods that will be discussed in more detail in the next chapter.

Evidence-Based Practice.   The term *evidence based* must be clarified for every evaluation, just as the reader was encouraged to clarify these other terms already covered in previous chapters: *evaluation; stakeholders; strengths; culture; ethical guidelines;* and *multiples systems levels. Evidence-based theory* and *evidence-based practice* are terms that are appearing in many RFPs, sometimes without any clear indication of how they are being applied in a given situation.

Evidence-based practice in social work has been advocated for a long time, especially in the writings of Gambrill and Gibbs (e.g., Gambrill, 1997, 1999, 2003; Gibbs, 1990, 2003; Gibbs & Gambrill, 1999, 2002). It is not my intent to summarize the sources that already exist on evidence-based practice. Interested readers can consult the "Further Readings" section of this chapter. Take the time to read the original source thoroughly if you are going to follow a specific author's application of evidence-based practice. Also, take the time to have stakeholders agree on the terms taken or adapted from the literature on this subject.

Evidence-based practice is the intervention that has, on the basis of the most rigorous data collection feasible, been demonstrated to be effective in the practice setting. Evidence-based literature should be consulted in the planning stage to guide the selection of intervention type. Even if an intervention has already been implemented, the literature can be utilized to help workers adapt or change the intervention.

Stakeholders may direct workers to consult specific sources for evidence-based theory and practice. One source mentioned later in this chapter is the Campbell Collaborative, a literature database sponsored by the University of Pennsylvania. This database currently contains only reports of evaluations and research that were conducted using experimental or quasi-experimental data-collection methods and may contain qualitative data collection in future reviews. The reports are categorized by problem focus. The criteria for inclusion in the database are given on the Web site.

In all evaluations, decisions are based on some type of evidence, whether it be evidence reported in the literature or evidence gained during the course of conducting the current evaluation. Stakeholders should agree on what evidence is acceptable. Discuss the following issues:

What are acceptable sources for locating literature as evidence?

Must the evidence reported in the literature have been collected through specific data-collection methods? Will stakeholders accept evidence collected through qualitative approaches or quasi-experimental designs?

What is unacceptable evidence? What are the guidelines for choosing or rejecting literature that is located through a search process?

Literature and Exploratory, Descriptive, and Explanatory Evaluation Questions. Students and social service workers consulting the literature at the beginning of a project are most likely reading reports of work that has taken years to complete. They must, therefore, be careful to remember that, while they themselves are still wrestling with formulating the scope of their evaluation and making complicated decisions with regard to theory and data collection, the authors to whom they are turning for guidance have that all behind them. Published reports reflect, not the early stages of negotiating with stakeholders, but the final stage, that at which negotiations have been concluded and the project itself completed.

Most published reports contain references to the literature the author consulted, reinforcing the point that social service workers and researchers are constantly testing past theories and building new ones. Get in the habit of understanding how the author of an article utilized past literature to guide the evaluation decisions and the inferences reported in the article. Authors sometimes discuss utilizing the literature differently depending on whether their reported evaluation or research was conducted to answer exploratory, descriptive, or explanatory questions.

Stakeholders ask *exploratory* questions when they want to know the experiences of persons connected to the social service system or when there is little published knowledge about a specific situation, setting, or stakeholder group. While those asking exploratory evaluation questions have usually formulated a working theory, they remain open to new theories encountered during the evaluation process, placing no limits on the scope of responses.

There are times in the program planning stage when agencies are able to build theory and develop innovative programs based on exploratory evaluation questions. Examples of exploratory questions listed in chapter 1 were the following:

What is it like to have worked in child welfare for over ten years? (Brode, 1990)

What happens after families leave a homeless shelter? (Tingler, 2000)

How do parents predicted to be at risk for child abuse and neglect successfully raise their children? (Brun, 1993, 1997)

Tingler's exploratory question was, "What happens after families leave a homeless shelter?" An undergraduate social work intern posed this study question because there was a perception among agency staff that, once families left a homeless shelter, they were stable. Through open-ended interviews with five families one and two months after they left a shelter, the student learned the following:

Families did not always secure housing.

Many of the families had positive outlooks in spite of having no housing.

An important source of support was family and friends.

Support from social service programs was not always available to prevent the family from reentering a shelter at a later date.

The study led to recommendations that guided the shelter's new proposal to offer follow-up services to clients leaving the shelter, a service not previously provided (Tingler, 2000).

Brun's exploratory question was, "How do parents predicted to be at risk for child abuse and neglect successfully raise their children?" The agency logic model was the following: The strategy of providing in-home outreach interventions will result in a decrease in the incidence of child abuse and neglect. When conducting the open-ended, qualitative interviews, the student researcher never heard participants use the words *abuse, neglect,* or *at risk.* Instead, the six participants, all women, described the strengths they called on within themselves, their friends, and their formal supports to help them raise their children. Throughout the study, the researcher consulted literature that supported the effectiveness of the strengths described by parents. Figure 4.3 shows the Interactive Model of Coping with Life's Demands that emerged from the parent stories and the literature. This model has been used to train social workers to support family strengths when providing in-home services (Brun, 1993, 1997).

Stakeholders ask *descriptive* questions when they are planning or implementing interventions based on some preconceived theoretical relationship between the intervention and desired changes in the targeted clients. Those asking descriptive evaluation questions limit the scope of responses by focusing questions. Sometimes they follow open-ended, qualitative approaches and allow participants to answer in their own words, and sometimes they follow closed-ended, quantitative approaches and give participants specific responses from which to choose.

Be clear which approach is being used in the literature you review and how that approach applies to your current evaluation. The case example in figure 1.2 followed an open-ended, qualitative approach. The evaluators were open to the themes that emerged from the participants' responses. These themes were compared to the literature on similar interventions (Brun & Rapp, 2001). One case example in figure 1.5 (that of direct-care mental health workers' competencies) followed a closed-ended, quantitative approach. Participants' responses were compared to the literature base from which the survey was constructed (Clasen et al., 2003).

Figure 4.3.   Case example: Theory building from exploratory research question.

Interactive Model of Coping with Life's Demands: Common Themes in the Exploratory Study with Six Parents

Fighting Oppression/Facing Discrimination

Being the target for blame	The children's father
Balancing work, school, and child care	Being African American
Being on welfare	Being young
Choice about pregnancy	Strong women role models

Relying on Inner Drive	Meeting the Child's Needs
Spirituality	Child's behavior
Slogans for change	Special needs
Recovery	Protecting them
	Discipline
	It's different from abuse

Experiencing Feelings Associated with Being a Parent	Sorting out Advice
Mixed feelings	Wanted advice
Depression	Unwanted advice
	Conflicting advice

Negotiating Resources

Supportive social agents
Social agents in the way

In both these examples, the literature was reported at the beginning of the final published articles and also in the "Findings" section. For other case examples of how the literature was utilized to guide planning, practice, and evaluation decisions to answer descriptive evaluation questions, see figure 4.4.

Stakeholders ask *explanatory* questions to determine whether an intervention produced the results predicted by theories systematically tested in previous evaluations or research. Persons testing explanatory hypotheses rely on specific, preconceived theories as those theories apply to the current situation. During the testing process, much attention is devoted to replicating or repeating the implementation and evaluation of the intervention as it was reported in the literature. In such evaluations, explanatory statements or hypotheses are used rather than evaluation questions. In the case example given in figure 1.3, a hypothesis tested was, "Consumers of the FSIs will significantly improve family functioning."

Figure 4.4.   Case examples: Utilizing literature to answer descriptive evaluation or research questions.

One descriptive question in the evaluation of family support interventions was, "How do different stakeholders [at each of the thirty-eight local sites] perceive success of the programs?" (see fig. 1.3). A position paper by Kagan (1995) was included in the original evaluation request for proposal. The paper conceptualized that results for school readiness interventions could be targeted for changes in children, families, agencies, or communities. The evaluators used this multiple systems conceptual model to categorize the narrative results from the site visits. This model was presented earlier in figures 3.12 and 3.13.

The descriptive question in the United Way planning evaluation of prior community reports was, "What are the targeted populations and interventions described in the four analyzed studies?" (see fig. 1.5). A position paper published by United Way (1998) was used by the evaluators to code the content in the analyzed studies according to the categories *vision, impact, or geographic targets; strategies;* and *outcomes.*

The descriptive question in the teenage pregnancy prevention planning evaluation was, "What are the best interventions for preventing teenage pregnancy?" The evaluator conducted a search of effective interventions on the topic and presented those results to the stakeholders. One of the products of that evaluation was a folder containing the original articles consulted and the evaluator's summary of the findings. As the evaluator reported in a published article, the stakeholders made the final decision of how this literature base was utilized (Brun & Giga, 1999).

Explanatory evaluations predict that certain relationships between the intervention and changes in the consumers will be found, whereas descriptive evaluations make no such predictions. Explanatory evaluation questions not only target certain program characteristics but also pose answers to the question, "Why did the intervention produce the expected changes?" In the example given above, methods can be employed to further assess how separate components of the FSIs improved family functioning. Examples of intervention components were assessment, treatment planning, referral, and goal setting.

In the evaluation of FSIs, the literature review guided the following responses to explanatory questions:

The standardized instrument adapted and used to measure family functioning was called the Family Assessment Device (FAD) and was based on a substantial body of literature substantiating its validity and reliability (Epstein, Baldwin, & Bishop, 1982).

The results of the implementation of the FAD were compared to those of other studies and included in the final evaluation report (Brun et al., 1998).

The evaluators also conducted separate literature reviews to report the validity and reliability of instruments that measured child health, other measures of family functioning, and parent involvement with children's school performance.

The discussion now switches to the "how to" part of locating the literature. Consider the issues raised in this chapter so far that will guide where and how you select literature to guide your evaluation decisions.

Sources for Literature Reviews.   For a list of sources for evaluations and research studies pertinent to your current evaluation, see figure 4.5. A university library Web site is a valuable resource, allowing you to access most of the sources listed in figure 4.5. Many of the sources can be obtained electronically, which means that at least the initial search for relevant studies can be conducted from your home or office. Eventually, you may find some sources that you need that are available only in print. Universities pay a fee to obtain the rights to the electronic sources. For this reason, some university electronic resources may be available only to current students and

Figure 4.5.   Evaluation decisionmaking tip: Sources for a literature review.

Check all sources used to conduct a literature search for a current evaluation at your agency or practicum setting.

_____ university library services
_____ university research services
_____ abstract databases
_____ academic journals
_____ reference lists appearing at the ends of published articles
_____ national government offices
_____ state and local government offices
_____ Campbell Collaborative for Evidence-Based Research
_____ Internet search engines
_____ organization Web sites
_____ requests for proposals
_____ funders' Web sites
_____ books
_____ conference papers
_____ conference proceedings
_____ statistical databases
_____ popular press and media
_____ local and federal policies and legislation

faculty. Access to literature resources is, thus, an important benefit of university-agency evaluation partnerships.

A common way to locate evaluations and research studies is by conducting a key word search using an abstract database. An abstract database is a compilation of brief summaries, called *abstracts,* of published scholarship. The abstracts describe articles that appeared in academic sources (usually peer-reviewed journals), dissertations, and books. A peer-reviewed research article is one approved for publication by two or more researchers.

Each database lists the journals from which the abstracts were taken and the time period during which the journals were published. Since persons from different professions work collaboratively and across disciplines, it is best to use more than one database to conduct a key word search. Some common academic databases used for social service evaluations are listed below:

ERIC, which contains published and unpublished papers, microfiche, and presentations related to education

Lexis/Nexis Academic Universe, which contains state and federal legislation and analysis of legislation

PsycINFO, which contains abstracts of research studies found in psychology

Social Science Index, which contains abstracts of research studies found in sociology and social work

Social Work Abstracts, which contains abstracts of research studies found in social work

MEDLINE, which contains abstracts of research studies found in health and medicine.

Depending on the abstract database, the indexed scholarship will usually include results from exploratory, descriptive, and explanatory evaluations and research. It can also include editorials, descriptions of interventions, policy analyses, and case studies. Some databases include unpublished or non-peer-reviewed papers. Some include media and popular press sources. Clarify with all stakeholders which databases are acceptable.

Evaluation and research literature can also be located through the Internet. Some of the evaluation resources listed at the end of chapter 2 are private and public evaluation groups that include research and evaluation studies, both published and unpublished. There are several different search engines available with which to locate other sites not listed in this book that may relate to your evaluation. Popular search engines include Google, Yahoo!, and Lycos. The main limitation to literature located on the Internet is that the studies and results may not have gone through a peer review process. Again, be clear with stakeholders about the criteria for including or excluding literature located through the Internet.

Method for Conducting the Literature Review. A **key word search** is the process of locating abstracts by using the search function of an abstract database, online library book catalog, or other computerized system in which published scholarship has been compiled and categorized. The search function in most academic databases is conducted by author, title, key word, or subject. If you know the exact title of an article, then the search function will locate the abstract and publication information. The article itself may be available online through one of several, usually subscription, services. If it is not, or if you do not have access to the service carrying it, you will then need to locate it at a university library or obtain it through the publisher.

If you know the author of a published work related to your evaluation, the search function will locate all persons with that name, which should allow you to locate the correct author and article. The advantage to the author search is that you are likely to discover other, possibly more recent articles by that author that are related to your topic. An author search is much more easily conducted through an academic database than through an Internet database. An author search on the Internet will result in literally hundreds, if not thousands, few of which are likely to be related to your focus.

The most patience and time is required when conducting a key word or subject search. Enter the words into the search field that you think best describe the focus of your evaluation. The search function will look for the key words anywhere in the abstract, including the article title. In the evaluation of the family violence prevention planning grant, there were several different subcategories of family violence. The key words used in conducting a literature search were *family violence, domestic or partner violence, elder abuse, child abuse or neglect, rape or date rape,* and *dating violence.*

These key words were also matched with the key word *prevention.* Using the word *and* in a key word search results in abstracts that contain both sets of key words, for example, both *family violence* and *prevention.* There may be 1,000 references to family violence and 3,000 references to prevention but only 100 references that contain both sets of words. The word *or* in a key word search results in abstracts that contain either set of key words, for example, either *child abuse* or *neglect.* There may be 5,000 abstracts on child abuse and 3,000 abstracts on child neglect, resulting in 8,000 abstracts that contain either set of words.

The *or* command allows you to expand the number of possible articles, the *and* command to narrow the number. For the sake of feasibility, it is best to begin with a list of potential sources that is well under 100. Narrowing the search field to most recent years of publication will reduce the number. For other tips on conducting feasible literature searches, see the "Further Readings" section at the end of this chapter.

Figure 4.6 provides a description of the key word search conducted in the evaluation of Children's Health Insurance Program outreach programs. The example provides a nice connection to all the issues connected to conducting a literature review. Notice how the evaluators used as the criterion for including or excluding articles the goal of the literature review. They also stated why they used both academic and Internet search engines.

LOCATING THEORY THROUGH LOGIC MODELS

A logic model is an agency's clarification of the connection between intervention and program goals, strategies and expected results. It is a tool for developing program theory and adhering to that theory. Rodwell and Woody (1994) argued that an evaluation should not be conducted if it has no clearly stated purpose and no clearly stated program goals and objectives agreed on by key stakeholders. The latter point relates directly to the logic model. The assumption is that one cannot evaluate a program if there is not a clear plan for connecting the program to desired change. There is too much room for disagreement over the interpretation of the evaluation if stakeholders are not clear about the intended impact of the evaluation. On the other hand, Scriven (1991) claimed that a logic model is not necessary in evaluations, arguing that whether an agency connected interventions to goals is not as important as whether expected results were met.

As in every evaluation decision so far, clarify whether a logic model is necessary. If so, these questions then need to be answered:

1. Why is this logic model being constructed?
   a. To *explore* the need for an intervention?
   b. To *describe* an intervention?
   c. To *explain* an intervention's impact?
2. Is the logic model based on evidence-based theory reported in the literature?
3. Is the logic model based on stakeholders' perception of the relationship between the intervention and client change, even if these perceptions are not grounded in credible research?
4. What is the purpose for the logic model? How will it guide planning, practice, and evaluation decisions?
5. What are the actual components of a logic model? That is, what should a logic model look like?

There is much variation in the literature and in practice to help social service workers answer these questions. The previous discussion on locating theory through literature reviews relates directly to answering the first two. Donaldson has written about the utilization of evidence-base literature

Figure 4.6.   Case example: Conducting a literature and Web site review.

This example relates to the evaluation of statewide outreach efforts to enroll eligible children in the Children's Health Insurance Program (CHIP). One of the products agreed to by stakeholders was a literature and Web site review. The procedures described here are excerpts from the final grant report (Meyer, Yung, Ranbom, Cauley, Brun, Fuller, Clasen, & Mase, 2001, pp. 6–9):

The goal of the literature review was to investigate the results from empirical evaluations of outreach interventions that have proven to be effective or ineffective in increasing child enrollment into public insurance programs.

Sources and Methods for Key Word Search

The databases for the electronic search were: MEDLINE, HealthStar, Cumulative Index to Nursing and Allied Health Literature (CINAHL), LEXIS/NEXIS Academic Universe, and PsychINFO. The search terms combined "Medicaid" and "CHIP" with "outreach," "evaluation of research," and "enrollment." This search yielded more than fifty citations, the majority of which were not relevant to the narrow focus of the research. . . . Only three of the articles met the criteria of studies that had examined the impact of outreach strategies on child health insurance enrollment.

The Internet proved to be a much richer source of research data on this topic. Internet searches were performed to locate reports that had not yet been published in journals or books. Using similar terms as in the traditional literature review, we used major search engines including HotBot, AltaVista, Yahoo!, Google, Lycos, and Excite. We also visited government Web sites, including the Centers for Disease Control, state CHIP sites, the Health Care Financing Administration, the Health Resources and Services Administration, and the U.S. General Accounting Office. We also included in the search academic and private health policy and research centers, foundation Web sites, professional associations, state associations, and child advocacy organizations. Links to other resources were followed at all sites and proved to be a valuable source of downloadable research materials.

Using this method, an additional seventy-five documents were located. Of these, forty are included in the final bibliography. A slight majority of the studies reviewed came from academic or private research centers (twelve), followed by government agencies (ten), foundation-sponsored studies (ten), child advocacy organizations (six), and professional or state associations (two).

Types of Evaluations Included: Exploratory, Descriptive, or Explanatory

The authors excluded from the final bibliography those articles that had an overly broad focus on the topic or had general conceptual suggestions without some base of related research. In Internet publications we excluded articles that did not appear to come from a credible source. The bibliography did contain some studies that conveyed focus groups and structured interviews. Because outreach to engage populations not traditionally targeted is at such an early stage, it seemed important to include some of this qualitative research as a base for identifying hypotheses to be tested by outreach programs.

Utilization of Final Literature Review Report

As mentioned earlier, the evaluators found the Internet to be a valuable resource for results and implications from credible evaluation and result studies. So much so that they wrote a Web site resource guide as part of the final bibliography. The guide begins with the top five Web sites, selected on the basis of the credibility of the sponsor, the relevance of the site's information on Medicaid and CHIP outreach, ease of use, comprehensiveness, currency, and value of links to other sites. Thirty-two other sites from the sources listed above were also listed. For each listing we provide information on the sponsor, the Web address, the specific topic addressed at the site, a site overview, and a section describing application to Medicaid outreach.

---

and stakeholders' perceptions of program theory to construct logic models, which he states is necessary for conducting credible evaluations (see Donaldson & Gooler, 2002; Fitzpatrick, 2002; Donaldson, 2003). Fetterman (2001) combines worker perceptions and evidence-based literature to construct logic models for the purpose of evaluating the intervention and equally important, to help the stakeholders be empowered as active participants in the planning and information-gathering stages of the evaluation. For more references on the purpose and process of constructing logic models, see the "Further Readings" section at the end of this chapter.

Constructing a Logic Model.   There are four basic components to a logic model: (1) goals; (2) strategies; (3) short-term results; and (4) long-term results. Some stakeholders add a component called *inputs* that precedes the goals component. **Inputs** are the sources determining the logic model (e.g., needs assessment conducted with consumers and social service workers). The rationale behind the inclusion of an input component is demonstrating how the logic model was developed. In many cases, an entire report is necessary to document the process for determining the logic model.

Goals are general, abstract statements about the desired processes, outcomes, or results of an intervention or program. Three to five goals are usually preferred. Examples of goal statements for *planning* purposes are:

1. Develop a countywide family violence prevention plan.
2. Develop a five-year plan for funding priorities.
3. Develop a teenage pregnancy prevention curriculum.

Examples of goal statements for *practice* purposes are:

1. Decrease family violence throughout the county.
2. Improve school performance.
3. Decrease the number of teenage pregnancies.

Examples of goal statements for *evaluations* are:

1. Include multiple stakeholder groups in the evaluation planning.

2. Implement a standardized measure of family functioning.

3. Include qualitative and quantitative data collection of family functioning.

Goals describe the underlying purpose, values, or theory of an intervention. Some persons may use the term *mission* or *vision,* although intervention goals are most often a subset of a larger mission or vision statement. Some persons use the term *objectives.* Objectives are usually a subset of goals and are written in measurable terms. An example of a measurable objective is: "There will be a 2% decrease in the number of teenage pregnancies recorded at South Hospital." Goals are deliberately abstract to allow for different means of reaching the same results.

The key question to ask of goal statements is, "Are these the goals that are agreed on by the key stakeholders?" If you have the wrong goal statement, you will then have the wrong strategies and results. The correct goal statements are usually taken from the RFP or the final grant contract. If your goals differ from those outlined in those documents, add a written addendum signed by all stakeholders that the change in goals was approved.

Strategies are the actual interventions employed to reach the stated goals. As with goals, with strategies it is best to limit the number employed. Two strategies are usually optimal. Examples of strategies for each of the three previously stated goals for *planning* purposes are:

Goal 1. Develop a countywide family violence prevention plan.

Strategy 1. Conduct focus groups with workers from agencies throughout the county that provide services to prevent family violence.

Strategy 2. Analyze all domestic violence reports recorded over the year by police and sheriff's departments in the county.

Goal 2. Develop a five-year plan for funding priorities.

Strategy 1. Analyze the results of four needs assessments conducted in the county by different organizations over the last two years.

Strategy 2. Conduct a focus group with United Way board members asking about their targeted priority areas.

Goal 3. Develop a teenage pregnancy prevention plan.

Strategy 1. Consult the research literature to learn of the interventions that have been proven effective in reducing teenage pregnancy.

Strategy 2. Survey selected teens on their ideas for reducing pregnancy.

Examples of strategies for each of the three previously stated goals for *practice* purposes are:

Goal 1. Decrease family violence throughout the county.

Strategy 1. Implement a computerized management information system that records domestic violence reports across multiple agencies to improve the tracking of perpetrators.

Strategy 2. Provide dating violence prevention education in grades 8–12.

Goal 2. Improve school performance.

Strategy 1. Provide tutoring services to all youth attending schools that report proficiency rates below the expected norm.

Strategy 2. Provide assessment and referral services to health and mental health service providers to all youth attending schools that report proficiency rates below the expected norm.

Goal 3. Decrease the number of teenage pregnancies.

Strategy 1. Provide pregnancy prevention education during health education classes in grades 8–12.

Strategy 2. Provide pregnancy prevention education to families attending special workshops.

Examples of strategies for each of the previously stated goals for *evaluation* purposes are:

Goal 1. Include multiple stakeholder groups in the evaluation planning.

Strategy 1. Form an evaluation stakeholder advisory group.

Strategy 2. Submit six-month evaluation progress reports for this group's approval.

Goal 2. Implement a standardized measure of family functioning.

Strategy 1. Consult all literature that has tested the implementation of standardized measures of family functioning.

Strategy 2. Pilot-test the selected family functioning measure with members of the stakeholder advisory group.

Goal 3. Include qualitative and quantitative data collection of family functioning.

Strategy 1. Conduct qualitative, open-ended focus groups with clients, agency staff, and community representatives about their views on the best ways to improve family functioning.

Strategy 2. Conduct quantitative, standardized telephone surveys with client families measuring their level of family functioning.

Strategies are sometimes called *interventions, treatments, activities,* or *programs.* As long as all stakeholders agree, alternative terms can be used.

A more important issue is how specific the strategy needs to be. Examples of vague strategy statements are: "Conduct focus groups with key stake-holders"; "Coordinate countywide agencies"; "Collect qualitative and quantitative data." Sometimes it is not possible to be more specific, such as when writing the original RFP or when information with which to narrow the strategies is not yet available. Make sure that, as the strategy becomes fine-tuned, all stakeholders agree on the final strategy.

The key question to ask about a strategy listed in a logic model is, "Is it logically connected to the goals?" For example, if the goal is, "Develop a countywide family violence prevention plan," then the strategies must be re-lated to family violence prevention. This may seem simple enough, but it really is not. The place to start is to define the terms in the goal statement. For example, how is *prevention* defined? If *prevention* is defined as deliver-ing services to all members of a community who have not been victims of family violence, then a shelter for victims of family violence would not be part of that plan.

Results are the desired changes related to specific strategies. The term *results* is used to conceptualize change as being both processes and out-comes. Processes are how people do things, for example, "Changing the ways social service workers communicate with consumers of services." Out-comes are what people do differently after receiving an intervention, for ex-ample, "Stop using alcohol and illegal substances." Some stakeholders may specify that persons list only outcomes and that the outcomes be measur-able behaviors of the targeted group. The term *results* allows the evaluation question to shape whether processes, outcomes, or both are measured.

Another term that needs clarification is *desired changes*. In the planning stage, results are listed as the changes that stakeholders expect to occur. Since the intervention has not yet occurred, the changes have not yet oc-curred. During the implementation stage, these "desired" results are ex-pected to become "actual" results. Some stakeholders require that the results be written in very specific terms: "Fifty-five percent of the young people par-ticipating in the program will report increased assets"; "The reports of child abuse and neglect will be reduced by 5% at the end of the five-year period." Result statements hold great weight because continuation of the interven-tion and evaluation can hinge on whether the stated results are met. It is im-portant to clarify the consequences if the desired results are not met.

Another point about results is that there are often multiple systems at which change can be targeted and that stakeholders should agree on the sys-tems to be targeted. Kagan (1995), for example, argued that, depending on the evaluation question, school readiness results can be measured in several ways: in terms of changes in the child (e.g., child passes educational marker level); in terms of the family (e.g., parents help child with homework); in terms of the school (e.g., the school is more "parent friendly," providing transportation and inviting parents to participate in more school activities);

in terms of the community (e.g., older adults volunteer as tutors); and so on. In such situations, stakeholder agreement on the systems level that you plan to measure as results is essential.

Distinguish between short-term and long-term results. **Short-term results** are those desired changes predicted to occur immediately after the intervention has been implemented. Examples of short-term results for the *planning* strategies listed previously are:

> prioritization of five interventions for the final family violence prevention plan
>
> publication of domestic violence reports in the county
>
> prioritization of five target needs for future funding based on analysis of secondary documents
>
> prioritization of five target needs for future funding based on stakeholder focus groups
>
> list of evidence-based practices to prevent teenage pregnancy
>
> understanding of teens' knowledge and behaviors related to sexual practices and pregnancy prevention

Examples of short-term results for the *practice* strategies listed previously are:

> increase in arrests of multiple perpetrators of family violence
>
> decrease in the incidence of youth attending the education classes being victims of dating violence
>
> increase in academic performance among those students receiving tutoring
>
> increase in number of youth receiving needed health and mental health services
>
> decrease in teenage pregnancy among persons attending the classes
>
> decrease in pregnancy among teens attending the workshops

Examples of short-term results for the *evaluation* strategies listed previously are:

> agreement that the stakeholders need to advise the evaluation process
>
> advisory board approval of the evaluation activities
>
> standardized measure of family functioning selected
>
> application of a standardized measure of family functioning pilot-tested for its relevance and feasibility with the current project
>
> credible implementation of focus groups
>
> valid and reliable implementation of surveys

Short-term results are sometimes called program results because they are expected right after the program or intervention is delivered. The key question to ask of short-term results is, "Are they evidence that the goal has been achieved?" The simple fact that results have been achieved is not necessarily evidence that the goal itself has been achieved. Consider, for example, the goal statement, "Reduce family violence in the county." One strategy related to that goal may be, "Form a countywide coalition of social service agencies to coordinate efforts to prevent family violence." One short-term result of that strategy may be that the coalition is formed within a year of funding. But the fact that the coalition is in place is not evidence that family violence has been reduced; rather, it is simply evidence that the strategy has been implemented.

Long-term results are those desired changes predicted to occur after all strategies have been implemented. They demonstrate that the original goal has been reached. In most situations, it will take at least two years after the initial interventions are implemented for long-term results to become evident. Long-term results of program implementation are often called *impacts* or *indicators* because they are measurable evidence that the desired outcomes were reached. Examples of long-term results for the *planning* goals listed previously are:

> development and approval of family violence prevention plan
>
> development and approval of five-year priority target plan
>
> development and approval of teenage pregnancy prevention plan

Examples of long-term results for the *practice* goals listed previously are:

> decrease in the following reports of family violence: domestic violence arrests; child abuse and neglect cases founded; elder abuse cases founded
>
> increase in the following academic performance indicators: student attendance; pass rate of proficiency exams; graduation rate
>
> decrease in births reported for teens at the five county hospitals

Examples of long-term results for the *evaluation* goals listed previously are:

> stakeholder involvement in the evaluation plan
>
> valid and reliable implementation of standardized measure of family health
>
> credible implementation of qualitative and quantitative data collection

There are two key questions to ask of long-term results: (1) Are they connected to the overall goal? (2) Are all the strategies and short-term results logically connected to the long-term results? Long-term results statements are a good reality check for the scope of a given logic model. For example, if it does not seem feasible to reduce the county reporting rates of child abuse and neglect, then what part of the logic model needs to be restated?

Figure 4.7.   Evaluation decisionmaking tip: Political issues related to constructing logic models.

The handout reproduced below was distributed to the staff of the Office of Disability Services (ODS) at a public university. The staff were constructing a logic model of their programs as the first step toward identifying outcomes and ways to measure those outcomes.

I. Introductions

   Complete the following information:

   Person's name:

   Program name:

   The interventions I provide are:

   What I hope to achieve by these interventions are:

   The changes I'll see in the students based on my interventions are:

II. Evaluation

   Have I met my goals?

   How do I know?

   Student examples:

   Goal is to get _____ major; I will know when I am accepted into _____.

   Goal is to graduate; I will know when I receive my diploma.

III. Logic Model as a tool

   Statement of Goals, Means to Reach the Goals, Results

   Complete the information below:

   Program Name:

Goals	Strategies	Short-Term Results	Long-Term Results
1.			
2.			
3.			
4.			
5.			

Beginning ideas of how to measure the results:

IV. Key points to consider about choosing goals:

   1. Do you have the "right" general goals?
      Do the goals fit your job description? If not, are your goals still considered relevant by ODS? By Office of Student Affairs?

(figure continues)

2. Do your goals contain a measurable outcome? How will you know your goal was reached?

3. Do your goals have a specific time line?
Example: I will graduate in five years vs. I will graduate sometime.

V. Key points to choosing activities:

1. There should be a logical connection between goals and intervention.
Example: What would a person need to do to get accepted into a major? To graduate?

2. The logical connection between goals and activities needs to be "proven" by:

    a. the literature—research has been done to show that the activity is effective in reaching your stated goal;

    b. your own systematic assessment.

3. No longer acceptable answers to the question, "Why do you do _____?"

    a. "It's common sense," or, "It makes sense."

    b. "It's what I do best."

    c. "It's what we've always done."

4. A hard-to-swallow answer to the question, "Why do you do _____?"

    a. "Because _____ made me"
    Sometimes policies are made without having a clear conceptual connection between the program and desired results.
    Answer: Test the approach and report the results.

VI. Results

After I do _____, this is how the student is different. . . .
Have each person write these out.

VII. Key points when considering results

1. There should be a logical connection between goals, interventions, and results.

2. Acknowledge that more than one intervention and/or program is connected to the results. Most results are due to a collaborative effort!

3. Results can be divided into long-term and short-term.
Example: Long-term goal of getting accepted into a major may have the following short-term goals: learn the acceptance criteria; take required courses; fill out the application.
Allow enough time for long-term goals to feel the impact of your intervention. For example, if you implement a new program to improve graduation rates, allow three to five years to see a noticeable change.
Long-term results tend to be quantitative, measurable outcomes (e.g., number of majors or number of graduates).

Short-term results tend to be measures specific to the processes that led to the outcomes (e.g., improvement in grades after the intervention or improvement on a study skills survey).

4. Results can be processes or outcomes.

Examples of processes to get accepted into a major: successfully completed a course on choosing majors; attended informational meetings within a department; or completed a career inventory.

You must be able to "prove" the conceptual connection between the processes or short-term outcomes and the long-term outcomes.

5. Select reasonable long-term results.

"Unreachable" results will look like the interventions didn't work. "Too easy" results will look like the interventions were not necessary.

Result indicators become the benchmark by which your intervention is assessed.

VIII. The hard part is now done!

1. The logic model determines the method of assessment.
2. Take sufficient time to write a clear logic model.
3. Be visual—draw a causality chart. Use only pictures—no words.

Perhaps the results statement needs to be more realistic, for example, reducing incidences of child abuse only among families that received the specific intervention rather than using the county rate, which includes persons not receiving the intervention. Perhaps using child abuse reporting rates is not the best indicator that child abuse was reduced because there are incidences of child abuse that go unreported.

The relationship between the logic model and data collection will be discussed in more detail in the next chapter. Figure 4.7 offers a guide to help social service stakeholders address the political issues related to determining the goals, activities, and results of a logic model. Figure 4.8 offers a case example of a logic model of two programs in the office of disability services at a public university to develop an evaluation plan.

This discussion closes with the reminder that the construction of a logic model is of necessity influenced by the values guiding an evaluation. Here are questions to consider when constructing a planning, practice, or evaluation logic model that takes account of the SCREAM values discussed in chapter 3:

Do the goals, activities, and results include an increase or maintenance of stakeholder *strengths?*

Do the goals, activities, and results include recognition of the diverse *cultures* represented by the stakeholders?

Are the goals, activities, and results realistic for the *resources* that are available?

Figure 4.8.   Case example: Logic models.

Below are the logic models for two programs offered at a university office of disability services.

UNIVERSITY OFFICE OF DISABILITY SERVICES—PROGRAM: ADAPTIVE TECHNOLOGY

Goal	Strategies	Short-Term Results	Long-Term Result
Ensure computer labs are accessible to all disabled students	Purchase needed equipment Educate students about equipment	Improve labs Increase number of students using labs	In five years, 90% of disabled students will be using computer labs

Goal	Strategy	Short-Term Results	Long-Term Result
Disabled students will improve their computer skills	Train students to utilize technology	Increase the skill level of students using the labs	Over five years, 90% of disabled students using the labs will increase their skills

Goal	Strategies	Short-Term Results	Long-Term Results
Disabled students will generalize technology outside of campus	Help students buy equipment Train students in their residences	Increase the number of students with equipment in their residences Increase the skill level of those using equipment in their residences	Over five years, 50% of disabled students will have equipment in their residences and increase their skill level

UNIVERSITY OFFICE OF DISABILITY SERVICES—PROGRAM: ACADEMIC SUPPORT

Goal	Strategies	Short-Term Results	Long-Term Results
To ensure that students who are deaf or hard of hearing have access to the same spoken class material as hearing students	Sign-language interpreters, C-Print, real-time captioning, class notes	Accommodations available in every classroom situation	Students will have improved test scores and higher GPAs

Goal	Strategies	Short-Term Results	Long-Term Results
To ensure that visually impaired students have access to all required printed material for in-class and out-of-class work	Provide required text material in alternative formats Raised-line enhancements of maps, drawings, etc. or use of Talking Globe Reader/Writers in classes such as math, labs, etc. Copies of classmates' notes read or scanned	Students with visual impairments will have access to print material prior to each class	Students will have improved test scores and higher GPAs

Goal	Strategies	Short-Term Results	Long-Term Results
To ensure that students with learning disabilities have access to all academic accommodations and support for which they are eligible	Carefully review documentation and interview student to access extent of learning disability and accommodations needed Explain verbally and in writing how services are to be accessed Explain how students are required to notify instructors and keep in touch with instructors Remind students often in as many ways as possible what their responsibility is	Students with learning disabilities will know the services of the disability office Persons with learning disabilities will actively participate in class and all assignments, develop self advocacy skills, time management and organization skills	Students will have improved test scores and higher GPAs

(figure continues)

Goal	Strategies	Short-Term Results	Long-Term Results
To ensure students with physical disabilities can participate fully in the classroom experience	Books in alternative formats In-class reader/writers to assist with in-class assignments Out-of-class writers to assist with out-of-class assignments Arrangement of classroom furniture to accommodate wheelchairs	Improved attendance and participation in class Better preparedness for class Involvement in class projects and activities	Students will have improved test scores and higher GPAs

Beginning ideas of how to measure the results:
1. Check GPAs, retention, and graduation rates.
2. Measure *student satisfaction* with services.

Are the goals, activities, and results achievable within the boundaries of *ethical conduct* for evaluations?

Were the goals, activities, and results negotiated in such a manner that all stakeholders were in *agreement* about the final logic model?

Do the goals, activities, and results include changes at *multiple* systems levels?

MAJOR POINTS

Theory for evaluation purposes is not so much about building knowledge as it is about justifying the need for the intervention or making decisions about changing interventions. It is not uncommon to find the following questions in an RFP or in required reports for funders related to theory:

What is the program theory or theory of change?

What is the program logic model?

How is the intervention supported by evidence-based theory?

How is intervention based on best practices?

What are the expected outcomes of the program?

What all these questions have in common is that answering them requires connecting aspects of the program and changes in the targeted population. Literature reviews and logic models were the two tools discussed in this chapter to utilize in answering these questions. Both tools are utilized differently depending on whether the current evaluation is answering exploratory, descriptive, or explanatory questions.

This chapter discussed the general role of theory in social service evaluation and the specific ways in which literature reviews and logic models guide evaluation decisions. It also discussed in detail how to conduct literature reviews and how to construct logic models.

FURTHER READINGS

Evidence-Based Practice

Best Practices in Mental Health. Journal.

Briggs, H., & Rzepnicki, T. (Eds.). (2004). *Using evidence in social work practice: Behavioral perspectives*. Chicago: Lyceum Books.

Campbell Collaboration of University of Pennsylvania. Web site: www.campbell.gse .upcnn.edu. See Systematic reviews of social service research.

Corcoran, J. (2000). *Evidence-based social work practice with families: A lifespan approach*. New York: Springer.

Cournoyer, B. (2004). *The evidence-based social work skills book*. Boston: Allyn & Bacon.

Gambrill, E. (1997). *Social work practice: A critical thinkers' guide*. New York: Oxford University Press.

Gambrill, E. (1999). Evidence-based practice: An alternative to authority-based practice. *Families in Society: The Journal of Contemporary Human Services, 80,* 341–50.

Gibbs, L. (2003). *Evidence-based practice for the helping professions: A practical guide with integrated multimedia*. Pacific Grove, CA: Thomson Brooks/Cole.

Gibbs, L., & Gambrill, E. (1999). *Critical thinking for social workers: Exercises for the helping professions*. Thousand Oaks, CA: Sage.

Gibbs, L., & Gambrill, E. (2002). Evidence-based practice: Counter-arguments to objections. *Research on Social Work Practice, 12,* 452–76.

Gira, E., Kessler, M., & Poertner, J. (2004). Influencing social workers to use research evidence in practice: Lessons from medicine and the allied health professions. *Research on Social Work Practice, 14*(2), 68–79.

Macdonald, G. (2001). *Effective interventions for child abuse and neglect: An evidence-based approach to planning and evaluating interventions*. New York: Wiley.

Knowledge Utilization by Social Service Workers

Bronson, D. (2000). Progress and problems in social work research and evaluation in the United States. *Journal of Social Work Research and Evaluation, 1*(2), 125–37.

Henry, G., & Mark, M. (2003). Beyond use: Understanding evaluation's influence on attitudes and actions. *American Journal of Evaluation, 24*(3), 293–314.

Hess, P., & Mullen, E. (Eds.). (1995). *Practitioner-researcher partnerships: Building knowledge from, in, and for practice.* Washington, DC: NASW Press.

Kazi, M. (2002). Guest editorial: Evaluation for practice. *Journal of Social Work Research and Evaluation, 3*(2), 107–8. Part of a special issue on evaluation for practice.

Kirk, S. (Ed.). (1999). *Social work research methods: Building knowledge for practice.* Washington, DC: NASW Press.

Marsh, J. (2002). What knowledge is relevant to social work practice? The case of TANF reauthorization. *Social Work, 47*(3), 197–200.

Marsh, J. (2003). Chewing on cardboard and other pleasures of knowledge utilization. *Social Work, 48*(3), 293–94.

Marsh, J. (2004). Vanquish the backlog! And into the future—of social work. *Social Work, 49*(2), 149–50.

Patton, M.Q. (1997). *Utilization-focused evaluation: The new century text* (3rd ed.). Thousand Oaks, CA: Sage.

Potocky-Tripodi, M., & Tripodi, T. (Eds.). (1999). *New directions for social work practice research.* Washington, DC: NASW Press.

Smith, M. (1995). Utilization-focused evaluation of a family preservation program. *Families in Society, 76*(1), 11–19.

What is a useful evaluation [Special section]. *American Journal of Evaluation, 24*(4), 483–536.

Literature Reviews

Fortune, A., & Reid, W. (1999). *Research in social work* (3rd ed.). New York: Columbia University Press. (See esp. app. 1.)

Gibbs, L. (1990). Using online databases to guide research and practice. In R. Reinoehl & T. Hanna (Eds.), *Computer literacy in human services* (pp. 97–116). New York: Haworth.

Marlow, C. (2005). *Research methods for generalist social work* (4th ed.). Belmont, CA: Wadsworth/Thomson Learning. (See esp. app. A.)

Martinez, R., & Clark, C. (2001). *The social worker's guide to the Internet.* Boston: Allyn & Bacon.

Yegidis, B., & Weinbach, R. (2004). *Research methods for social workers* (5th ed.). Boston: Allyn & Bacon.

Logic Models

Donaldson, S., & Gooler, L. (2002). Theory-driven evaluation of the work and health initiative: A focus on winning new jobs. *American Journal of Evaluation, 23*(3), 341–46.

Donaldson, S. (2003). Theory-driven program evaluation in the new millennium. In S. Donaldson & M. Scriven (Eds.), *Evaluating social programs and problems: Visions for the new millennium* (pp. 109–41). Mahwah, NJ: Erlbaum.

Fetterman, D. (2001). *Foundations of empowerment evaluation.* Thousand Oaks, CA: Sage.

Patton, M. (1997). *Utilization-focused evaluation: The new century text* (3rd ed.). Thousand Oaks, CA: Sage. (See esp. chap. 10.)

Renger, R., & Titcomb, A. (2002). A three-step approach to teaching logic models. *American Journal of Evaluation, 23*(4), 493–503.

Wandersman, A. (2001). Program development, evaluation, and accountability. In L. Ginsberg (Ed.), *Social work evaluation: Principles and methods* (pp. 178–210). Boston: Allyn & Bacon.

W. K. Kellogg Foundation Web site: www.wkkf.org. See the following resources: *Evaluation in foundations: The unrealized potential* (1998); *W. K. Kellogg Foundation evaluation handbook* (1998); *Logic model development guide* (2001).

REFLECTIVE JOURNAL ACTIVITIES

1. Do you agree more with the quote from Marsh or Thyer that serves as an epigraph to this chapter? Why or why not? As social service worker or student, do you utilize theory in your daily interventions with clients? Why or why not?

2. What are your reactions to the discussion of literature reviews? Do you think literature reviews are necessary for planning, practice, and evaluation? Why or why not? Do the stakeholders of a current evaluation agree on the procedures for conducting a literature review? If no, why not?

3. What are your reactions to the discussion of logic models? Do you think logic models are necessary for planning, practice, and evaluation? Why or why not? Do the stakeholders of a current evaluation agree that a logic model is necessary? If no, why not?

4. Think of an evaluation where the program logic model is already determined. Which stakeholders most influenced the logic model? Is the logic model guiding decisions for planning, practice, evaluation, or a combination of all three? Are the goals of the logic model written as exploratory, descriptive, or explanatory statements? Do the activities and the measurement of results match the type of goal statement you specified?

5. What have been your experiences with constructing logic models? Have stakeholders struggled with agreement on what to include in them? Have stakeholders disagreed on how to select the specific goals, activities, and expected results?

PROCEDURAL JOURNAL ACTIVITY

1. Answer the Evaluation Decisionmaking Model questions in figure 4.9 related to the place of theory in a current evaluation.

Figure 4.9.   Evaluation decisionmaking model: Theory-driven evaluation decisions.

A literature review will be conducted by the following stakeholders: _____

by the following date: _____

The sources for the literature review will be (check all that apply):

____ Academic peer-reviewed print journals and books
____ Academic peer-reviewed Internet sites, journals, and books
____ Evaluation and program reports
____ Web sites
____ Other (specify)

Related research and evaluation answering the following types of questions will be reviewed (check all that apply):

____ Exploratory
____ Descriptive
____ Explanatory

A logic model will be developed by the following stakeholders: _____

along the following time line: _____

The logic model contains the following components (check all that apply):

____ Inputs   ____ Goals   ____ Strategies

____ Short-term results   ____ Long-term results

The logic model will be based on program theory learned from the following workers, community members, and clients: _____

using the following data collection methods: _____

The logic model will be based on evidence-based practice from the following research studies: _____

gathered from the following literature search process described above: _____

The goals of the evaluated intervention are: _____

The evaluated strategies expected to reach the above goals are: _____

____ Short-term results

The expected immediate results of the above strategies are: _____

____ Long-term results

The expected long-term results of the above strategies are: _____

CHAPTER 5

DATA-DRIVEN EVALUATION DECISIONS

Chapter 5 can help social service workers select the best methods for collecting information and transforming that information into data to be used to answer the evaluation questions agreed on by key stakeholders. Ideally, key stakeholders should agree on the following decisions before data collection begins because these decisions influence how the data are collected and analyzed:

scope and purpose of the evaluation (chap. 1)

evaluation stakeholder plan, including time line (chap. 2)

ethical and value guidelines (chap. 3)

use of literature review and logic model (chap. 4)

Evaluation is a fluid process that goes back and forth between each of the activities decscribed in the previous chapters and illustrated in figure 1.1. Becoming more involved in the data-collection activities may result in adjusting some of the earlier evaluation activities. Knowing the amount of time needed, for example, to conduct and analyze open-ended, qualitative focus groups with large numbers of participants may influence stakeholders to ask more narrowly focused descriptive rather than exploratory evaluation questions. Likewise, knowing the ethical dilemmas involved in utilizing a comparison group to increase the credibility of the administration of a closed-ended, quantitative written questionnaire may influence stakeholders to ask descriptive rather than explanatory evaluation questions.

The *learning outcomes* for chapter 5 are as follows:

1. Understand how information in a social service setting is transformed into data.

2. Understand the difference between qualitative, quantitative, and mixed approaches to data collection when employed in answering exploratory, descriptive, and explanatory evaluation questions.

3. Understand the difference between qualitative and quantitative approaches during the following steps of data collection:

   a. Selecting evaluation participants.

b. Selecting the data-collection method (interviews, surveys or instruments, observation, or collecting secondary documents).

c. Analyzing the data.

d. Ensuring the credibility of the data-collection methods.

4. Implement a data-collection plan.

TRANSFORMING INFORMATION INTO DATA

Social service workers collect information all the time: when they write case notes; when they check a box on an intake form; when they enter numbers into a computerized management information system. **Data** it is information systematically collected for specific evaluation and research purposes. The evaluation purposes discussed in this book are (1) planning new programs; (2) evaluating programs that have been implemented; (3) providing evidence that program characteristics do exist (e.g., for accreditation); and (4) answering exploratory, descriptive, or explanatory evaluation questions. The term *information* has been deliberately used up to this point in the book because the discussion had not yet focused on which information would be collected as *data* to answer specific evaluation questions.

Data collection is the last set of decisions in the Evaluation Decision-making Model. Stakeholder agreement on the prior tasks in the evaluation leads to the selection of the most appropriate data-collection method. For example, clarifying the value *respect culture* as "include consumer participants from all racial backgrounds represented at the agency" may lead to selecting participants according to racial background rather than randomly from the population of all clients. As another example, choosing the theoretical model of implementing and evaluating evidence-based interventions will most likely lead to the application of quantitative, closed-ended data-collection approaches to test whether the intervention is effective in the current setting.

A vague evaluation question can lead to stakeholder disagreement about whether the question is exploratory, descriptive, or explanatory. Some may assume that the purpose of the evaluation is to test the impact of an intervention (i.e., answering an explanatory evaluation question). Others may assume that the purpose is to report different aspects of the intervention without testing its impact (i.e., answering a descriptive evaluation question). The assumption that the evaluation is for explanatory purposes could lead to decisions to end an intervention if the findings are that it did not achieve the expected changes in client results. In contrast, the assumption that the evaluation is for descriptive purposes could lead to changes in the intervention but not necessarily the decision to end it.

Stakeholders should clarify their definition of *data,* just as they are encouraged to clarify other evaluation terms previously covered in this book. Stakeholders come into a current evaluation with different knowledge and

Figure 5.1.   Evaluation decisionmaking tip: Clarifying myths about data.

Check the data myths that are being followed in a current evaluation at your agency or practicum setting.

_____ *Data* is synonymous with the term *survey.*

_____ *Data* is synonymous with the term *focus groups.*

_____ *Data* is synonymous with the term *statistics.*

_____ *Data* is synonymous with the term *objective.*

_____ *Data* is synonymous with the term *outcomes.*

_____ *Data* alone drive evaluations.

_____ *Data* are utilized only if they are valid and reliable.

_____ *Data* are invisible until there is an evaluation.

experiences of evaluation. For this reason, the discussion here briefly covers some common myths about data. These myths are summarized in figure 5.1

Myth 1: *Data* is synonymous with the term *survey*.   It is common for social service stakeholders to ask. "We need to evaluate our program. What is the best survey to use?" Collecting information or data by conducting a survey is only one of four basic data-collection methods, which are:

1. Asking questions through face-to-face interviews with individuals and groups

2. Observing people, places, and objects

3. Analyzing data collected and documented by someone other than the current evaluators

Even if a written survey is used to collect data, there are many different ways of asking questions: conducting individual interviews; allowing a participant to answer a mailed survey; and so on. Additionally, the results from data collection have more meaning for the stakeholders and are more credible if similar findings are obtained from at least one other data-collection method. Implementing multiple data-collection methods is called **triangulation.**

Myth 2: *Data* is synonymous with the term *focus groups*.   Focus groups are becoming a popular method of engaging key stakeholders (e.g., clients, agency workers, or persons from the community) as evaluation participants because more than one person can be interviewed at a time. Again, focus groups are only one type of data-collection method. As will be explained later, focus groups, interviews, and written questions can be designed according to a closed-ended, quantitative format or an open-ended, qualitative format. Each approach will produce different types of results.

Myth 3: *Data* is synonymous with the term *statistics*.   Statistical analysis is one method of analyzing data. **Data analysis** is making sense of and meaning out of the information gathered in an evaluation. Statistical analysis converts information into numerical values in order to reduce large amounts of information into a format that can be more easily understood and applied. There are different types of statistical analysis. **Descriptive statistics** is the numerical meaning attributed to the distribution of data collected quantitatively. **Inferential statistics** is the numerical meaning attributed to the relationship between data collected quantitatively. A **theme** is the meaning attributed to the narrative data collected qualitatively.

Learning basic methods of quantitative statistical analyses is a Council on Social Work Education (CSWE) requirement for undergraduate and graduate programs. There are excellent social work research texts that cover statistical analysis in easy-to-follow and easy-to-apply contexts for students and social service workers. Some of those texts are listed in the "Further Readings" section of this chapter.

Myth 4: *Data* is synonymous with the term *objective*.   Just because data were collected for evaluation purposes does not mean that they were collected in an objective, impartial way. Some evaluators begin with the assumption that the collection, analysis, and interpretation of data are of necessity biased by the subjective experiences of the evaluators and the other stakeholders involved in the evaluation process. Evaluators can document how they construct the evaluation process in the midst of the different influences on the evaluation decisions (Rodwell, 1998). The reflective journal exercises at the end of each chapter in this book help evaluation stakeholders become aware of subjective views that affect the evaluation.

Myth 5: *Data* is synonymous with the term *outcomes*.   A repeated theme of this book is that the process of evaluation and data collection is as important as the results measured. This is so for several reasons. First, stakeholders who actively participate in making evaluation decisions are prepared to take more control in future evaluations. Second, knowledge and insight obtained during the evaluation process can be applied immediately, long before the entire evaluation process is completed and the results finally analyzed and interpreted. Finally, results are just one component of an evaluation and do not necessarily drive program planning and practice decisions. From the current evaluation process stakeholders can learn reflectively and procedurally how to ensure that future evaluations are better utilized (Smith, 1995).

Myth 6: Data alone drive evaluations.   Clarifying the scope, values, and theories of an evaluation with key stakeholders was discussed first because, in many evaluations, decisions are influenced as much, if not more, by those components. In every evaluation it is ideal to take the time necessary to:

1. Clarify the problem, focus, or evaluation questions.
2. Conduct a search of the literature to learn how others have approached similar questions.
3. *Then and only then* determine the best data-collection methods to resolve the questions.

A related myth is that data drive agency decisionmaking. The discussion at the beginning of this book pointed out that evaluation is only one tool for influencing agency planning, practice, and policy decisions. Many agency decisions are made without consulting evaluation data. At the same time, the more social service workers use evaluation to improve practice and accountability, the more evaluation can be used to influence agency decisions in the future.

Myth 7: Data are utilized only if they are valid and reliable.   The terms *validity* and *reliability* have specific meanings for quantitative approaches to data collection. The term *credibility* is used in this book because it can be applied to quantitative and qualitative data collection. **Credibility** is the rigorous and systematic collection of qualitative and quantitative data according to the most widely accepted procedures cited in the research and evaluation literature. The credibility of the evaluation results depends on the credibility of the evaluation planning and implementation process.

The results of evaluations that employ credible quantitative approaches reduce the threats to validity and reliability. **Validity** refers to describing or explaining the intended concepts and generalizing from the sample to the larger population. **Reliability** is the consistent measurement of the same concept.

The results of evaluations that employ credible qualitative approaches reduce the threats to the trustworthiness of the data. **Trustworthiness** is the accurate description of the concepts and realities as intended by the participants in the evaluation. The established norms for ensuring the trustworthiness of qualitative data will be discussed later in this chapter, as will those for ensuring the validity and reliability of quantitative data. The "Further Readings" section at the end of this chapter contains several references on ensuring the credibility of data collection.

Myth 8: Data are invisible until there is an evaluation.   Potential data are everywhere. Numerical data exist in agency management information systems, consumer responses to standardized assessment tools and satisfaction surveys, and communitywide databases. Narrative data exist in workers' case records, consumers' verbal or written goal statements, and agency and community meeting minutes.

As social workers integrate evaluation more routinely into daily interactions with consumers and other stakeholders, the roles of information and data will become interchangeable. Only the data that answer specific evaluation questions should be collected and reported for a specific evaluation. Avoid getting bogged down with information that is not relevant to the specific evaluation questions. Make sure that the important stakeholders are involved in selecting the right evaluation questions since those questions are what will guide planning and practice decisions.

Figure 4.1 showed that *the evaluation question was the real transformer of information into data.* The evaluation question guided the data-collection process, connecting the current data with theory learned from other studies. Exploratory questions build theory through qualitative means. Descriptive questions build and test theory through qualitative and quantitative means. And explanatory questions test theory through quantitative processes. The following discussion expands on qualitative and quantitative data-collection approaches.

QUALITATIVE, QUANTITATIVE, AND MIXED APPROACHES

The terms *qualitative approach* and *quantitative approach* are used rather than the terms *qualitative method* and *quantitative method.* The term *approach* connotes how decisions are made throughout the entire evaluation process. The terms *qualitative method* and *quantitative method* often refer to only one component of the entire evaluation, that is, the information-gathering process, more often called *data collection.* The term *method* implies a practical, procedural process devoid of underlying values and theoretical premises shaping the planning, practice, and evaluation decisions.

The entire data-collection process is conducted differently from qualitative and quantitative approaches. The steps to data collection discussed in this chapter from both approaches are as follows:

1. Choosing the procedure for selecting participants:
   a. Purposive sample (qualitative approach);
   b. Random sample (quantitative approach).
2. Selecting the data-collection method:
   a. Interviews (qualitative or quantitative);
   b. Written surveys (qualitative or quantitative) or instruments (quantitative);
   c. Observation (qualitative or quantitative);
   d. Document analysis (qualitative or quantitative).
3. Selecting the methods for analyzing the results:
   a. Narrative and theme analysis (qualitative);

b. Statistical analysis (quantitative).

4. Selecting the methods for ensuring the credibility of the results:

    a. Reducing threats to trustworthiness (qualitative);

    b. Reducing threats to validity and reliability (quantitative).

Before discussing each data-collection step, I briefly cover the general differences between qualitative, quantitative, and mixed approaches to data collection. Mixed approaches or mixed methods refers to the use of both quantitative and qualitative data-collection approaches in the same evaluation.

Qualitative Approaches. **Qualitative approaches** refers to gathering information in an open-ended manner to answer exploratory or descriptive evaluation questions. As mentioned in the previous chapter, qualitative approaches are used to answer *exploratory* or *descriptive* evaluation questions. Stakeholders want to know the experiences of persons connected to the program or are seeking information about a specific situation, setting, or stakeholder group on which very little has been published.

In qualitative approaches, stakeholders are open to the responses given in the participants' own words and spend much time planning the best way to systematically and rigorously capture the important characteristics that emerge from the participants. The participants—including consumers of services because consumers know best their own perceptions of the intervention—become the experts on the evaluation question. In the dissertation study discussed throughout this book, only the perceptions of parents were collected as data, whereas, in the Strengths-Based Case Management (SBCM) program, perceptions of clients and workers were collected as data. Be clear in qualitative approaches how the data, including the literature reviewed, lend authority to the interpretation of results.

Qualitative approaches generate new or affirm current program theory on the basis of the information gathered. Theory generated from qualitative approaches to data collection were discussed in chapter 4. Qualitative approaches to answering exploratory questions are open to theory that is learned throughout the evaluation. Qualitative approaches to answering descriptive questions already have in place some beginning theoretical framework. The open-ended responses to the qualitative focus groups with family support intervention (FSI) stakeholders were grouped according to the following predetermined, targeted systems for change: individuals; families; the agency; or and the community (see figs. 3.11 and 3.12).

Quantitative Approaches. **Quantitative approaches** refers to gathering information in a closed-ended manner to answer descriptive or explanatory evaluation questions. As mentioned in the previous chapter, some evaluations are conducted to determine whether an intervention produced the results predicted by theories empirically tested in previous evaluations or research. In such evaluations, explanatory statements or hypotheses are used rather than evaluation questions. In the evaluation of FSIs, one hypothesis tested was, "Consumers of the FSIs will significantly improve family functioning."

In quantitative approaches, stakeholders predetermine ahead of time the closed-ended responses that the participants can choose during the data-collection procedures. The process of narrowing the foci of the evaluation through quantitative processes before collecting information from participants results in different evaluation decisions than are made in qualitative designs. In quantitative approaches, much time is spent planning the best evaluation to systematically and rigorously measure predetermined characteristics.

Recall the discussion in chapter 4 of logic models. There, quantitative approaches describe or test program theory that already exists before collecting more information. The experts guiding explanatory evaluation questions are most often the authors of the theories that have been tested in other settings. The research literature becomes the basis for designing the evaluation and intervention. Social service workers are held accountable for carrying out the intervention and evaluation according to the theorized relations supported by prior research. The evidence-based research literature takes priority over the social service workers' and consumers' experiences.

Mixed Approaches.   Many advocate the application of mixed approaches, that is, both qualitative and quantitative data collection, to evaluation (Bisman and Hardcastle, 1999; Frechtling & Sharp, 1997; Padgett, 2004a; Patton, 1997; USGAO, 1998). Four reasons for the use of mixed-methods data collection are discussed here. The discussion ends by noting the confusion that can occur when mixing qualitative and quantitative approaches to answer more than one type of evaluation question.

First, mixed approaches are used because narrative responses from qualitative, open-ended data-collection methods can affirm responses from quantitative, closed-ended methods. In the descriptive evaluation of direct-care mental health worker competencies, the responses to the qualitative focus group questions matched some of the same competencies prioritized in the quantitative mail survey. Many evaluations use direct-participant quotes to illustrate the results presented in statistical terms. For example, in King et al. (2001, p. 239), a study of evaluators' ratings of expected competencies for evaluation, the authors reported: "It is noteworthy that there was nearly unanimous agreement on the perceived importance of two competencies. The first of these competencies was 'Framing the evaluation question(s),' for which the mean was 99.97 with a range of 99 to 100. One participant's comment summed up what participants consistently expressed across sessions:

'If you don't have a good evaluation question, nothing else matters.' The direct quote collected qualitatively emphasized the finding collected quantitatively.

Second, responses to open-ended questions on a qualitative data-collection instrument can shed light on unexpected responses to closed-ended questions on a quantitative instrument. For example, in the evaluation of FSIs, a telephone survey using a standardized instrument measuring family functioning was used to test the explanatory evaluation hypothesis that consumers receiving FSIs would see significant improvement in family functioning compared to those not receiving FSIs. The expected results were not obtained. Responses by staff to open-ended interviews conducted in the same evaluation demonstrated that stakeholders from the various FSIs did not necessarily conceptualize the term *family functioning* or the underlying program theory in the same way. Such variation could explain why there were no significant changes in the quantitative measures.

Third, the combination of both qualitative and quantitative approaches helps bridge planning, practice, and evaluation. Qualitative approaches were administered in the evaluation of an SBCM intervention that had previously been proven effective through quantitative methods. One of the findings of the qualitative interviews was that some participants did not trust the case worker's focus on strengths. This finding sparked the practice question: "How can we implement the SBCM in such a manner as to identify this possible obstacle?"

Fourth, quantitative approaches can be used to verify qualitative findings. Nichols-Casebolt and Spakes (1995) collected qualitative data from women participants in a three-day town hall forum focused on the topic "families in crisis." The authors wanted to ensure that these qualitative data would be considered when policy decisions related to families were made in the future. They used a two-tiered, qualitative and quantitative evaluation design to meet these concerns:

> Although committed to using qualitative techniques, we were confronted by several competing concerns that often prevent policy analysts from pursuing the use of qualitative methods. First, we needed to ensure that we presented some information that was representative of the diverse population in the state. Second, the town hall research committee required that the background document provide information on trends over time and comparisons with national data. And finally, the data needed to be presented in such a way that generalizations would assist in the development of policy recommendations. (Nichols-Casebolt & Spakes, 1995, p. 50)

Mixed data-collection methods can provide comprehensive information to answer descriptive evaluation questions. Both quantitative and qualitative approaches were used in the descriptive evaluation to determine core competencies for direct-care mental health workers. In this evaluation, the follow-

Figure 5.2.   Evaluation decisionmaking tip: Recognizing qualitative and quantitative approaches throughout the evaluation decisionmaking process.

As you begin to develop the evaluation, this chart can be used to identify whether you will use qualitative or quantitative approaches to each decision discussed throughout this book. Place an x in the appropriate column for each row.

	Qualitative	Quantitative	Not Applicable
SCOPE			
Exploratory evaluation questions	x		
Descriptive evaluation questions			
Explanatory evaluation questions		x	
Evaluation with individuals			
Evaluation with families			
Evaluation with organizations			
Evaluation with communities			
Can guide planning decisions			
Can guide practice decisions			
VALUES			
Measurement of strengths			
Culturally competent evaluation			
Resources needed			
Ethical guidelines			
Agreement with stakeholders			
Multiple systems measurement			
THEORY			
Literature review			
Logic model			
DATA COLLECTION			
Interviews			
Written surveys/instruments			
Observation			
Secondary documents			
Data analysis			
Data credibility			

ing stakeholders completed a closed-ended-format survey that listed twenty-six competencies formulated on the basis of the literature and the evaluation advisory group: administrators, direct-care workers, supervisors, and consumer advocates. In that same evaluation, follow-up open-ended focus groups were conducted with representatives from the same constituencies. The open-ended focus group questions allowed the participants to explain in more detail the meaning of the prioritized competencies. Future required training of mental health workers in the participating agencies was based on the selection of the top five competencies and the comments from the focus groups.

Mixed data-collection methods may not be appropriate in an evaluation that contains both exploratory and explanatory questions:

> One might be able to combine both quantitative and qualitative methods while still attending to the rigor requirements built on the epistemological assumptions of each position. But how can one assume both single and multiple realities at the same time? How can one trust the separation between the researcher and the object of inquiry while supporting their interaction? (Rodwell, 1998, p. 13)

Stated another way, how can practitioners explore multiple emergent possibilities and at the same time test a predetermined relation between intervention and results? Padgett (2004a) disagrees with the polarization created between constructivist and positivist views of research and evaluation. Instead, she calls for qualitative methods from a pragmatist perspective.

The differences between qualitative and quantitative approaches will now be discussed across each step of data collection. Readers will need to determine for themselves whether different combinations of each approach can be applied to their current evaluation questions. Use the chart in figure 5.2 to assist in documenting whether qualitative or quantitative approaches will be used for each evaluation decision discussed in this book.

PARTICIPANT SELECTION

The first data-collection decision is, "Who will be invited to participate in the evaluation and why?" Evaluation participants are those persons from whom data are collected for research or evaluation purposes. The use of the term *participants,* rather than the research term *subjects,* illustrates that people, not objects, are the source of information. Even when the sources of information are secondary documents such as case records, the documents are about human behavior. The term *participants* is also a reminder that there are special ethical considerations in social service evaluation because it involves human subjects.

As discussed in chapter 2, stakeholders can advise the evaluation process and also be participants from whom data are collected. In the needs assessment conducted for the purpose of developing a countywide family violence prevention plan, social service directors of family violence prevention agencies served on the planning and evaluation advisory board. Some of these same persons became participants when they completed a provider survey about the services offered at their agencies. Stakeholders, including the funding source, were aware of this dual role of some stakeholders. In final reports, and even in media accounts of the information collected during the planning process, the sources of information were clearly acknowledged.

There was never an intent to hide the overlapping roles that some persons played in advising and providing data for the planning and evaluation process.

QUALITATIVE APPROACHES TO PARTICIPANT SELECTION

In evaluations that answer *exploratory* questions, participants who best fit the experiences specified in the question are selected. In the exploratory study with parents, the overall question asked was, "How do parents predicted to be at risk for child abuse and neglect successfully raise their children?" This exploratory question was chosen because there was minimal empirical research literature on this specific question. **Empirical research** refers to the published, peer-reviewed dissemination of the results of studies that applied credible data-collection methods. Empirical research includes credible qualitative and quantitative approaches.

Practitioners should be critical of authors' interpretations of evaluations found in reports, conference presentations, and journal articles, including connections made between the results of an evaluation and the empirical literature. For items that should be included when reporting the results of qualitative approaches to evaluations, see Drisko (1997) and Padgett (2004b).

Most of the empirical research consulted for the example above related to risk factors for child abuse and neglect concentrated on social service workers' and researchers' conceptualization of the causes of child abuse. Some of those theories focused on parent characteristics as the primary cause of abuse and neglect. Some focused on institution characteristics. The study's final research question focused on how those parents identified as at risk for child abuse and neglect perceived their own parenting skills. The data thus obtained—parents' experiences related in their own words—were then compared to the existing empirical literature to see whether they matched reported data.

Alternative selection decisions would have resulted in a different group of participants and, thus, different results. Some of the alternative decisions that could have been made were (1) to invite participants from one or more agencies; (2) to select participants in such a way that diversity was ensured in terms of gender, race, and age; or (3) to solicit participants from the general public through advertisements run in newspapers or posted in public places such as doctors' offices, social service agencies, grocery stores, and laundromats.

The procedural journal can offer important proof that participants were selected purposively. **Purposive** participant selection means that participants were selected on the basis of specific criteria addressed in the evaluation question, that is, not randomly. Keeping a record of evaluation decisions—why specific data-collection methods were chosen, whether procedural changes were questioned, the negotiation process by which such questions were resolved—ensures the credibility of qualitative approaches.

Another important decision made in the above example was who *not* to select for information gathering. The researcher chose to interview only parents. He deliberately chose *not* to interview social service workers because he did not want their perceptions to deflect attention from the experiences of the parents.

The results of the research were reported in a doctoral dissertation (Brun, 1993), and at the national Head Start conference from which an article was published (Brun, 1997). All these reports discussed the fact that the participant selection process resulted in a sample—six women, five of whom were African American, and all of whom were between the ages of twenty-one and thirty-five—that was small and not necessarily representative. Still, however, the reports were useful because of the rich, contextual information about participants that each supplied. A separate chapter offering detailed case studies of all participants appeared in the dissertation (Brun, 1993). Connections were also made between common themes expressed by the participants and the discussion, or lack thereof, of these same themes in the empirical literature. Readers of these reports could be critical of the interpretation of results and determine whether the findings apply to consumers of their social services.

In the example given in figure 1.2, qualitative approaches were used to answer the overall descriptive evaluation question, "How do consumers experience SBCM?" Prior empirical research reported in the literature and obtained from evaluations previously conducted at the agency demonstrated the effectiveness of SBCM with substance abuse populations. The results of this evaluation provided experiences from the consumers' perspective that may or may not support the effectiveness of the SBCM. The participants gave information about areas of SBCM not analyzed in prior empirical research.

The participants were selected purposively because a key stakeholder, the director of the intervention, wanted to limit the evaluation to persons currently participating in SBCM. Because of limited available funding, only persons referred to SBCM within a six-month period were invited to participate in the evaluation. The stakeholders agreed that the evaluator would interview the three caseworkers who delivered the services to assess the match between the workers' and the consumers' perceptions of the intervention.

The interpretation of the results from this evaluation appeared in a final report, a presentation given at a national conference, and an article published in a peer-reviewed journal (Brun & Rapp, 2001). The authors noted the limitations imposed by the small sample size but noted the high percentage of participants who participated in all three interviews. The results—presented as common themes with brief social histories given about some of the participants—offered information not reported in previous research (namely, the consumers' mistrust of the approach) as well as consumers' descriptions of the positive impact of SBCM. Approximately one-third of the participants reported no substance use during the six-month

Figure 5.3.   Evaluation decisionmaking tip: Qualitative participant selection.

1. Clarify the exploratory evaluation question. Examples of exploratory questions are

 a. What is it like to have worked in child welfare for over ten years? (Brode, 1990)

 b. What happens after families leave a homeless shelter? (Tingler, 2000)

 c. How do parents predicted to be at risk for child abuse and neglect successfully raise their children? (Brun, 1993)

2. Think of all the possible contexts that surround the question. State why you want to include persons with certain backgrounds. You should have an answer grounded either in the literature or in the agency purpose for the evaluation to justify your decisions to purposively include persons with specific characteristics.

Using example *a,* do you want workers from one agency? Why? If more than one agency, do you want persons who work in urban agencies or rural? Why? Do you want persons who have similar demographics? Why? Do you want men and women, older and younger persons, or persons from different cultural backgrounds? Why? What other characteristics should the participants possess? Why?

3. How will you purposively select persons who meet your contextual definition in step 2?

Will you invite participants from a particular intervention? Why? Will you select persons who are involved in the intervention for a certain time period? Why? Will you advertise for persons by posting announcements in the agency or in other public places? Why? Will you ask participants to recommend other persons to participate (this is called a *snowball sample*)? Why? What other methods will you use to invite participants? Why?

4. How will you decide that theme redundancy has occurred and that there is, therefore, no need to invite more participants?

You should be able to convince stakeholders that persons with the same contextual background as the persons selected in steps 2 and 3 will result in no new themes.

---

evaluation period, a result that matched the findings of prior research in this same setting. Persons attending the presentation or reading the reports must assess the results critically to determine whether the knowledge gained from the evaluation can be applied to the stakeholders to whom they provide similar services.

How many participants are needed in evaluations using qualitative approaches? Methodologically speaking, qualitative and quantitative approaches differ in terms of the number of participants needed to answer the evaluation question. When the approach is qualitative, participants are selected until theme redundancy is reached. **Theme redundancy** is when conceptual ideas will be repeated if persons possessing the same characteristics are selected. In the study of parents considered to be at risk, the dissertation committee and additional peer reviewers agreed that theme redundancy had occurred across the six women interviewed because of the similarities in their backgrounds and experiences. Had the researcher chosen to change the research focus to comparing mothers' and fathers' perceptions of parenting, then he would have had purposively to include fathers in the research. Still, the exclusion of fathers was not itself purposive. The researcher began the selection process without limiting his focus to women. But, while there were fathers in the homes of five of the six women interviewed, none chose to participate.

In the SBCM evaluation, no new themes were reported from men selected in the third month of the evaluation period compared to the first two months. Throughout the evaluation period, no women were referred to the program, in which only about three women participate annually.

Figure 5.3 summarizes the points to consider when selecting participants through qualitative, purposive, and nonrandom approaches.

QUANTITATIVE APPROACHES TO PARTICIPANT SELECTION

In quantitative approaches, when the target population is too large to be sampled in its entirety, participants are selected in such a way that their responses will be generalizable or representative. The basic approach, a **random sample** (also called a probability sample), is based on the theory that a sample chosen systematically, but randomly, from a larger population— that is, a sample chosen in such a way that every member of the larger population has an equal chance of being selected—will represent that larger population accurately.

Consider, for example, a population of 10,000 consumers from among whom a 10% random sample of 1,000 is to be selected. According to probability theory, 95% of those 1,000 participants will report results consistent with those of the larger population of consumers. The reasoning here is based on the theory that results obtained from large populations will be naturally distributed along a bell-shaped curve, with 95% falling within a range that runs from two standard deviations above to two standard deviations below the average or mean, a range that is commonly accepted as indicating the credibility of results.

Also according to probability theory, 5% of those 1,000 participants will report outlier results, results that are not consistent with 95% of the larger population of consumers. In quantitative approaches, stakeholders have the option of ignoring the outlier results. But, in some qualitative approaches, stakeholders often chose to investigate those outlier results further. Brode (1990), for example, wanted to explore why such a large number of child welfare workers leave their jobs within two years. Initially, she focused on the experiences of those workers who left their jobs. Ultimately, however, she chose to explore the experiences of those workers who stayed on the job, some for ten years or longer. Thus, instead of ruling out the outliers, she was able to learn from them.

Because of the generalizability of the results obtained, there are pressures to use random sampling, especially on state or federal programs. Some stakeholders may desire a stratified random selection process, one in which persons from each of the identified demographic groups (e.g., the same percentage of women and men as is found in the population list) are randomly selected. Some stakeholders may desire a purposive selection process too if they want to make sure that at least one person from each of the identified demographic groups (e.g., racial groups) participates in the evaluation.

In the evaluation of direct-care mental health workers' competencies described in figure 1.5, the descriptive evaluation question was answered by inviting the entire studied population (approximately 3,500 employees) to participate in the mail survey. Stakeholders and evaluators agreed that the resources were available to invite all workers to participate in the evaluation. All employees were given the data-collection instrument along with their monthly pay stub. An accompanying letter encouraged them to complete the survey and return it (in the self-addressed envelope that they were also given) to the evaluation team. Ultimately, 438 surveys were returned, for a response rate of 13%.

The limitations of the participant selection process were stated in the final report. While the response rate was low, surveys were received from employees at each of the nine participating behavioral health organizations and in each of the job categories and education levels, and 65% of the respondents had worked in mental health for more than ten years (Clasen et al., 2003, p. 12). The prioritized competencies in this evaluation matched the findings of prior empirical research. This evaluation contributed to future empirical research by constructing a valid and reliable instrument that other persons can implement to prioritize mental health competencies. This evaluation described the competencies. The purpose was not to test a relationship between possessing the competencies and achieving desired consumer results. Critical readers of the published evaluation must determine for themselves if the results apply to the mental health setting in which they work.

Evaluations that answer explanatory questions begin with a **hypothesis,** that is a statement predicting a causal relationship between the intervention and desired results. In the evaluation of FSIs, the explanatory hypothesis tested through quantitative approaches was, "Consumers of the FSIs . . . will significantly improve family functioning. . . ." The hypothesis was based on the following goal in the logic model that was contained in the RFP for all the funded programs: "A goal of the family support interventions is to strengthen family functioning." The general functioning scale of the Family Assessment Device (Epstein et al., 1982) was selected to measure the outcome *family functioning* after a thorough search of the empirical literature was conducted.

The original evaluation plan was to randomly select persons from each of the thirty-eight evaluated programs who were consumers of a program during a specified six-month period. There was sufficient funding to conduct telephone interviews with up to 1,000 consumers and 1,000 persons from a comparison group at three different times, figures based on the assumption many more than 1,000 consumers would be available across the thirty-eight programs.

It turned out that the number of potential consumers was actually much smaller, for several reasons. First, each FSI had different operational definitions of *consumers*. Some programs considered consumers to be those individuals or families who received direct services. Others considered consumers to be all members of the community—these were programs targeted at community level change. In these community level programs, the number of potential participants was much lower because some agencies did not have intake information (names, addresses, and phone numbers) for recipients of community level interventions (e.g., health fairs or presentations at a hospital).

Second, none of the FSIs included a consent form to provide their names for possible evaluations. The agency directors wrote a letter explaining the evaluation and asking permission to release contact information to the evaluators. Once a consumer signed and returned the letter, his or her contact information was turned over to the evaluators. The telephone interviewers then contacted the consumer and sought verbal informed consent before proceeding to administer the questions on the family functioning scale.

Third, many of the potential participants could not be reached by telephone. Unfortunately, only telephone interviews could be conducted because the expense of traveling to each of the thirty-eight sites and interviewing even a sample of consumers was beyond the budget.

Still, efforts were made to reach the entire population of FSI consumers. Of the 1,261 telephone numbers provided by the FSI staff, 626 were usable at time 1, resulting in an initial clean rate of 49.6%. A clean sample rate is the number of participants who can be contacted (626) divided by the total number of participants on the original sample list (1,261). At time 1,533 of the FSI participants on the cleaned list were interviewed, a response rate of 85.1%. The **response rate** is the number of persons who complete the survey (533) divided by the number of persons who were given the survey (626). Of those 533 participants, 318 were retained at time 2 and 205 at time 3, for a final retention rate of 38.5%. The retention rate is the number of persons who continued to participate in all three surveys (205) divided by the number of persons originally given the survey (626). The number of FSI participants responding to all three surveys also represented 32.7% of the cleaned FSI population (205 of 626).

A sample of persons in a comparison group also completed the survey. A **comparison group** is made up of persons who do not receive the intervention, in this case, persons who were not consumers of FSIs. The procedure for the random selection of the comparison group was as follows:

1. In each of the thirty-eight sites, the zip codes of persons answering the telephone survey were obtained.
2. Phone numbers for the appropriate area codes were purchased from Survey Sampling Incorporated, a company that provides this service for large-sample-size studies.
3. The evaluators entered those names into a computer software program that randomly selects for the comparison group the same number of persons who participated in the consumer interview.
4. The evaluators checked to make sure that none of the persons in the consumer interviews were also in the comparison group.

For the FSI comparison group (FSIC), 549 persons were contacted at time 1, of whom 333 were retained at time 2 and 248 at time 3. The retention rate for the number of original FSIC participants who completed all three surveys was 45.2% (248 of 549).

The interpretation of the results was provided in a final report, at a state level conference and, later, at a national conference, and in a manuscript submitted for publication in a peer-reviewed journal. In these presentations and reports, the authors stated the limitations of the sampling procedures described above. But they claimed that, despite these limitations, the results from the sample could be generalized to the original population, which was all consumers of the thirty-eight evaluated FSIs.

The authors provided possible explanations for why there was not a significant change in family functioning for the consumers, including the reality that family functioning was not conceptualized consistently across evaluated programs. Thus, the instrument selected from past research may not have been the best measure of all evaluated programs. Readers of these reports should be critical of the methodology and determine whether the interpretation of the results can apply to their own settings. For criteria to use when reading findings of quantitative evaluations reported in journals, see Thyer (2002).

The desired participant size and response rate should be agreed on prior to beginning data collection. First determine the population size, following the steps outlined in figure 5.4. The evaluators of the FSIs erred by writing into the evaluation contract that they would interview 1,000 consumers, not anticipating the problems that they would encounter. They were, however, able to negotiate the number of participants with the fun-

Figure 5.4.   Evaluation decisionmaking tip: Quantitative participant selection.

In order to select a participant group that represents a larger population, follow these steps:

1. Clarify who composes the population.
2. Compose a population list of all persons who fit the clarified definition.
3. Clean the list by removing persons whose name appears more than once or persons whom it is not feasible to contact (e.g., persons without addresses or phone numbers).
4. Choose whether to conduct a random or a nonrandom sample. If conducting a random sample, follow the appropriate steps to increase the power of statistical analysis (see Potocky-Tripodi & Tripodi, 2003).
5. Contact all persons selected from the "clean list." Record how many of these persons respond. This number will now become the response rate of the persons chosen to be in the random sample (e.g., if 250 persons are contacted from the clean list and 125 respond, the response rate is 50%).

ders. In retrospect, they should have stated a percentage of the total population rather than an arbitrary number based on limited knowledge of the setting.

DATA-COLLECTION METHODS

The three general ways to collect data are (1) to *ask questions* through face-to-face interviews or self-administered surveys and instruments; (2) to *observe people,* places, and objects; and (3) to *collect secondary documents,* that is, information and data collected, analyzed, and reported by someone else. All three data-collection methods can be implemented through qualitative or quantitative approaches. The discussion here makes no assumptions as to which approach readers are implementing in their current evaluation. Some texts listed in the "Further Readings" section follow data collection exclusively from a qualitative approach (e.g., Patton, 2002; Rodwell, 1998), others exclusively from a quantitative approach (e.g., Bloom et al., 2003).

Questions can be asked through a face-to-face interview with one or more persons. Individuals can answer written questions handed to them, mailed to them, asked of them over the phone, or asked of them via the Internet. The questions can have set, predetermined answers (quantitative), or they can be the type that respondents can answer in their own words (qualitative). The results can be reported individually by question (qualitative or quantitative) or collectively for all questions (quantitative). Responses can be reported as statistics (quantitative) or as themes and actual quotes (qualitative). The evaluators and local stakeholders can write the questions (qualitative or quantitative), or a standardized instrument can be implemented

Figure 5.5.   Case example: Triangulation of data-collection methods and approaches.

I was part of an evaluation team that was asked to answer the descriptive question, "What are the competencies expected of all direct-care mental health workers?" We began by reviewing the published literature related to the topic and syllabi of courses teaching mental health worker competencies. More than 135 separate competencies were found during the analyses of these secondary documents. We reduced these down to twenty-six by condensing similar competencies into one. The final list was agreed to by an evaluation stakeholder advisory group. We then quantitatively constructed a survey containing closed-ended questions about agreement or disagreement on the importance of these twenty-six competencies. The survey also contained qualitative, open-ended questions asking the respondents whether they recommended additional competencies. There were open-ended and closed-ended questions seeking respondent feedback on ways to learn the competencies. The surveys were distributed to approximately 3,300 employees with their pay stub in the same time period. The response rate was 13%, with 438 surveys returned. The responses to the twenty-six competencies were analyzed quantitatively for validity and reliability among respondents. The twenty-six competencies were ranked in the order in which the respondents collectively prioritized the competencies. Answers to the qualitative questions were summarized according to common responses.

Focus groups were then conducted with stakeholders at nine different behavioral health organizations throughout the state. Representatives of different stakeholder groups were invited to the focus groups. These stakeholders included direct-care workers, supervisors, administrators, staff trainers, union representatives, and client advocates. Each focus group had between five and fifteen participants. Some, but not all, of the focus group participants had also completed the previous survey. The purpose of the focus groups was to compare answers to data gathered from the self-administered surveys.

Persons in the focus group were asked to quantitatively prioritize the top five competencies from the list of twenty-six that were contained on the survey. Persons were also able to qualitatively add other competencies that were not contained in the survey and to discuss the best ways to learn the competencies. A productive discussion that occurred across all focus groups was how several of the individual competencies were actually covered together in individual training sessions.

The final evaluation report combined findings triangulated across all data collection methods: (1) review of the literature; (2) self-administered surveys; and (3) focus groups.

(quantitative). Many evaluators construct surveys that combine questions from standardized instruments with questions of local interest.

Observations of a person's behaviors can be self-reported, reported by a person familiar with the person observed, or reported by a person having no relationship with the participant. Observations can also be made of places and objects. For example, persons conducting a home visit often routinely record their observations of the physical environment. The observational documentation could take the form of a written, open-ended narrative description based on general categories (e.g., cleanliness, safety, and neatness) or no categories (qualitative approach) or of a closed-ended observation sheet on which boxes are checked off (quantitative approach).

Secondary documents are sources of information recorded by someone else prior to the current evaluation that are used to help answer the current evaluation questions. Secondary documents are not restricted to written materials. They can include video and audio recordings, photographs, images on a Web site, dance, music, theater, and other expressions of thoughts and feelings. Secondary documents need not necessarily contain an analysis of the information. An agency annual report that includes evaluation outcomes is one document, and another person's written critique of that report is a separate document.

As discussed earlier, triangulation is the process of implementing multiple data-collection methods in the same evaluation. Methodologically, triangulation increases the credibility of the results because the same evaluation questions are answered by more than one data-collection strategy. This increased credibility is a big reason there has been the call for mixed-methods evaluations. For an example of an evaluation that used multiple data-collection methods and both qualitative and quantitative approaches, see figure 5.5.

QUALITATIVE APPROACHES TO ASKING QUESTIONS

Individual Interviews.   Qualitative, face-to-face interviews can be conducted with individuals or groups to answer exploratory or descriptive evaluation questions. Qualitative individual interviews were conducted in the research study that answered the exploratory question, "How do parents predicted to be at risk for child abuse and neglect successfully raise their children?" Qualitative individual interviews were conducted in the evaluation that answered the descriptive question, "How do consumers experience SBCM?" In both examples, the participants were *purposively* selected in consultation with key stakeholders because their backgrounds fit the exploratory question.

The interviews took place in the participants' natural settings, that is, a place that was familiar to the participants and, thus, not distracting. In the first example, all the interviews took place in participants' homes at a time they chose. In the second example, the first interview took place when the SBCM participants were in a residential facility and had not yet begun SBCM. This facility served as a thirty-day transition from the hospital where they received substance abuse detoxification treatment to their eventual independent or semi-independent housing in the community. The second interview took place in a private office in the SBCM care manager's building. The third interview took place in participants' community residences.

In both examples, the same person asked the questions of each participant and followed the same **interview guide,** which is a set of general questions that allow participants to describe their experiences about a subject in their own words. Go to figures 5.6 and 5.7, and notice the difference between the interview guides used in both examples. The questions in the interview guide in figure 5.6 were asked in a conversational manner to help the parents feel comfortable discussing any and all aspects of parenting. After the first interview was conducted with all six participants, a follow-up set of questions was developed to address themes that arose during the previous interviews but were not previously discussed with all participants. The second and third interviews allowed the interviewer to clarify the content of previous interviews, a process called **member checking** (discussed later in this chapter).

The questions in the interview guide in figure 5.7 allowed for open-ended responses from the participants but were asked in a much more probing and directive manner than were the questions in figure 5.6. They were descriptive rather than exploratory because the program staff wanted to know client perceptions about specific aspects of the intervention. The stakeholders were not as interested in other information not related to the intervention that the clients might share from a more exploratory format.

Focus Groups.   **Focus groups** are interviews conducted with more than one person at a time. The term *focus groups* has become one of those evaluation terms that many stakeholders use generically without specifying whether the method will be implemented qualitatively or quantitatively. Qualitative focus groups follow a general, open-ended interview guide. Focus groups require special practical considerations, considerations that set them apart from face-to-face interviews. For example, two evaluators should conduct the focus groups, one to facilitate the interview, the other to record the information gathered.

The facilitators should follow a script that contains the following:

1. Introductions of the evaluators and a statement of the purpose of the focus group.
2. Conditions of informed consent stated verbally (with each person asked) to sign the written permission-to-participate form.
3. An explanation of the format of the focus group (e.g., "I will give each of you a chance to answer a question before I go on to the next one"; "Please save all of your questions for me until the end").
4. The actual interview guide questions.
5. Instructions to leave time for questions from the participants and then to thank them and let them know how they can request the results of the evaluation.

Figure 5.6.   Case example: Qualitative interview guide to answer an exploratory research question.

The following interview guide was used in the exploratory study with six parents:

To be asked in first interview:

The purpose of my interview is to learn in your own words the experiences you have had as a parent. Parenting is often defined by the researchers rather than the parents. I want this interview to be a mutual effort where we both choose the topics to talk about.

If it is OK, I would like to turn on the tape recorder now in order to get all of the information from the interview.

The study is for parents ages 21–35, with three or fewer children living with them, the children are eleven years old or younger, and they have not had a finding of child abuse or neglect report since July 1, 1992.

Next, let me go over the details of the interviews by going over the consent form.

Specify that the report will be in the library and that it will be read by other social workers and researchers.

Let me start by asking you, "How has it been to raise your child(ren)? What has it been like to be a parent?"

What has been enjoyable about being a parent?

How would you have liked to do things differently?

How have you changed since becoming a parent?

What does it mean to be a successful parent?

What tips would you give a new parent?

What has influenced you the most as a parent? Who are the persons who have influenced your parenting?

In the second interview, the focus was mainly on follow-up questions from the first interview and/or topics that arose from the participants:

How have things been since I saw you last?

Is there anything you thought of that we talked about when I was here last?

Is there anything from the transcription of the last interview that you wanted to talk about?

How was it for you growing up?

Describe how it was during your pregnancy with your child?

How have you handled child care?

How have you handled finances?

How has it been to raise your children in this neighborhood? Describe your neighborhood.

How does being African American affect taking care of your children?

Would you talk more about the children's father?

In the third interview, the beginning questions asked were the same as at the beginning of interview 2. The main part of this last interview was to go over material

(figure continues)

from the first interviews. I read the parents my summary of this material and asked them if they had anything else to add. Then the following questions were asked because they were relevant themes across participants from the first two interviews:

> How would you like your story told?
> Whom would you like to read it?
> Has alcoholism ever been a problem in your family?
> Has child welfare services ever been involved with your children?
> How would you define *child neglect?* How would you define *child abuse?*
> What else would you like to talk about?
> Do you have any questions of me?
> Do you have any suggestions for when I meet other parents?
> How has it been to do the interviews?
> Explain that I will mail the third transcription with follow-up questions.

Figure 5.7.   Case example: Qualitative interview guide to answer a descriptive evaluation question.

This interview guide was used to answer the descriptive question, "How do consumers experience SBCM?"

Interview at the Rehabilitation Unit after the SBCM Intake Interview

1. What was it like to meet the worker from SBCM?
2. What was the purpose of the meeting with the SBCM caseworker?
3. What other things did the two of you discuss?
4. Please describe the meeting from beginning to end.
5. Is there anything else you would like to tell me about the reasons you are in the rehabilitation program?
6. Is there anything else you would like to tell me?
7. Do you have any questions of me?

Interview at One Month and Three Months after Discharge from the Rehabilitation Unit

1. Have you met the case manager at the SBCM site?
2. What was the first meeting like?
3. What was the purpose of that first meeting?
4. Please describe the meeting from beginning to end.
5. What do you like about the meeting at the SBCM site?
6. How are the meetings with the workers at SBCM different from meetings with other workers you have had?
7. Is there anything you would like to change about the meetings with the case-worker?
8. Is there anything else you would like to tell me about the reasons you are in case management?
9. Is there anything else you would like to tell me?
10. Do you have any questions for me?

The two evaluators should establish a protocol for how they will work together. The recorder may ask follow-up questions based on his or her observation of the focus group. For an example of a qualitative focus group protocol, see figure 5.8.

If practitioners audiotape the focus group, the facilitator may need to instruct participants to speak slowly and clearly and, at times, to repeat their statements. Transcribing an audiotape is very difficult, especially if persons' voices or tones are similar. Sometimes, the facilitator can announce that a new person is responding to the question to aid the person transcribing the interview. Videotaping the focus group helps in keeping observational notes, especially if one wants to capture participants' nonverbal reactions. The transcriber needs to enter initials or other symbols onto the transcription for each respondent on the tape. More discussion about transcription occurs later in this chapter.

It is helpful to display key words via a flip chart or a projection device of some sort so that all respondents can see the collective responses. If one expects detailed notes from the evaluator who is serving as the recorder, then do not have the recorder also be the scribe for the flip charts. It is nearly impossible to facilitate and scribe at the same time. In order to ensure their full participation in the focus group, do not expect one of the participants to serve as scribe. The flip chart sheets of paper peppered with permanent marker words can be a source of information to compare to the recorder's notes and later transcriptions.

Train all persons who are conducting focus groups to increase the consistency and reliability of data collection and reporting, especially when more than one team of evaluators is conducting the focus groups at different sites. Training should cover points such as

How directive should the facilitator be?

Is the audiotape the main source of data or a support to the notes of the recorder?

How should the facilitator respond to questions about the purpose of the evaluation?

Provide a checklist of items for all teams to have before they jump in their cars and travel to the focus group site. Train all evaluators regarding the format of and depth of information to include in the summary of the focus group.

Krueger and Casey's (2000) book on focus groups is an excellent resource for conducting qualitative focus groups for exploratory and descriptive purposes. The authors conceptualize the qualitative focus group as an interactive, flexible, open-ended interview process. They provide suggestions for preparing and conducting the interviews as well as recording the information collected during the interviews.

Figure 5.8. Case example: Qualitative focus group interview guide to answer a descriptive evaluation question.

Consumer Focus Group Questions

The following is an informal checklist of items to cover before starting the focus group. Cover the content in the words that work best for you. (Allot 15 minutes)

Introductions

____ My name is _____. I'll be asking the questions today.

____ My name is _____. I'll be taking notes today.

Details about the Consent Form

____ This focus group discussion is part of a two-year study being conducted by _____ evaluating the outreach efforts of counties to enroll children who are eligible for the Medicaid Expansion program commonly called Healthy Start or CHIP.

____ This focus group will be taped. Please talk slowly and clearly so my colleague can take good notes.

____ Your participation is voluntary and confidential. Also, please respect the confidentiality of the other persons in the room. Do not repeat their comments to anyone else outside of this room. Please take time to read the consent to participate form before we go any further.

____ At the end of this interview, you will receive a $15 gift certificate to _____ grocery.

____ The entire focus group will last no longer than one hour.

____ Are there any questions?

____ If not, please sign the consent form if you agree to participate in this focus group. If you do not agree with the form, you do not have to participate in this focus group.

Format of the Focus Group

____ I will read one question at a time. Each person will have the chance to answer the question. Please, only one person respond at a time. I may need to limit how much time we give to each question.

____ I understand it may be difficult to hold your responses, but I need to structure the responses so that I can record them accurately. We have provided you with paper and pencils to write down your thoughts while waiting to respond so that you don't forget the important points you want to say.

____ If there is something you did not have a chance to say, we will have a few minutes at the end of the focus group to go over your responses.

____ Any questions before I go on?

Consumer Focus Group Questions

The interviewer will ask each question with one person at a time. (Allot 15 minutes for question 1)

1. How did you first find out about the health insurance program for your children called Healthy Start or CHIP? For example, did you hear about Healthy Start from a caseworker? Health advocate? Hospital staff? Friends or family? Advertisements?

   How did you apply for Healthy Start (or CHIP)?

   What persons helped you apply for Healthy Start (or CHIP)?

   Was your child accepted into the program? If no, why not?

   Is your child still in the program? If no, why not?

2. What or who helped you the most to enroll your child(ren) in Healthy Start? (Allot 5 minutes)

3. What were the obstacles to enrolling your child(ren) in Healthy Start? (Allot 5 minutes)

4. Are you aware of specific outreach efforts in your area to enroll minority groups in Healthy Start? (Allot 5 minutes)

   (If yes, the interviewer lists the strategies and the target minority group on the flip chart.)

5. Were there any posters, billboards, or flyers you saw describing Healthy Start? (Allot 10 minutes)

   If yes, what and where were they? Did these flyers influence you to call Healthy Start?

   Were there any commercials you heard describing Healthy Start?

   If yes, what and where were they? Did these commercials influence you to call Healthy Start?

   Were there any _____ (other efforts in the plan that have not yet been discussed)?

   If yes, what and where were they? Did these efforts influence you to call Healthy Start?

6. Were you part of an evaluation of _____? (Allot 5 minutes)

   If yes, please explain.

7. That covers all of my questions. Do you have anything else to add about Healthy Start or CHIP and your outreach strategies? (Allot 5 minutes for questions 7 and 8)

8. Do you have any questions for me?

Thank you for your participation!

Written Surveys.   Participants can be asked to answer written qualitative questions on a survey. A **survey** or questionnaire is a set of questions developed by the evaluation stakeholders to collect locally specific information. The entire survey can contain only qualitative, open-ended questions, or it can contain both qualitative and quantitative questions.

One common way in which stakeholders use surveys is as part of a *needs* or *assets assessment* to determine respondents' perceptions of areas that need an intervention. Provider surveys are surveys sent to representatives of a social service agency asking questions about the services delivered. For example, during one community's efforts to develop a teenage pregnancy prevention plan, written provider surveys were sent to learn which agencies were providing teenage pregnancy prevention services (Brun & Giga, 1999).

Another common way in which stakeholders use surveys is to get feedback about an event, intervention, or program. The instruments employed for this purpose are called satisfaction surveys. Satisfaction surveys help persons adapt the intervention but do not provide data about whether the intervention created the desired results.

The following list details ways in which to administer surveys. Methods are listed in the order most likely to produce the best response rates, from highest to lowest. Ways in which potential participants are missed are listed too:

1. Hand deliver a survey, and wait for it to be completed. Examples of potential participants missed: persons not present owing to illness or some other reason; persons who are present but do not like to answer surveys; persons who do not give serious thought to their answers to the surveys; and persons who do not understand the questions, a possible occurrence for persons from cultural backgrounds different from the evaluators'.

2. Conduct a telephone survey. Examples of potential participants missed: same as method 1 as well as persons without phones; persons not home when the phone call is made; and persons who have caller ID or screen calls for solicitors or phone surveys.

3. Conduct an Internet survey. Examples of potential participants missed: same as method 1 as well as persons without access to the Internet and persons who do have access but do not like to answer Internet surveys.

4. Mail a survey, and request its return. Examples of potential participants missed: same as method 1 as well as persons without a mailing address; persons who moved without a forwarding address; and persons who do not like to respond to mail surveys.

QUANTITATIVE APPROACHES TO ASKING QUESTIONS

Constructed Surveys.   Quantitative survey questions come supplied with predetermined answers from which the respondent is asked to choose.

The predetermined answers may be based on theory or practical administrative program needs. The twenty-six competencies listed in the quantitative survey described earlier in figure 5.5 were written by the evaluators on the basis of theories described in the literature and course syllabi. The underlying descriptive theory was that workers possessing certain competencies deliver effective interventions to mental health clients. Closed-ended questions were also asked about the respondent's preferences for training on these competencies, such as whether he or she preferred receiving college course credit for the training or taking the courses on the weekend. For the quantitative survey developed in this evaluation, see figure 5.9.

Standardized Instruments.   Persons can implement **standardized instruments,** that is, evaluation and research data-collection tools, tested and reported in the literature. Corcoran and Fischer (2000) provide a two-volume set of actual instruments used most often by social service workers in clinical settings. The authors begin the first volume with an overview of the issues to consider when choosing a standardized instrument. They provide additional sources for locating published instruments (see vol. 1, pp. 53–57) and discuss questions to ask when reviewing instruments (see vol. 1, pp. 56–72). Royse et al. (2001) and Bloom et al. (2003) also provide a discussion on the use of standardized measures and include selected instruments.

During the course of the literature review, you will locate journal and Web site references that contain either actual instruments or reviews of instruments. During the evaluation of FSIs, reviews of family and child instruments were consulted (Pecora, Fraser, Nelson, McCroskey, & Meezan, 1995; Sawin, Harrigan, & Woog, 1995; USDHHS, 1993). Authors often publish articles demonstrating the reliability and validity of standardized instruments in evaluation and research journals.

When reading reviews of specific instruments, look for the following information:

general description of the instrument

description of the theory underlying the instrument

evidence of the instrument's validity and reliability

evidence of the instrument being used across different cultural groups

results of using the instrument

procedure for implementing and scoring the instrument

information on how to obtain the instrument, including costs

Stakeholders may prefer using quantitative instruments rather than qualitative surveys, arguing that quantitative instruments are more efficient, credible, and accountable. First, from an efficiency standpoint, someone

Figure 5.9.   Case example: Quantitative survey.

	How *important* do you think it is for a direct-care mental health worker to have the following skills and/or knowledge?					How much would you (or the workers you supervise) *benefit* from additional education in the following?				
	Not important	Somewhat important	Important	Very important	Extremely important	Definitely not important	Probably not important	Don't know	Probably benefit	Definitely benefit
1. Treating clients with respect, dignity, and as equal partners in their treatment.	①	②	③	④	⑤	①	②	③	④	⑤
2. Including family members and other supportive people/groups in the client's treatment.	①	②	③	④	⑤	①	②	③	④	⑤
3. Knowing the symptoms/ characteristics of mental illness.	①	②	③	④	⑤	①	②	③	④	⑤
4. Responding to cultural, racial, and gender issues that affect clients.	①	②	③	④	⑤	①	②	③	④	⑤
5. Knowing the uses and side effects of psychiatric medications.	①	②	③	④	⑤	①	②	③	④	⑤
6. Knowing the biological nature of mental illness.	①	②	③	④	⑤	①	②	③	④	⑤
7. Knowing and using the best types of therapy for general mental illness.	①	②	③	④	⑤	①	②	③	④	⑤
8. Knowing and using the best types of therapy for people with a forensic status.	①	②	③	④	⑤	①	②	③	④	⑤
9. Knowing and using the best types of therapy for people with a substance abuse/ mental illness (SA/MI) diagnosis.	①	②	③	④	⑤	①	②	③	④	⑤

	How *important* do you think it is for a direct-care mental health worker to have the following skills and/or knowledge?						How much would you (or the workers you supervise) *benefit* from additional education in the following?				
	Not important	Somewhat important	Important	Very important	Extremely important		Definitely not important	Probably not important	Don't know	Probably benefit	Definitely benefit
10. Knowing and using the best types of therapy for people with a mental illness/ mentally retarded (MI/MR) diagnosis.	①	②	③	④	⑤		①	②	③	④	⑤
11. Knowing and using the best types of therapy for children/adolescents affected by severe emotional disorders (SED).	①	②	③	④	⑤		①	②	③	④	⑤
12. Knowing and using crisis interventions.	①	②	③	④	⑤		①	②	③	④	⑤
13. Knowing and using recovery principles.	①	②	③	④	⑤		①	②	③	④	⑤
14. Developing and putting into practice Individual Service Plans (ISP) and Individual Treatment Plans (ITP).	①	②	③	④	⑤		①	②	③	④	⑤
15. Using community resources effectively.	①	②	③	④	⑤		①	②	③	④	⑤
16. Being a client advocate.	①	②	③	④	⑤		①	②	③	④	⑤
17. Knowing about legal issues, client rights, and ethical issues.	①	②	③	④	⑤		①	②	③	④	⑤
18. Working well as a member of an interdisciplinary team.	①	②	③	④	⑤		①	②	③	④	⑤

(figure continues)

	How *important* do you think it is for a direct-care mental health worker to have the following skills and/or knowledge?					How much would you (or the workers you supervise) *benefit* from additional education in the following?				
	Not important	Somewhat important	Important	Very important	Extremely important	Definitely not important	Probably not important	Don't know	Probably benefit	Definitely benefit
19. Working in a professional way.	①	②	③	④	⑤	①	②	③	④	⑤
20. Evaluating one's own work performance.	①	②	③	④	⑤	①	②	③	④	⑤
21. Keeping accurate work records.	①	②	③	④	⑤	①	②	③	④	⑤
22. Knowing and being able to use first aid, CPR, and other ways to keep clients and workers safe.	①	②	③	④	⑤	①	②	③	④	⑤
23. Providing basic nursing care, including taking vital signs and helping clients use the bathroom.	①	②	③	④	⑤	①	②	③	④	⑤
24. Using different ways to reduce worker stress.	①	②	③	④	⑤	①	②	③	④	⑤
25. Knowing basic facts of good nutrition.	①	②	③	④	⑤	①	②	③	④	⑤
26. Using computer technology.	①	②	③	④	⑤	①	②	③	④	⑤

else has already done the hard and laborious work of constructing the instrument. It does take a lot of time to construct a well-thought-out, closed-ended set of questions. Finding an instrument that measures exactly what one wants to describe or explain is a great time-saver. Make sure that the instrument does address the stakeholders' evaluation questions. In the evaluation of FSIs, it turned out that each FSI had a different conception of how its interventions affected family functioning. Thus, in retrospect, the evaluators may not have used the most valid instrument for the concepts tested.

From a credibility standpoint, evidence can be found that an instrument is valid and reliable. *Validity* in this sense means that the instrument measures the intended concepts. The General Family Functioning questions of the Family Assessment Device (Epstein et al., 1982) administered in the evaluation of FSIs was based on systems, role, and communication theories. There was extensive evidence available in the literature that this instrument did measure the theorized concepts as well as related concepts contained in other standardized instruments (Sawin et al., 1995). *Reliability* here means that the instrument measures these concepts consistently and repeatedly across participants. For more discussion of instrument validity and reliability, see the references to quantitative data collection listed in the "Further Readings" section of this chapter.

When reviewing the literature, look for descriptions of the validity and reliability of the instrument across different populations. Has it been used with different cultural groups? Do its concepts have the same meaning across cultures or across genders? Has it been translated into different languages? Has it been normed for different cultural groups? That is, does a particular score have the same meaning for different groups?

Focus Groups.   Quantitative focus group questions require more than one respondent to select closed-ended responses. In the example in figure 5.5, the focus group respondents were asked to answer the survey that some members had already completed individually. This format was followed partly to observe whether the focus group responses would be reliable, that is, consistent with the results from the written survey. Also, time did not permit discussion related to the prioritization of the competencies in the focus groups, only discussion meant to ascertain participants' descriptions of other competencies deemed important and preferences for training on the competencies.

The earlier discussion about different ways to administer qualitative surveys (e.g., face-to-face, mail, telephone, and Internet) also applies to quantitative surveys and instruments. To learn more about constructing and implementing surveys, see Fink (2003). To learn about implementing instruments through single system designs, see Bloom et al. (2003).

QUALITATIVE APPROACHES TO OBSERVATION

The purpose of the open-ended, qualitative recording of observations is to provide rich, contextual descriptions surrounding the evaluation and research questions. In the exploratory study with parents, the researcher recorded open-ended observations of the environment in which each interview occurred. Five of the six interviews took place in participants' homes, the sixth in the office of an agency worker.

The observations were hand recorded immediately after each interview and included descriptions of the following:

The participant and any other persons present (adults and children).

Items in the home that related to experiences the parents shared. One parent described how her faith helped her raise her child positively. The observation notes included descriptions of religious items.

Observations of the parents' nonverbal behavior. It was noted that one parent established eye contact with the child by getting down on the floor.

Observations of the surrounding neighborhood. One day's case notes were: "The home was located on a street with high traffic. The home was a two-story, four-unit apartment building that was part of a larger apartment complex."

Observations of the researcher's behaviors that were not evident on the audiotape. It was noted that "the researcher turned off the tape recorder during the time Ms. Smith received a telephone call."

The researcher also took verbatim notes of a parenting support group that he attended with one of the participants. The purpose of observing the group was to experience an activity at the suggestion of one of the participants. The parent perceived the group as a positive support. The researcher's observation affirmed that the participant and other parents in the group offered support and advice to each other.

The qualitative observation approach in the descriptive evaluation of the SBCM program was similar. Observational notes were taken of the interview settings. The first two interviews took place in an agency setting, the last in the participant's home. The evaluator also documented his observation of an Alcoholics Anonymous group in the transitional living program and an SBCM assessment and case-planning session. The purpose of the observations was to observe events that the participants experienced. The evaluator's observations were triangulated with the participants' descriptions of the same events.

QUANTITATIVE APPROACHES TO OBSERVATION

The purpose of the closed-ended, quantitative recording of observations is to provide valid and reliable measures of the desired results needed to answer descriptive and explanatory evaluation and research questions. In the research study of a parent behavioral modification intervention, a closed-ended observation tool was developed that allowed the social service worker to measure specific behaviors of the two parents and their two boys.

An observation instrument was also developed that allowed each parent to measure desired (e.g., playing without hitting) and inappropriate (e.g., hitting) child behavior.

The *first step* in developing this observation tool was to operationalize the target behavior for change, in this case, *hitting*. The parents and the social service worker identified all hitting behaviors (pushing, biting, tripping, punching, etc.). They also defined different parent responses to the hitting (yelling, hitting, ignoring, placing in time-out, etc.). The process of defining the observed behaviors itself led to the desired outcome of less hitting because the parents became aware of their responses that actually increased the hitting.

The *second step* was to agree on the observation procedure. The parents agreed to record their children's behavior during the following thirty-minute intervals because these were the times the children fought the most: (1) 7:20–8:00 a.m.; (2) 2:30–3.00 p.m.; and (3) 7:30–8.00 p.m. They placed a sheet of paper on the refrigerator door for each boy that listed both appropriate behavior (playing without hitting) and what constituted hitting. Each time period was broken down into five-minute intervals. A check was placed in any interval in which any hitting behavior by either boy occurred, a star in any interval in which no hitting behavior occurred. This *interval observation* procedure was chosen because it was easier than recording *frequency* (i.e., every single time one boy hit), because the fighting was occurring so often, and also easier than recording *duration* (i.e., how long the hitting lasted) because the length of hitting bouts varied.

The *third step* was to ensure the reliability of the observation procedures. *Intrarater reliability* is achieved when an individual observer follows observation procedures consistently, *interrater reliability* when all observers follow observation procedures consistently. In this case interrater reliability was achieved in two ways. First, each parent recorded the children's behaviors at the same times for a two-week period and then compared measurements. Once there was consistency (i.e., 80% agreement) in their ratings, then either parent could reliably record the child's behavior alone. The social service worker also conducted several observations of the children during the 2:30–3:00 p.m. time slot and also achieved agreement with the parents' ratings.

Intrarater reliability was checked only through self-reporting. No outside observer took measurements frequently enough to enable comparison with the parents' measurements. The parents also recorded their responses to the children's behavior, such as reinforcing nonhitting behavior and employing a time-out when one of the boys did hit. There are threats to the credibility of self-reporting. In this example, the parents kept well-organized records of their observations and did reflect on whether they felt they were consistent in their measurements.

Quantitative observation ratings, both standardized and self-written instruments, are often administered in a single system evaluation or research design. A **single system design** is an evaluation or research study in which the desired results are measured both before and after an intervention has been administered to a single system, which can be an individual, family, group, organization, or community. Thus, the *fourth step* was to have a baseline measure of the children's hitting and the parents' responses before the social worker discussed alternate ways for the parents to interact with the children. This study used an AB design which consists of a baseline measure of target behaviors and then a measure of those same behaviors after the intervention has been delivered. *A* refers to the baseline period before intervention and *B* refers to the intervention period. The intervention in this case was a ten-week parent-training course that supported the use of reinforcement for nonhitting behavior (e.g., verbal praise and weekly rewards such as trips to the park) and time-out for hitting behavior (e.g., two minutes at the kitchen table). There was a noticeable change in the boys' behavior during this intervention phase. Thus, the *fifth step* in the example was agreeing to the consistent and reliable implementation of the intervention and single system design evaluation.

The charting of the children's noticeable change through this basic AB single system design showed the parents that changes in their own behavior resulted in the desired changes in the boys' behavior. From an evaluation credibility standpoint (discussed later in this chapter), the single system designs listed below could be considered to provide more valid evidence that, in fact, the social worker's intervention with the parents was a main influence in the change of desired behaviors:

An ABA design consists of expecting the inappropriate behavior to return to baseline level when the intervention is withdrawn. The parents were encouraged to continue to chart their children's behavior after the intervention with the social worker ended. The expectation, however, was that the parents would continue to use the skills they learned in the intervention and be able to *maintain* the children's appropriate behavior at the desired B level or better. A refers to the baseline period before the intervention, B refers to the intervention period, and A refers to the period after the intervention has ended.

A multiple-baseline design consists of measuring the impact of the intervention across different behaviors, persons, or settings. The effectiveness of the intervention is demonstrated if the desired changes can be generalized to other conditions. In our example, the parents could chart other target behaviors, such as finishing chores or going to bed on time. In other settings, social service workers may want to measure the same intervention across different clients. In one of the case examples in figure 1.7, two master's level students conducted a multiple-baseline design using the Goal Attainment Scale with youth attending a drop-in center. The results demonstrated that setting goals in an informal manner was effective in helping the youth reach their goals.

For a more thorough discussion of quantitative approaches to observation and the use of single system design, consult the references in the "Further Readings" section. The single system design is a common tool taught in undergraduate and graduate social service programs to meet the CSWE learning objective that students be able to evaluate their own practice.

Here are some final tips on the use of quantitative approaches to observation and of single system design:

1. Do not underestimate clients' ability to record their own behavior and that of others. People respond to seeing changes in behavior graphically displayed in frequency tables and charts. Records of behavior are especially effective when attempting to change unhealthy habits, such as smoking and overeating.

2. Do not underestimate the change in perceptions that usually accompanies a change in behavior. In the parent-training example, during the fifth week the mother threw the charts on the table and said, "This stuff does *not* work," even though the charts were showing a positive change in behavior. When the social work intern explored this statement more, the mother disclosed that her friends and relatives continued to say that the only way to discipline children is through physical force. Thus, the mother was trying to change behavior in a way that did not coincide with long-held attitudes. Many behavioral interventions often add a cognitive change component.

3. Some change will occur before the actual treatment or intervention stage. From a design credibility standpoint, that means that there may be some distortion between the baseline and the intervention stages. The point emphasized throughout this text is that the process of the evaluation is as important as the outcome. Thus, change can occur from the very beginning of the evaluation.

4. Train all persons to carry out the observation as consistently as possible. It takes a lot of time to specify the target behaviors in a way that is conducive to consistent recording. Again, the process of identifying target behaviors, intervention, and the procedures for recording baseline and intervention data can lead to desired changes.

QUALITATIVE APPROACHES TO COLLECTING SECONDARY DOCUMENTS

Secondary documents are sources of information recorded by someone else prior to the current evaluation that are used to help answer the current evaluation questions. In qualitative approaches, secondary documents are conceptualized as contextual descriptions of the experiences being explored or described. In the exploratory study with six parents, each participant was asked the question, "Was there anything you read that helped you as a parent?" The answers to this question became one source of documents collected for this study. One parent provided posters she was given by the doctor at a local health clinic. The posters contained information on proper pre- and postnatal care. Another parent directed the researcher to a book she had read on Christian child raising. Another provided handouts from a parenting class. Qualitatively, these documents showed the range of materials that had shaped the way these parents raised their children.

There were two examples used earlier in this book in which secondary documents were collected qualitatively during agency site visits (1) to describe the perceived success of FSIs by staff and clients and (2) to describe the perceived success of the Children's Health Insurance Program (CHIP) outreach efforts. In both examples, the participants controlled which documents were presented to the evaluation team. The evaluation team was open to all documents the participants chose.

Examples of secondary documents provided in the two examples are the following:

agency written material, such as a mission statement as it appeared on a Web page or in an agency brochure

agency promotional material distributed at community health fairs, such as pens, buttons, and other items carrying the agency name and services

media accounts of an event or situation, whether from newspapers, journals, or telecasts

reports from self-evaluations

data collected for annual reports, such as the number of consumers served or results from satisfaction surveys

curriculum used for community presentations

From a qualitative approach, the documents listed reflected the participants' perceptions of evidence of success. Reviewing the list, however, the reader can see that the documents included descriptions of the intervention as well as possible results. Some reading the final evaluation report may, therefore, not agree that the documents do, in fact, demonstrate actual success. Consumer utilization data, for example, reflect usage but not necessarily client change. The same is true for client satisfaction data. At the same time, the evaluators now have a preliminary view of how participants view program success. They and other key stakeholders can help participants collect data more in line with descriptive and explanatory evaluation questions.

The major disadvantage of using secondary documents as data is that the documents were written to meet goals different from those of the current evaluation. For example, a local United Way provided the reports of four separate needs assessments as the basis for an evaluation to determine the priority target areas when writing a five-year strategic plan. Each report was based on different evaluation questions, data-collection procedures, and foci. The difficult task for the evaluation team was to compose a data-analysis scheme (described later in this chapter) that applied across the different reports.

QUANTITATIVE APPROACHES TO COLLECTING SECONDARY DOCUMENTS

In quantitative approaches, documents are collected that answer predetermined descriptive or explanatory questions. In evaluations for accreditation or auditing purposes, persons know ahead of time the criteria for reports that need to be submitted. That is, the form that the reports are to take has been predetermined. In addition to the documents selected by the participants qualitatively in the two previous examples, the evaluators also collected RFPs filed by the participating agency with the state funding agency. Quantitatively, it was assumed that there would be some consistency in how the RFPs were written since all agencies were responding to the same, predetermined guidelines.

Another major source for secondary documents from a quantitative approach is reports of data collected by other agencies that have some relevance to the current evaluation questions. The evaluation team helping key stakeholders develop a countrywide family violence prevention plan analyzed reports of family violence, including:

National Incident-Based Reporting System cases of domestic violence reported to the country sheriff's office in a one-year period

annual reports of domestic violence from the countrywide family violence shelter

the number of founded cases of child abuse and neglect reported in the county

the number of abuse reports for persons over sixty-five years old in the county

These reports, studies of family violence reported in the literature, and new data collected by the evaluation team all became part of a report titled "Status of Family Violence." This report was the primary tool used to guide the strategic planning process.

Since the evaluators had no control over the data-collection process, they could not guarantee the validity or reliability of the secondary documents. Persons should review the methods used to collect the data reported in secondary documents critically. Even if they agree that the data were collected reliably, they can still challenge the data's validity, at least as far as the current evaluation question is concerned. In the family violence prevention planning evaluation, the elder abuse reports were primarily of victims in institutional settings. The numbers reported could be even higher when reports of elder abuse in the home are also included.

DATA ANALYSIS

Data analysis is the process of making sense and meaning of information gathered in an evaluation. Data analysis is first a process of *reducing* the original information into a form that can be more easily managed and understood within the theoretical context of the evaluation. Once the original information is reduced, data analysis becomes a process of *interpreting* the connection between the findings and the evaluation questions.

In very general terms, qualitative approaches to data analysis are open to the theories that emerge from the data as well as the theories that social service workers and other stakeholders already have before beginning the evaluation. Such approaches begin with predetermined theories that guide the data analysis. As the reader will see from the discussion that follows, there is during data analysis (as at other stages of data collection) a distinct difference between a qualitative and a quantitative approach. In the qualitative approach, there is a constant comparison between possible perceived relationships between the intervention or program and client change. In the quantitative approach, there is a specific perceived relationship that is tested. This connection between the evaluation question, theory building, and theory testing, on the one hand, and qualitative and quantitative approaches, on the other, was illustrated in figure 4.2.

The approach to data analysis can be different from the approach used to collect the data. The results of open-ended focus groups (qualitative approach) can be organized into predetermined categories on the basis of a specific theory or model (quantitative approach). Similarly, documents that participants select and choose to give to the evaluators (qualitative approach) can be analyzed by category on the basis of a specific theory or model (quantitative approach). Surveys that contain closed-ended questions (quantitative approach) often also contain open-ended questions (qualitative approach). The data analysis can compare the answers that were narrowly focused by the evaluators (quantitative approach) to the answers that emerged from the participants (qualitative approach). Figure 5.2 recognizes that, except for purely exploratory and purely explanatory evaluations, the entire evaluation process can be a combination of qualitative and quantitative approaches.

The data-analysis process is less cumbersome when persons collect only information relating to the evaluation questions. This avoids the presence of data that distract from the original questions. Keeping the focus narrow is always difficult because of natural human curiosity.

Keeping the focus narrow is even more difficult in qualitative approaches. A goal of qualitative data collection is to learn what is relevant or important to the participants. The possible boundaries or categories are not exhausted until the practitioner has had prolonged engagement in the natural setting of the participants, that is, until the researcher has observed and interviewed the participants to the point of theme redundancy. Those themes narrow the focus, compared to the wide range of possible foci that were present when the researcher or evaluator first entered the setting.

The focus in quantitative approaches is on answering descriptive and explanatory questions and is already narrowed down to certain specified categories. Thus, the data collected should be pertinent to the characteristics already identified in the literature and by key evaluation stakeholders. The evaluation becomes the place to test whether those characteristics are present in the current setting.

This chapter started by making the point that information available to an agency worker is transferred into data when key stakeholders collect that information to answer exploratory, descriptive, or explanatory evaluation questions. The data can be collected in an open-ended, qualitative or a closed-ended, quantitative manner by asking questions, observing, or collecting secondary documents. The discussion that follows describes how the data are further transformed into *findings* reported as qualitative themes or quantitative statistics. These findings become the basis for *interpreting* the data. It is important to understand how the original information has taken on new meaning during the data-reduction and -analysis steps.

The data-analysis procedures must also match the evaluation questions being asked. Thus, qualitative approaches to data analysis will not answer explanatory questions, and quantitative approaches will not answer exploratory questions. The middle-ground descriptive questions can be answered through qualitative and quantitative approaches. Keep your original evaluation questions in mind as you read the material that follows.

QUALITATIVE APPROACHES TO DATA ANALYSIS

The qualitative approach to data analysis can be applied to data collected and recorded in all three methods discussed earlier: (1) asking questions; (2) making observations; and (3) collecting secondary data. The goal of qualitative data analysis is to reduce the large amounts of open-ended narrative data into manageable codes, categories, and themes that credibly capture the experiences and descriptions of the participants and settings. The examples given below relate specifically to transforming interview data, but they can also apply to reported observations and secondary documents.

All ethical guidelines for the protection of participants must be followed during all parts of the evaluation process. The analysis of qualitative data can involve the selection of direct quotes that appear in final reports or journal articles. The evaluator needs to notify participants of this possibility and assure them that confidentiality will be maintained. No identifying information should be provided in final reports. It should not be possible to trace any direct quotes back to their sources. The only exception to this policy is when permission is given for reports to contain identifying information. For an example of empowering participants by including their names in the final publication, see Lather (1991).

Several case examples reported earlier followed the procedures for reducing the data generated by open-ended interviews:

1. The interviewer *tape-recorded* the interview.

2. The interviewer wrote *notes* on the interview guide, highlighting points to review closely later.

3. After the interview was over, the interviewer recorded his comments about the interview in the *reflective journal*. Within one to three days, he typed up his handwritten notes, postinterview taped comments, and any other insights he had about the interview.

4. The interviewer, or a person hired by him, *transcribed* the tape-recorded interview verbatim.

5. The transcription was organized by *themes* and corresponding quotes.

The important point to note is that each of these steps resulted in a transformation of the original information, which was the words spoken by the participants in the interviews. In theory, the verbatim transcription should be just that, verbatim. In actuality, transcribers make mistakes, which are influenced by their own predispositions, theoretical or otherwise. Below are some tips to consider about the mutual influence between evaluator and participants in each of the steps listed above. For more detailed discussion of qualitative approaches to data reduction and analysis, consult the texts on qualitative methods in the "Further Readings" section.

Tape Recording.   Buy, borrow, or rent a quality tape recorder. It should be one that has a microphone sensitive enough to capture the words of persons sitting far away. It should also be one that can be battery operated so that it can be used in those situations in which there is no access to an electrical outlet. Practice operating the recorder before the interview. Position the microphone away from such distracting sounds as a blaring television, a crying child, traffic, sirens, and loud voices. If distracting sounds cannot be avoided, ask to move to another location, or politely rearrange the interview time. Ask people to repeat their answers if needed. Some persons choose to videotape interviews. The main reason to videotape is to include observational data. If you plan to use only the words spoken, then video-recording inundates you with information, more information than you need. A poor-quality tape-recording affects all the remaining steps of the interview.

Note Taking.   Be clear about the purpose of taking notes during the interview. Are the notes the primary source of recording the data, or are they serving as a secondary method of collecting data or as a reliability check? Notes can serve as cues to double-check specific themes when reviewing the tape or transcription. Tape-recording the interview allows the evaluator to give the participant all his or her attention and not be distracted by the note-taking process. If practitioners are not able to tape-record the interview, then they may need to take more extensive notes.

Reflective Notes.   Take notes after an interview to reflect on issues, values, biases, and reactions that arise during the interview. The reflective journal is an important vehicle for identifying how your thoughts and actions intertwined with the participants' words. The awareness thereby attained helps the evaluator get out of the way of the participants (Lather, 1991) and make the final interpretation a close approximation of their experiences. The analogy to direct practice is that the reflective journal serves a similar purpose as process notes. Both are used to analyze the interviewer's (e.g., the evaluator's or the therapist's) role in the interviewee/interviewer dialogue.

Transcribing the Interview.   Typing the recorded words of a person is no easy task! A one-hour, verbatim-transcribed interview will consume twelve to fifteen typed pages. Buy, borrow, or rent a quality transcribing machine. It should be able to play back the tape through both headphones and speakers. The tape-recording is sometimes easier to hear using the speaker, but, if you must transcribe the tape in a public place (e.g., your office), it is essential that you use the headphones to protect the participants' privacy. The transcribing machine should also have a foot pedal that allows you to stop, rewind, and go forward on the tape. With practice, practitioners hope to achieve the ability to type at the same pace one is able to stop and forward the tape without rewinding. Finally, the transcribing machine should have speed control. This allows practitioners to adjust the speed of the tape to the point that one can type as one listens to the tape. A slower speed also allows one to better understand words that may be hard to hear at regular speed.

Establish clear guidelines for yourself or others you hire to type the transcriptions. Not every transcription needs to be typed verbatim, although it is best to transcribe the first one or two interviews verbatim until you become familiar with the topics of the interview. Write down rules about typing utterances (e.g., *uh, oh*)

whether to retype a statement if the participant repeats himself

what to paraphrase if you are not transcribing verbatim

having clear indicators of which statements were made by the interviewer (e.g., *Int:*) and which by the respondent (e.g., *Res:*)

putting the participants' actual words in quotation marks to distinguish them from your paraphrasing

having guidelines of when to start new paragraphs (e.g., when a person switches to a new topic)

numbering the pages and, sometimes, the lines

Enter the transcription into computer software that is compatible with the theme-analysis software you plan to use. For example, some types of qualitative software require the transcription to be in rich text format. Most qualitative software applications have a process to convert files into a format appropriate to that application. Practitioners may be able to save valuable time if they enter the transcribed data directly into the software application to be used for the theme analysis. For a discussion of qualitative data-analysis software, see Drisko (2004), Richards (1999), Weitzman (1999) and Weitzman and Miles (1995).

Have someone other than the transcriber conduct a reliability check of the transcribed data. Reliability here refers to the accuracy and consistency of reducing and interpreting the data. In one evaluation, reliability was reached by having a second person listen to the taped interview while reading the transcription. The purpose of the reliability check was to ensure accuracy of transcription. In another evaluation, instead of reviewing the entire tape, the second person listened to one-minute snippets of the tape at fifteen-minute intervals. Major discrepancies between the transcription and the tape would indicate that the evaluator needed to compare the entire transcription against the tape.

Theme Analysis of the Transcription.   Theme analysis reduces the transcription to codes, categories, and themes. In qualitative processes, **codes** are symbols or labels given to words or phrases that compose a single idea. In the exploratory study of six parents, *GM* was the code given to references that participants made to their grandmothers. Categories are the labels given to groupings of codes addressing similar topics. In the same study, two categories were *advice* and *family*. Statements coded *GM* could fall under both these categories. **Themes** are more general, conceptual ideas that capture related categories. In the interactive model of parenting that emerged from this study and is shown in figure 4.3, the five general themes were *spirituality, slogans for change, agencies in my way, agencies that were* *supportive,* and *knowing my child.* Conceptually, these themes were the common strengths on which the participants relied to raise their children. The words coded *GM* may have fallen under the themes *spirituality* and *slogans for change.* For more discussion of the mechanics of assigning words and phrases to codes and categories, see Rodwell (1995).

You can create codes and categories directly on the transcription. Use different colored pens to write different categories or themes in the margins. Save the original transcription as your raw, untouched data so that an outside person can see the original words before coding. Coded hard copies of qualitative transcriptions can be quite colorful. The originally straightforward dialogue of the transcription has now been transformed into multiple shades of highlighter pen with strange coded words or combinations of letters and numbers in the margins. Arrows can be drawn connecting codes and sentences to each other. Categories can be crossed out, and new labels can replace old ones. Drawing an accompanying flow chart or theme chart helps lend some order to the seemingly chaotic array of words and symbols.

Exploratory and descriptive evaluation questions that follow primarily qualitative data-collection and data-analysis processes contribute to new knowledge through the process of the evaluation as much as the final product does. The evaluator and, one hopes, other stakeholders constantly move back and forth between gathering information and making critical assumptions about the interpretation of that information. Multiple interpretations are sought, including the analysis of the participants and the evaluator. Connections are made to relevant theories and empirical findings reported in the research literature. This notion of being critical of emerging and existing theories throughout the data-analysis process is adapted from the grounded theory approach (Strauss & Corbin, 1998).

Writing down coding rules in the procedural journal is essential to the reliability of the coding process. An example of a coding rule is, "Each time a person describes any member of his or her family, place that coded group of words into the category titled *family.*" For more discussion of qualitative coding rules, see Rodwell (1995).

Entering the coded data into a computer software package is the next step for qualitative analysis. Qualitative analysis software packages allow you to move data out of the transcribed form into new files arranged by themes. You can then compare the similar themes and provide direct quotes that reflect those themes. There are many additional analyses that you can conduct with qualitative software, including frequency counts (how often codes appear) and the graphic display of themes (Miles & Huberman, 1994), interactive PowerPoint presentations of the thematic data (Richards, 1999), and mapping of results reported in client narratives (Kibel, 1999). For an example of results collected from a qualitative, open-ended, focus group and reported both qualitatively and quantitatively, see figure 5.10.

Figure 5.10.   Case example: Reporting of qualitative and quantitative data analysis in the final evaluation report.

The results of the focus groups with stakeholders from ten Ohio counties about their successful outreach efforts to enroll eligible children in CHIP were reported both qualitatively and quantitatively.

Qualitative Reporting of Qualitative Focus Group Data

In the final report, direct quotes from direct-care staff, administrators, and consumers that exemplified the successful strategies listed above were provided. Below are some excerpts from *direct-care staff* related to the successful strategy of *agency collaboration:*

> We work with Head Start a lot. They go do a home visit and they enroll a child there. They'll find out this family doesn't have medical insurance and they'll ask the parents first if we can give CHIP outreach your name and address to contact you. And we work with doctors. They give us referrals. The doctors say, "They're having trouble getting medical insurance." We'll go chase the clients down and help them fill out the application. . . . They don't even have to come to Human Services.

> We entered into a contract with neighborhood agencies, because we felt that would be a good way to get applications with the community. Not everybody would want to come into our agency to apply or to mail in the application. We felt that, if they were centered in the community they could work with that community. The contract stipulated they would only be paid for the application if it was an application we were able to approve.

> I work at the Health Department and have called people at Human Services and asked them about what I need to get this person to be eligible either for their pregnancy or their child to go through services here. Maybe I even work with somebody in WIC.

> The parents did not want to come into our agency. For whatever reason, maybe transportation because I was far from school. So the school said, and I agreed with them wholeheartedly because it was their neighborhood, if the parent comes to school, we will fax the completed application to you.

> And I think one other thing that's helping that all of us sitting in this room today are doing is we use the same family assessment. Wherever they go first. Whether it's Head Start or the Health Department or Human Services. One of the questions on there is "Do you have insurance?" This triggers the person that's doing the assessment [to make the referral]. (Meyer et al., 2001, pp. 125–26)

Quantitative Reporting of Qualitative Focus Group Data

Following is a list of the *most common outreach strategies* across the ten counties as discussed in the *direct-care staff focus groups*. The numbers in parentheses refer to the number of the ten counties in which the strategy was mentioned:

> print and broadcast media (10)
>
> providing direct assistance to help persons fill out the application (10)
>
> collaborating with other referral agencies to inform potential clients about CHIP (10)

distributing promotional items at a public fair (7)

word-of-mouth referrals (7)

providing workshops, presentations, or meetings with other agencies about CHIP (5)

home visits (2)

The most successful outreach activities were

direct assistance to help potential clients fill out the application (7)

collaboration with agencies (6)

broadcast media, including broadcasts from adjoining counties (3)

The least successful outreach activities were

print resources, specifically a mass mailing or mass distribution of brochures at a fair (3)

broadcast media (3) (Meyer et al., 2001, pp. 21–22)

Take the time necessary to research the different qualitative software programs available before you begin to collect information. There are conceptual and practical considerations involved in choosing the software. The manual coding step is not always necessary. It is possible to code transcribed data as you read it on the computer screen. Some persons, myself included, keep the manual coding process to feel more in control of the comparative theory coding process (Strauss & Corbin, 1998). Some feel confident that they can meet the same rigorous grounded theory process without manually coding hard data.

In summary:

Have a data-management protocol.

Decide where the evaluators send the tapes, notes, and summaries.

Decide who summarizes the collective data and conducts the theme analysis.

Decide where the data-analysis notes will be kept.

Decide how these notes are then entered into a qualitative software package and by whom.

Decide how the final themes are then developed.

Remember, the idea is to keep such detailed notes that an outside person can audit your steps backward—from the interpretations in the final report all the way to the original words spoken by the participant. The evaluators are the keepers of the raw data (e.g., field notes, transcriptions, and software files), but the stakeholders have the right to know how the raw data was transformed.

QUANTITATIVE APPROACHES TO DATA ANALYSIS

The quantitative approach to data analysis can be applied to data collected and recorded via all three methods discussed earlier: (1) asking questions; (2) making observations; and (3) collecting secondary data. The goal of quantitative data analysis is to reduce the large amounts of data to manageable descriptive and inferential statistical analyses that credibly describe the participants and settings and, when appropriate, test relationships between studied characteristics of the participants and settings. The examples given below relate specifically to transforming interview data, but the same tips apply to reported observations and to secondary documents. Again, ethical guidelines protecting participant confidentiality must be followed. Whether you conduct these analyses or hire someone to conduct them for you, rely on your past research classes to develop an understanding of the theory and uses of quantitative analyses that will allow you to be a critical user of the information.

The quantitative data-reduction process of the descriptive evaluation that led to the development of a tool to prioritize competencies for mental health workers followed these steps:

1. A thorough review of the literature and interviews with key stakeholders led to the development of the closed-ended *interview survey*.

2. The survey was *delivered* to all direct-care mental health workers of identified behavioral health organizations in one state.

3. The responses to the returned surveys were entered into a computer software program for *statistical analysis* related to the descriptive or explanatory evaluation questions.

For a full description of the quantitative approach to data analysis that will be described below, see Clasen et al. (2003).

Instrument Development or Selection.   Instruments are used in quantitative approaches to test theories that guide the planning and implementation of interventions. The closed-ended format of a quantitative instrument allows responses to be entered into a computer software program for analysis. The process for developing the Competency Assessment Tool–Mental Health (CAT-MH) was discussed earlier in the section covering the literature review process. Twenty-one competencies were selected on the basis of a thorough review of the theoretical and empirical literature available about mental health worker competencies. The evaluation advisory group added four competencies related to specialized populations (e.g., people with a substance abuse/mental illness diagnosis) and one related to the ability to apply computer technology in their jobs.

This instrument was developed because the evaluators could not locate a standardized instrument measuring mental health worker competencies.

Once the competencies were agreed on, the evaluation team consulted with a statistical service that developed the actual Scantron survey. A Scantron survey allows participants to circle one answer to each question. Once the completed surveys are electronically scanned, numerical responses to each question by each respondent can be calculated and analyzed. "The instrument was piloted with twelve mental health employees for comprehension, readability, understanding, content validity, and clarity" (Clasen et al., 2003, p. 12). For the final instrument, see figure 5.9.

Statistical analyses of the returned instruments allowed the evaluators to assess the reliability of the two subscales for the instrument. For each question, the respondents were asked, "How *important* do you think it is for a direct-care mental health worker to have the following skills and/or knowledge?" This was called the *Knowledge* subscale. For each question, the respondents were asked, "How much would you (or the workers you supervise) *benefit* from additional education in the following?" This was called the *Benefit* subscale (Clasen et al., 2003, p. 12). The authors reported internal reliability for the two scales using a statistical analysis called *Cronbach's alpha*. They also reported correlation between items on the Knowledge and Benefit scales. "These correlations were conducted to determine if respondents thought a skill or knowledge was important, they would also think training in that area would be beneficial. Every correlation was significant" (Clasen et al., 2003, p. 13).

Whether an instrument is reliable and valid is important information for persons who intend to replicate that instrument in another evaluation or research setting. "Since all the competencies were rated by respondents as important, it seems clear that the CAT-MH successfully identified core competencies needed by mental health care workers. . . . In addition, assessments of the importance of a competency were significantly correlated to the benefit of training for that competency. The focus groups gathered narrative information that supported the validity of the constructed instrument, in that the competencies that ranked highest on both subscales were confirmed in the focus groups" (Clasen et al., 2003, p. 13). Future evaluations can further test the reliability and validity of this instrument, and its validity can be compared to other instruments that measure either or both subscales.

For more information on validity and reliability, whether it be of an instrument you construct or of a standardized instrument that you take from another source, see the references in this chapter's "Further Readings" section.

Instrument Delivery.   One goal of data collection is to reach the highest response rate possible in order to strengthen the generalizability of the results to the larger population. Previous discussion already covered the different ways instruments are usually delivered. The highest response rate occurs when the instrument is delivered face-to-face and returned at the same time it is delivered. The construction of the instrument also contributes to persons completing it. If the questions are too confusing, too long, or not relevant to respondents, it is not likely that they will complete the instrument. Well-constructed quantitative instruments make it easier for the respondents to complete the survey.

Another goal of data collection is that the results be credible or believable. From a quantitative approach, credible findings are reached by reducing the threats to internal and external validity through comparison group designs (Campbell & Stanley, 1963; Cook & Campbell, 1979). **Internal validity** is the ability to attribute results to the evaluated intervention or program. In research language, the outcomes are referred to as the *dependent variables*. Change in the client system is *dependent on* the intervention. The intervention is called the *independent variable*. The influence of factors other than the intervention, called *extraneous variables,* on the desired client system change is controlled through single system designs and group comparison designs, which are described below under "Quantitative Approaches to Credibility." **External validity** is the ability to generalize evaluation results to the larger population. Increasing the ability to generalize the results is also reached through single system designs and comparison group designs. The discussion of statistical analysis that follows is dependent on the controls contained in the evaluation design. There will be a discussion of reducing threats to validity through comparison group designs below.

Computerized Descriptive Statistical Analyses.   Responses to data collected quantitatively must now be coded and tabulated. Easy-to-use software has made data coding, entry, and tabulation much more user friendly than ever before. It allows social service workers to manage large amounts of data more reliably than when tabulating results and analyses manually. The most common statistical software taught in social work courses and used in social service agencies is SPSS. The most recent versions of SPSS are compatible with most personal computers. A good source for learning how to master SPSS is Babbie, Halley, and Zaino (2003).

The first step to quantitative computer software analysis is to develop a codebook. The codebook will identify the numerical values that you will assign to each variable entered for analysis. Each question or item on a survey usually represents a variable. The answers to each question represent different values for that variable. One purpose of entering the values into a computer software program is to describe the occurrence of different values across respondents. These descriptive statistics report and graph the frequency, percentages, and distributions of responses. Another purpose is to describe the relationship between values of one variable and values of other variables. These inferential statistics allow the social service worker to test whether the hypothesized relationship between independent and dependent variables occurred.

Levels of measurement are the variables used for statistical analysis grouped by the ability to make inferences from the data. The levels are listed here in terms of the strength of the inferences they allow you to make, from weakest to strongest: nominal, ordinal, interval, and ratio. It does not matter which is labeled 1 and which 2 since these values are nominal. Nominal values are simply numbers used to name a value. The assignment of one value rather than another implies no rank ordering. The variable *gender* will have two possible values: *male* or *female.* Ordinal values are numbers that assign more value to some responses than to others. These values can be placed in a meaningful order. In the focus groups with workers and client advocates in a mental health setting, the respondents were instructed to rank order their top five competencies from the list of twenty-six competencies shown in figure 5.9. The highest numerical values were given to those competencies listed as first, the second highest values to those listed as second, and so on. All the values were added to determine the top five competencies.

Interval values go a step beyond ordinal values by rank ordering along equal intervals. Age is an interval variable because it is measured the same way by everyone, in terms of years. The same can be said of income, which is measured in total dollar amounts. Age and income become ordinal variables if they are given in terms of categories, such as (a) twenty-five to twenty-nine, (b) thirty to thirty-four, and (c) thirty-five to thirty-nine; or (a) $25,000 to $29,999, (b) $30,000 to $34,999, and (c) $35,000 to $39,999. In terms of the ordinal variable examples, one can simply say that persons marking *c* were older or richer than persons marking *b* or *a*. In terms of the interval variable examples, however, one can report how much older and how much richer respondents are. Age and income are also examples of the highest level of measurement, ratio values, because there is an absolute zero point. This means that *0* connotes total absence of the variable: not born or no money.

The higher the level of measurement, the more one is able to move from descriptive to inferential statistical analysis. In this age of accountability, there is much pressure from stakeholders to show (by answering descriptive evaluation questions) or even prove (by answering explanatory evaluation questions) that the evaluated intervention resulted in the desired outcomes. Thus, in quantitative approaches to answering evaluation questions, it is important to construct instruments that have variables and values at ordinal, interval, or ratio levels.

It is also important to construct instruments whose variables are all conceptualized at the same level of measurement. It is common to arrange responses to a question along a Likert scale, on which the values go from high to low or low to high. There is, however, disagreement as to whether Likert-type variables should be treated as ordinal, interval, or ratio (see Mark, 1996, pp. 278–81).

Look at the values for the Knowledge and Benefit scales of the CAT-MH listed in figure 5.9. Would you say that these values are ordinal, interval, or ratio? The authors presented the results as ordinal—as descriptive statistics of a mean or average for each competency—allowing the reader to see the ranking from highest to lowest (Clasen et al., 2003, table 1, p. 14). "The lowest mean was 3.62, ranking between important (value of 3) and very important (value of 4). For most items means were over 4.00 (out of a possible 5.00 for extremely important)" (Clasen et al., 2003, p. 13). The authors were interested, not in how much higher competencies were rated (which would be interval level), but simply in the fact that some competencies were rated higher than others. Later, they acknowledged that there were differences in the two subscales because the Benefit subscale had a "don't know" option and the Knowledge subscale did not. "At the present, don't know represents the center option." A similar center option was not available for the Knowledge subscale. Thus, there was not an absolute 0 to allow the variable to be treated as ratio level data (Clasen et al., 2003, p. 13).

The descriptive statistics most commonly reported in evaluations are frequencies, percentages, measures of central tendency, and measures of variability. Frequencies are the number of times the value for a variable occurred. Frequencies alone can be misleading because the statistic does not report how many times the value *could* have occurred. For example, a school can report the number of students who passed proficiency exams, but that number alone is meaningless unless it is also reported how many students took proficiency exams. Similarly, reporting how many people used a service over the past year tells us nothing about how many people could potentially have used the service. Percentages are the number of times the value was selected divided by the number of participants responding to the variable measured. It is best to provide frequency and percentage for each value reported.

Measures of central tendency are statistics that illustrate how values are distributed among respondents. The mean or average is computed by dividing the sum of variable responses by the total number of respondents. The median is the value that is midpoint. There are an equal number of values above and below the median. Means and medians cannot be calculated for nominal data because the numbers only categorize the variable. One numerical value is no higher than another. The mode is the value that occurs the most often. The mean is a deceptive measure if the values are highly skewed toward one end. In such cases, it is best to use the median or to report all three measures of central tendency.

Measures of variability are statistics that illustrate how spread out the values are. They are used for interval- and ratio-level variables. The range lists values from lowest to highest and indicates the distance between those values. Ranges are usually reported for age and income. The variance (the squared difference of all scores from the mean) and the standard deviation (the square root of the variance) illustrate how much the values are spread out from the mean. The higher the standard deviation, the higher the variation in values. As we saw earlier, values are, according to probability theory, distributed along a bell-shaped curve, with 95% falling within two standard deviations of the mean. Thus, results with a standard deviation higher than 3 have highly spread out values.

So far the discussion has covered statistics that describe one variable at a time, called univariate analysis. What if you want to analyze two or more variables at a time, for example, whether gender or worker position (e.g., mental health aide, social worker, or psychologist) was related to score on the CAT-MH? One bivariate analysis, cross-tabulations or contingency tables, can be calculated with SPSS and other statistical software programs. Cross-tabulations are conducted with the two or more variables and display the frequency and percentages of responses in each cell. Using gender and response for each competency on the CAT-MH, the ten cells in a cross-tabulation for the Knowledge subscale for each competency would be (a) men who responded 1, 2, 3, 4, and 5 and (b) women who responded 1, 2, 3, 4, and 5. The table and percentages provide a visual comparison of scores but do not indicate whether those differences are statistically significant. Cross-tabulations can be used with any level of measurement, but other analyses are more appropriate when testing relations between ordinal, interval, or ratio variables.

Another descriptive statistic used with interval and ratio levels of measurement is correlations. Correlations show how values on one variable change in relation to values on a second variable. That is, they show the direction (positive or negative) and strength (ranging from 0 to 1, with 1 being a perfect correlation) of the relation. Scattergrams visually display the correlation between variables. Scattergrams and correlations are useful descriptive statistics in single system designs. In the parent training intervention, there was a positive correlation when an increase in the parents' use of reinforcement was related to an increase in the children's appropriate play. There was a negative correlation when an increase in the parents' use of reinforcement was related to a decrease in the children's inappropriate hitting.

Explanatory Statistical Analyses.   There is much pressure today from some stakeholders, especially funders, to demonstrate a causal relationship between the intervention or program and desired changes or outcomes in targeted client systems. For example, stakeholders wanted to describe or explain a relationship between the FSIs and an improvement in family functioning and school performance outcomes. They wanted to know what interventions successfully increased enrollments of eligible children in CHIP.

Quantitative approaches to data collection, data analysis, and controls for credibility are all necessary in order to explain that interventions are responsible for the measured outcomes. The following four conditions are minimally necessary to test explanatory evaluation hypotheses:

1. The hypothesized relationships must be grounded in theories and interventions that have been tested in other settings and reported in the literature.

2. Participants must be selected randomly so that the measured outcomes can be compared to a normal, naturally occurring distribution.

3. Reliable and valid instruments must be used to rule out error as a possible explanation for the results.

4. Outcomes must be measured at the interval and ratio levels to allow for statistical analyses that test the relationship between values.

Once these conditions are in place, then one must accurately select the appropriate statistical test, basing the selection process on the following four criteria:

1. Match the statistical test with nondirectional hypotheses (e.g., there is a relationship between FSIs and family functioning) or unidirectional hypotheses (e.g., FSIs increase family health) as appropriate. Inferential statistical analyses are calculated to reject the null hypothesis, which is the statement that the relationships between variables do not exist.

2. Match the statistical analysis to the level of measurement (nominal, ordinal, interval, or ratio) as appropriate:

Chi-square test can be used to test the null hypothesis between variables measured at all levels, but other tests may be more appropriate for nonnominal data. Chi-square is often used in social service evaluations where a comparison group sample is not available and the nominal level variables available for analysis all come from one sample.

t test tests whether to reject the null hypothesis by comparing the means of two samples (e.g., participants receiving intervention and those in a comparison group). The measure of desired results (i.e., the dependent variable) must be at least at the ordinal level and the intervention (i.e., the independent variable) at the nominal level.

Analysis of variance (ANOVA) tests whether to reject the null hypothesis by comparing the means of more than two samples. The levels of measurement are the same as with t tests.

Regression analysis tests the strength of change predicted to occur as a result of the intervention. The desired results and the intervention must be at the interval level or higher. The participants must be selected or assigned to the samples randomly.

3. **Statistical significance** is the existence of a relationship between the intervention and results outside an acceptable level for chance. When conducting statistical analyses to test the predictive, explanatory evaluation

question, select the level of statistical significance before conducting the analysis. The .05 level is most commonly used and implies that the evaluator will accept that five times out of one hundred the results were due to chance rather than the intervention. Statistical significance is relevant only if the participants were selected or assigned to intervention or comparison groups randomly. These conditions are not often feasible for social service evaluations (Potocky-Tripodi & Tripodi, 2003).

4. When computing the statistical significance of differences between samples, conduct a power analysis. "Power is the ability of a statistical test to correctly reject the null hypothesis (i.e., the probability of not making a Type II error). It is the function of three parameters: the effect size, the sample size, and the p value (which is the probability of making a Type I error)" (Potocky-Tripodi & Tripodi, 2003, p. 140). A Type I error occurs when the null hypothesis is rejected and, thus, an erroneous claim is made that there was a relationship between intervention and change. A Type II error occurs when the null hypothesis is not rejected and a true relationship between intervention and change is not identified.

The p value used in the power analysis is directly related to sample size. "Thus it is essential for researchers to understand this fundamental truth: with small sample sizes, even very large effects (i.e., strong relationships) will not be statistically significant; conversely, with large sample sizes, even very small effect sizes (i.e., weak relationships) will be statistically significant" (Potocky-Tripodi & Tripodi, 2003, p. 140).

As much as one may want to utilize what stakeholders consider to be the more important or powerful statistical analyses, a social service evaluation must use the analyses that are appropriate for the evaluation questions asked, the method of participant selection followed, and the level of measurement of the data collected. For an example of reporting the quantitative statistical analyses used and the limitations of those analyses, see figure 5.11.

DATA CREDIBILITY

There are many techniques that the evaluator can employ to increase the credibility of the data-collection and -analysis process. Credibility is the rigorous and systematic collection of qualitative and quantitative data according to the most accepted procedures cited in the evaluation and research literature. In qualitative approaches, credibility is achieved through techniques that increase the trustworthiness that data reported is the accurate description of the concepts and realities as intended by the evaluation participants. In quantitative approaches, credibility is achieved through techniques that increase the ability to reliably and validly connect the results to the intervention.

Figure 5.11.   Case example: Reporting of statistical analysis in the final
evaluation report.

The excerpt below is taken from the final FSI evaluation report (Brun et al., 1998):

> Frequencies and cross-tabulations were calculated for most of the questions asked in
> the telephone survey. Cross-tabulations were conducted so the frequencies could be
> broken down by group (e.g., FSI Intervention, time 1) and dependent variable (e.g.,
> Use of Social Services). For instance a cross-tabulation was run so information about
> participants of the FSI intervention group in time 1 would display along with their
> responses for use of social services.
>
> The mean was calculated for several unique variables and one aggregated vari-
> able (the FAD). To calculate the mean FAD score, the sum of the twelve FAD, general
> functioning questions was calculated. The sum was divided by the number of ques-
> tions answered. If 40% or fewer of the questions were answered by a respondent, the
> entire FAD score for that respondent was eliminated. Overall a mean was calculated
> based on the mean score for each participant.
>
> Different statistical analyses were calculated to present the findings appropri-
> ately. Over time, when discussing the respondents of the same group (FSI time 1
> and FSI time 3), the data are presented descriptively. Statistical analysis is not appro-
> priate to compare all of the respondents in time 1 and all of the respondents in time
> 3 because there is not an equal comparison (i.e., not all of the people that
> responded in time 1 responded in time 3). However, when comparing two separate
> groups, for instance FSI Intervention and FSI Comparison for the same time, two sta-
> tistical tests were conducted. When comparing the percentages of two different
> groups, the Pearson chi-square was conducted, and when comparing the means,
> the independent-samples t test was conducted. It should be noted that since the FSI
> intervention sample used in the telephone survey was a convenience sample, these
> statistics should only be used to generalize to all FSIs with caution. (Brun et al.,
> 1998, pp. 24–25)

QUALITATIVE APPROACHES TO CREDIBILITY

The previous discussion of qualitative approaches to data collection emphasized that data go through multiple transformations. The methods used
to increase the trustworthiness of the data during these transformations are
summarized in figure 5.12. These methods were used in the qualitative approach to answering the exploratory question, "How do parents predicted
to be at risk for child abuse and neglect successfully raise their children?"
and in the qualitative approach to answering the descriptive question, "How
do consumers experience SBCM?" **Trustworthiness** means remaining true
to the original source of data. All the methods in figure 5.12 were implemented to keep the researcher/evaluator focused on the original evaluation
purpose, which was to learn the participants' experiences.

Figure 5.12 demonstrates how one evaluator's interaction with the information collected produced the interpretations reported. Another person

conducting the same evaluation will mostly likely interpret the findings differently. The reality is that two people following identical procedures will not necessarily arrive at identical interpretations. In the exploratory study with parents, the researcher was a white man and all six participants women, five African American. The participants would have interacted much differently with an African American female researcher than they did with the white male researcher. The cultural differences between the researcher and the participants produced results specific to the participants and the setting.

The major benefit of collecting information systematically through rigorous qualitative approaches is that participants' experiences can be reported to stakeholders credibly. Findings from qualitative approaches are more than just, "This is what the client said," or, "This is what the workers think," or, "This is what I as the evaluator claim." They are the collective knowledge about program decisions that is gained through a systematic analysis of all data collected, including the empirical results of other research reported in the literature.

Another way in which to reach data trustworthiness is to employ a procedure called **member checking.** This is the feedback from the participants about the evaluator's reporting, and in some cases interpretation, of the information collected. In the exploratory study with parents, the researcher made the decision that, to best be true to the participants, he should give

Figure 5.12.   Evaluation decisionmaking tip: Procedures to increase credibility of qualitative approaches to data collection.

Check whether any of these qualitative data-collection approaches are being followed in a current evaluation at your agency or practicum setting.

____ Conduct open-ended, almost *conversational interviews.*

____ Conduct the interviews in the participant's *natural environment.*

____ Select the participants *purposively* on the basis of the experiences that are being explored or described.

____ *Triangulate* at least three different data-collection strategies.

____ Document in a *reflective journal* the evaluator's influence on the data-collection process.

____ Document in a *procedural journal* the evaluation decisions made and the reasons for making those decisions based on stakeholder input and following rigorous procedures recommended in the research and evaluation literature.

____ Establish *prolonged engagement* with the participants and in their natural setting, to the point that theme redundancy is reached.

____ Follow rigorous methods to identify *emergent themes* from the participants' experiences.

____ Connect the emergent themes to *empirical theories* reported in the literature.

each one the full fifteen pages of transcribed interviews. Thus, at the beginning of the second interview, he gave each participant a copy of the transcription of her first interview. This process was overwhelming for all the participants. As one participant said: "I never thought I talked that way." She was referring to her observation that the transcribed interview contained many unfinished sentences and repeated remarks and appeared to her to be unorganized. Verbatim conversations do not have the luxury of being edited for grammar or clarity.

Learning from this experience, before conducting the third interview, the evaluator prepared for each participant two-page summaries of the main topics discussed in the previous two interviews. He first read the summaries to the participants and then gave them hard copies to keep. The participants found the summaries much more manageable. Similarly, in the exploratory study with parents, the researcher gave each participant her final story as it appeared in her dissertation.

The purpose of the member checking in both examples was to ensure the accuracy of the data reported. If a point was inaccurately reported (e.g., a wrong age, location, or event), participants did correct the researcher/evaluator, who noted any differences of interpretation between the evaluator and the participant.

If practitioners and evaluators use member checking, consider the following three decisions prior to conducting the interviews:

1. What written document, if any, are you going to give to the participants (e.g., full verbatim transcription or a summary of the interview)?

2. How are you going to use the participants' feedback about the information? (For an example of including the member checking comments in the published description of a qualitative interview, see Lather [1991].)

3. How will you protect the confidentiality of the participants in the final report and other publications? If possible, show the participants how you reworded background information to preserve their confidentiality.

Yet another way in which to reach data trustworthiness is **peer debriefing.** This is consultation about the evaluation process from persons selected for their expertise. In the exploratory study with parents, three different African American women who were doctoral classmates of the researcher's served as peer debriefers at three different times in the research process. The first debriefer read selected transcriptions of the first interviews and provided suggestions for improved interactions in the second and third interviews. The second debriefer provided literature references specific to African American families from an Afrocentric perspective. The third debriefer reviewed the final six stories that would appear in the dissertation and suggested including, not verbatim quotations from the interviews, but edited quotations so that there would be no grammatical errors to distract from the meaning behind the words. All the feedback from the peer de-briefers was incorporated into the final dissertation.

Data trustworthiness can also be achieved by conducting an **evaluation audit,** a review of the evaluation decisions by a person not connected to the evaluation. Minimally, the reviewer can conduct a procedural audit, commenting on whether the evaluator followed rigorous and accurate qual-itative data-collection approaches. The evaluator, stakeholders, and auditor should agree if there are any other points that should be the focus of the au-dit. For more discussion of qualitative audits and other methods for reach-ing credibility of qualitative approaches see Denzin and Lincoln (1994), Guba and Lincoln (1989), Lather (2003), Lincoln and Guba (1985), Patton (1999), and Rodwell (1995, 1998). **Objectivity** is the process of identifying evaluator biases and influences that distort the data-collection process. Qualitative and quantitative approaches address evaluator bias differently. Evaluator bias cannot be completely controlled. Evaluators are human be-ings who have views and biases that guide their decisions. Qualitative eval-uators and researchers can document these biases in a reflective journal and report the actions taken to reduce the risks to the credibility of the final re-sults (e.g., member checking and peer debriefing).

QUANTITATIVE APPROACHES TO CREDIBILITY

The larger, centralized, publicly funded evaluation examples used in this book lent themselves more easily to quantitative processes than did the smaller, localized, single-agency evaluation case examples. First, stakehold-ers wanted the report to contain brief, easy-to-understand statistical findings from quantitative data analysis. Second, because more than one intervention was being evaluated, collecting data from a sample of a larger population of participants was the most efficient selection approach. Third, implementing consistent data-collection approaches across all localized interventions using the same closed-ended questions produced comparative findings that helped the funder make planning and implementation decisions similarly across all programs. Fourth, one of the conceptual assumptions underlying quantitative data-collection processes is the goal to collect data as objec-tively as possible.

One very specific quantitative approach to reducing evaluator bias dis-cussed earlier in this chapter is the implementation of a reliable, valid, stan-dardized, closed-ended survey instrument with all evaluation participants. The assumption is that using the same, closed-ended instrument will reduce the influence of the evaluator's own views and values on the findings and interpretations.

Another way to control for evaluator bias, again already discussed, is to train all persons collecting and analyzing data to do so in the same manner, thereby increasing inter- and intrarater reliability. Objectivity can be enhanced by following data-collection procedures already demonstrated in the literature to be effective. This includes choosing an instrument that is valid for the evaluation question and measures the concepts being studied.

A primary way in which credibility is achieved through quantitative approaches is to implement the appropriate evaluation design that controls the threats to internal and external validity. **Internal validity** is the ability to attribute desired results to the evaluated intervention or program controlling for other factors that might be affecting changes. Controlling the testing conditions to rule out alternative explanations for findings is the best way to reduce threats to internal validity. In addition to implementing the measurements consistently, also try to reduce the amount of time between measurements to reduce attrition in sample size.

External validity is the ability to generalize evaluation results from the participants to the larger population. Selecting participants randomly and having a comparison group is the most effective way to quantitatively increase the generalizability of the findings. The assumption is that the findings will apply to the larger population because all members of that population had an equal chance of participating. Thus, the sample should be a fair representation of the population. Further, controls for skewed characteristics in the sample can be implemented during the statistical analysis.

The **classic experimental design** is one in which participants are randomly selected and assigned to intervention and comparison groups and pre- and postintervention ordinal level and higher measures of results are given to both groups. Inferential statistical analysis determines whether the observed changes in clients receiving the intervention are statistically significant on the pre- and posttest measures relative to the comparison group. The classic experimental design produces the most control for threats to both types of validity.

Random selection of participants and random assignment to comparison groups are often not feasible, nor are they always ethical in an agency setting since the procedure involves some people in need of an intervention possibly not receiving it. If an agency has a normal waiting period for clients, the waiting list can be used as the comparison group since these clients are not currently receiving the intervention and will not be receiving it for some time. Persons receiving different forms of the same intervention can also serve as a comparison group, allowing all participants to receive some form of intervention. Finally, individuals in the community who have similar demographic backgrounds but are not in need of and, therefore, did not receive the intervention can serve as a comparison group. This method was used for the evaluation of FSIs. It was expensive, however, because it involved purchasing telephone numbers from a research firm.

Different versions of an experimental design are often implemented in an agency setting because of feasibility and ethical issues. These quasi-experimental designs are listed in order below from most control to least control of threats to validity:

Posttest Only, Comparison Group Design. Here, there is an intervention and a comparison group but no pretest measures. Without baseline data, that is, a measure before the client receives intervention, there is no way to know how much, if any, the participants changed. In the FSI evaluation, there was no baseline measure on the Family Assessment Device (FAD). Many of the participants may have already been high on the scale measuring family functioning before the first telephone survey, thus leaving no room for improvement. Random selection to intervention and comparison groups increases the controls for threats to external validity in this design.

Pretest and Posttest, No Comparison Group Design. Without comparison groups, the generalizability of results beyond the participants is reduced. But having a pre- and a posttest measure helps control for alternate explanations for reported changes in the clients. There are some statistical analyses that can still test the relationship between intervention and client change.

Time-Series Design. Here, the measures are given multiple times, preferably several times before and several times after the intervention is implemented. Having multiple measures should control for threats to internal validity related to poor administration of the instrument. Drastic changes in preintervention measures may be due to factors unrelated to the intervention. Measures of desired change after the intervention demonstrate maintenance of the desired outcome. Time-series designs can be used with or without comparison groups.

Posttest Only, No Comparison Group Design. This design has the least control for threats to validity. A posttest measure is given after the intervention. Without baseline data and a comparison group, it is very difficult to attribute client change solely to the intervention.

If you are following any of the comparison group designs listed, consult the references under quantitative approaches in the "Further Readings" section of this chapter. Consult the appropriate references also when following single system designs or qualitative approaches.

MAJOR POINTS

The ultimate learning outcome for this chapter is for you to develop and implement a data-collection plan for an evaluation in your agency or practicum setting. This chapter began with the reminder that selecting the appropriate methods for transforming information into data to answer evaluation questions builds on all the decisions that have been discussed in the previous chapters. Stakeholders should discuss how the SCREAM values guide the data-collection approaches: measuring participants' *strengths;* respecting their *cultural* diversity; selecting procedures that are feasible with the *resources* available; following *ethical* guidelines to protect the participants; reaching an *agreement* that all stakeholders will accept; and measuring *multiple* systems related to the evaluation questions. Stakeholders should utilize a literature review of academic and evaluation sources to see the interactive role between theory building and theory testing when answering different types of evaluation questions (see fig. 4.2). Logic models are another tool to assist in answering descriptive and explanatory questions by stating the intervention or program goals, activities, and desired short- and long-term results.

The discussion in this chapter focused on the important data-collection decisions from an open-ended, qualitative approach and a closed-ended, quantitative approach. The major point is that each decision leads to different ways to accomplish the following tasks:

- selecting the participants purposively (qualitative) or randomly (quantitative)
- collecting the data by asking questions, observing, or reviewing secondary documents in an open-ended (qualitative) or closed-ended (quantitative) manner
- analyzing the narrative (qualitative) or numerical (quantitative) data
- ensuring the credibility of the data through methods to reach data trustworthiness (qualitative) or methods to reduce threats to the internal and external validity of the evaluation results (quantitative)

The discussion throughout the entire chapter illustrated that qualitative and quantitative approaches can be used exclusively or together in the same evaluation. In evaluations that rely solely on qualitative approaches, the evaluator's early goals are to learn what is important from the participants and to have this information guide all other decisions, including the role of theory from other evaluations and research. In evaluations that rely solely on quantitative approaches, the evaluator's early goals are to learn what has been shown in the research literature to be the most valid and reliable way to collect evidence of the evaluated interventions. Then compare whether the results measured in the current evaluation match the findings of the prior research. In all evaluations, there is an interplay between learning new information from data you collect and comparing that information to old and new theories read during the evaluation.

FURTHER READINGS

Qualitative Approaches

Anastas, J. (2004). Quality in qualitative evaluation: Issues and possible answer. *Research on Social Work Practice, 14*(1), 57–65.

Brinkerhoff, R. (2003). *The success case method: Find out quickly what's working and what's not.* San Francisco: Berrett-Koehler.

Creswell, J. (2003). *Research design: Qualitative, quantitative, and mixed methods approaches* (2nd ed.). Thousand Oaks, CA: Sage.

Frechtling, J., & Sharp, L. (1997). *User-friendly handbook for mixed method evaluations.* Washington, DC: National Science Foundation.

Gubrium, J., & Sankar, A. (Eds.). (1994). *Qualitative methods in aging research.* Thousand Oaks, CA: Sage.

Krueger, R., & Casey, M. (2000). *Focus groups: A practical guide for applied research* (3rd ed.). Thousand Oaks, CA: Sage.

Lather, P. (1991). *Getting smart: Feminist research and pedagogy with/in the postmodern.* New York: Routledge.

Padgett, D. (Ed.). (2004). *The qualitative research experience.* Belmont, CA: Wadsworth/Thomson Learning.

Patton, M. (2002). *Qualitative evaluation and research methods* (3rd ed.). Thousand Oaks, CA: Sage.

Qualitative Inquiry. Journal.

Qualitative Social Work: Research and Practice. Journal.

Reissman, C. (Ed.). (1994). *Qualitative studies in social work research.* Thousand Oaks, CA: Sage.

Sherman, E., & Reid, W. (Eds.). (1994). *Qualitative research in social work.* New York: Columbia University Press.

Snowdon, D. (2001). *Aging with grace: What the nun study teaches us about leading longer, healthier, and more meaningful lives.* New York: Bantam. (an example of a qualitative study)

Taylor, S., & Bogdan, R. (1998). *Introduction to qualitative research methods: A guidebook and resources* (3rd ed.). New York: Wiley.

Standardized Instruments and Quantitative Analyses

Babbie, E., Halley, F., & Zaino, J. (2003). *Adventures in social research: Data analysis using SPSS 11.0/11.5 for Windows.* Chicago: Pine Forge.

Corcoran, K., & Fischer, J. (2003). *Measures for clinical practice: A sourcebook* (3rd ed., Vols. 1–2). New York: Free Press.

Grinnell, R. (1997). *Social work research and evaluation: Quantitative and qualitative approaches* (5th ed.). Itasca, IL: F. E. Peacock.

Mark, R. (1996). *Research made simple: A handbook for social workers.* Thousand Oaks, CA: Sage.

Marlow, C. (2005). *Research methods for generalist social work* (4th ed.). Belmont, CA: Wadsworth/Thomson Learning.

Montcalm, D., & Royse, D. (2002). *Data analysis for social workers.* Boston: Allyn & Bacon.

Royse, D. (2004). *Research methods in social work* (4th ed.). Chicago: Nelson-Hall.

Royse, D., Thyer, B., Padgett, D., & Logan, T. (2001). *Program evaluation: An introduction* (3rd ed.). Belmont, CA: Brooks/Cole.

Rubin, A., & Babbie, E. (2001). *Research methods for social work* (4th ed.). Belmont, CA: Wadsworth/Thomson Learning.

Schutt, R. (2001). *Investigating the social world: The process and practice of research* (3rd ed.). Thousand Oaks, CA: Pine Forge.

Thyer, B. (Ed.). (2001a). *The handbook of social work research methods.* Thousand Oaks, CA: Sage.

Yegidis, B., & Weinbach, R. (2002). *Research methods for social workers* (4th ed.). Itasca, IL: F. E. Peacock.

Single System Design

Bloom, M., Fischer, J., & Orme, J. (2003). *Evaluating practice: Guidelines for the accountable professional* (4th ed.). Boston: Allyn & Bacon.

Kazi, M. (1998). *Single-case evaluation by social workers.* Aldershot: Ashgate.

Tripodi, T. (1994). *A primer on single-subject design for clinical social workers.* Washington, DC: NASW Press.

Measuring Outcomes

Ginsberg, L. (2001). *Social work evaluation: Principles and methods.* Boston: Allyn & Bacon.

Mika, K. (1996). *Program outcome evaluation: A step-by-step handbook.* Milwaukee, WI: Family International.

Mullen, E., & Magnabosco, J. (Eds.). (1997). *Outcomes measurement in the human services: Cross-cutting issues and methods.* Washington, DC: NASW Press.

United Way of America. (1996). *Measuring program outcomes: A practical approach.* Alexandria, VA: United Way.

REFLECTIVE JOURNAL ACTIVITIES

1. What are your reactions to the myths about data contained in figure 5.1? Do you agree with any of the myths? Do you feel that some of them should actually guide evaluations?

2. What are your reactions to the discussion about qualitative and quantitative approaches to data collection? Which approach do you favor and why? What skills or knowledge do you need to better master for either or both approaches?

3. Which methods of participant selection—random or purposive—do you support more and why?

4. What data-collection methods discussed in this chapter do you want to learn more about? Set a contract with yourself to read one of the books cited in this chapter related to those methods.

5. What data-analysis methods discussed in this chapter do you want to learn more about? Set a contract with yourself to read one of the books cited in this chapter related to those methods.

6. Do you feel that evaluators can control the setting and, thereby, remain objective and keep their biases from influencing the evaluation? Do you feel that evaluators always influence the evaluation participants and results? Which methods of obtaining evaluation credibility do you have the most confidence in?

PROCEDURAL JOURNAL ACTIVITIES

1. Think of an evaluation at your agency or practicum setting and complete the chart in figure 5.2.

2. Answer the Evaluation Decisionmaking Model questions in figure 5.13 related to data collection. *Remember, it's all about the evaluation question!*

3. Document how different stakeholders have been included in making these data-collection decisions.

4. Document a review process for ensuring the ethical implementation of these data-collection procedures.

Figure 5.13.   Evaluation Decisionmaking Model: Data-driven evaluation decisions.

The types of *evaluation questions* being asked are:

_____ Exploratory

This evaluation will explore the experiences of the following individuals, groups, organizations, or communities:

The overall exploratory questions are:

The questions will be answered through the following data-collection methods:

_____ qualitative individual interviews

_____ qualitative group interviews

_____ qualitative constructed surveys

_____ qualitative individual observations

_____ qualitative group observations

_____ qualitative document analysis

Completed with the following participants:

The methods to analyze the results are:

(figure continues)

The methods to ensure trustworthiness of the data are:

_____

_____

____ Descriptive

This evaluation will describe specific aspects of the following individuals, groups, organizations, or communities:

The overall descriptive questions are:

These questions will be answered through the following data-collection methods:

____ qualitative individual interviews
____ quantitative individual interviews
____ qualitative group interviews
____ quantitative group interviews
____ qualitative constructed surveys
____ quantitative constructed surveys
____ quantitative standardized instruments
____ qualitative individual observations
____ quantitative individual observations
____ qualitative group observations
____ quantitative group observations
____ qualitative document analysis
____ quantitative document analysis

Completed with the following participants:

The methods to analyze the results are:

_____

_____

The methods used to ensure trustworthiness of the qualitative data are:

_____

_____

The methods used to ensure validity of the quantitative data are:

_____

_____

The methods used to ensure reliability of the quantitative data are:

_____

_____

_____ Explanatory

This evaluation will explain a connection between specific aspects of the following individuals, groups, organizations, or communities:

The overall explanatory statements being tested are:

These questions will be answered through the following data-collection methods:

_____ quantitative individual interviews

_____ quantitative group interviews

_____ quantitative constructed surveys

_____ quantitative standardized instruments

_____ quantitative individual observations

_____ quantitative group observations

_____ quantitative document analysis

Completed with the following participants:

The methods to analyze the results are:

_____

_____

The methods used to ensure validity of the data are:

_____

_____

The methods used to ensure reliability of the data are:

_____

_____

CHAPTER 6

REPORTING EVALUATION DECISIONS:
COMING FULL CIRCLE

The material in this book—especially the case examples and the evaluation tips—is meant to help the reader make evaluation decisions from the origination of the evaluation question to the final data analysis, decisions related to

> negotiating with stakeholders about the scope of the evaluation (chaps. 1 and 2)
>
> reinforcing key values that drive evaluation decisions (chap. 3)
>
> identifying relevant theories that drive evaluation decisions through a literature review and logic model (chap. 4)
>
> choosing the best approaches to data collection that drive evaluation decisions (chap. 5)

The reflective and procedural journal exercises at the end of each chapter are meant to help the reader document these decisions.

This chapter can help the reader document the connection between all the previous evaluation decisions made. Documentation is a necessary part of the accountability that social service workers owe the key stakeholders because it records the original evaluation plan and any changes made to that plan. Documentation demonstrates to stakeholders how the findings, interpretations, and conclusions contained in the final report were related to the evaluation questions. It demonstrates how important values and theories were considered during the course of answering the evaluation questions. With this chapter we come full circle. Documentation should occur at every step of the evaluation, not just at the end.

Remember the list of potential reports summarized in figure 2.6 that were part of the stakeholder agreement? Only one of those documents was the final evaluation report. All the others are produced at different stages of the evaluation, beginning with the evaluation plan written in the original request for proposal (RFP) to receive funding for an intervention.

This chapter serves as a review of the previous material by demonstrating how documentation conveys the evaluation decisions agreed on by key stakeholders. Evaluation reports are necessary to show how conclusions are based on the evaluation decisions addressed in the procedural journal activities at the end of each chapter. All those decisions are combined and summarized in the Evaluation Decisionmaking Model in appendix C.

The *learning outcomes* for this chapter are as follows:

1. Understand the importance of documenting evaluation decisions and, thus, being accountable to stakeholders.
2. Determine what should be contained in the final report.
3. Put evaluation reports to their full use.
4. Share the results of evaluations with others through such venues as paper presentations and journal submissions.

REPORTING DECISIONS ALONG THE EVALUATION CYCLE

The evaluation decisions discussed throughout this book happen along a plan-implement-evaluate-change continuum discussed in chapter 4 and illustrated in figure 4.2: (1) evaluation decisions are *planned;* (2) evaluation procedures are *implemented;* (3) the implementation of evaluation decisions is itself *evaluated;* and (4) the evaluation itself undergoes *change.* This cycle is repeated until the previously agreed-on ending of the evaluation period. There needs to be an ending point to determine whether the goals of the evaluation were met and the evaluation questions were answered. Most evaluations are funded by internal and external sources that have deadlines. Social service workers can always apply for more funding and support to conduct additional evaluations to further promote the changes and knowledge gained from the previous evaluation and to address the limitations of prior evaluation decisions.

The evaluation of family support interventions (FSIs) will be the case example highlighted in this chapter to discuss documentation and the evaluation cycle. This example is used because the issues it raises are relevant to many different types of evaluations. Attempt to find all the examples, however, material that applies to your own agency setting.

DOCUMENTATING THE EVALUATION PLAN

Ideally, the development of a new evaluation plan follows this sequence:

1. Social service workers *identify a concern* among clients that needs intervention (e.g., eligible children are not being enrolled in CHIP).
2. They *review the academic and professional literature* to learn about interventions and evaluations that have addressed these concerns.

3. They *develop simultaneously the most appropriate implementation and evaluation plans* on the basis of the review of the literature and discussion with supportive stakeholders.

4. Then, they *submit an RFP* created from the information learned in the first three steps.

More common, however are the following scenarios:

1. *Social service workers submit an RFP to receive funding to implement an intervention.* They include a general evaluation plan, as required by the funder. An outside person may even be named to conduct the evaluation, but the evaluation is not yet fully developed. The primary focus is on describing the intervention. The evaluation will be further planned and developed if the RFP is accepted. The evaluation is an *afterthought,* not a plan integrated into the intervention.

   Take the evaluation seriously. Take the time to get feedback from the proposed evaluator. His or her attention to the evaluation plan can improve the presentation of the need for the intervention. The best evaluation plans are those developed alongside intervention plans, and vice versa. Both evaluation and implementation plans should be based on a thorough review of the evaluation and research literature related to the proposed intervention and desired client changes. Be able to answer the question, "How do you know this intervention will work?" One credible answer to that question requires a review of the literature, a clarification of the logic model behind the proposed intervention, and a clear plan to measure those desired results. Another credible answer is to develop an evaluation to explore client experiences related to the studied concern. Propose a feasible plan within the funding available and the time line stated in the RFP.

2. *An evaluation team responds to an RFP to evaluate an intervention, a program, or multiple programs.* The RFP is often announced by the program funding source. The evaluators propose a plan based on their review of the literature related to the interventions and client systems and on their own experiences with similar programs and populations. The evaluators may propose an evaluation plan based on the theories, literature, and logic models stated in the RFP, which are in turn based on the conditions of the agency contracts. The assumption of an evaluation plan in this case is that the programs are implemented according to the terms of the grant contracts the agency workers signed with the funding source.

   Take the evaluation seriously. If you are in an agency that is asked to participate in this type of externally driven evaluation, become active in the planning, implementation, and review of the evaluation. Clarify the purpose of the evaluation and how the results will affect future funding. Clarify any changes the agency has made to the original RFP, and get documented approval of any changes made to the intervention and evaluation plans in the contract. Learn from the evaluation, and take the initiative to plan future internally driven evaluations.

3. *A student develops an evaluation activity or an entire evaluation plan for a class assignment, thesis, or dissertation.* The student is conducting the evaluation activities for academic purposes. She gets permission to conduct the activity but does not really see her activities as leading to agency planning and program decisions.

Take the evaluation activity seriously. Evaluating one's own practice is a learning outcome expected under the CSWE EPAS and also an ethical practice mandated in the National Association of Social Workers (NASW) Code of Ethics. Integrate the student's learning process with that of agency improvement. How can the agency best utilize her application of evaluation skills? What data-collection tasks and overall evaluation plans can she assist the agency in conducting?

4. *An individual social service worker wants to evaluate an intervention with one or more clients.* The evaluation plan is not connected to a funding source. The worker wants to truly understand whether and how his intervention is helping clients. He may want to explore the experiences of different client systems.

Take the evaluation seriously. Give the worker time to develop the evaluation plan. Reinforce his efforts to evaluate practice. Encourage single system design evaluations to help workers evaluate intervention with one client at a time. Build the agency's capacity to encourage more employees to conduct evaluations. Have evaluation support groups. Have literature review and reading groups. Financially reward evaluation planning.

The planning period starts with the RFP, a class assignment, or some other motivating event and continues until the evaluation activities are implemented. Ideally, data-collection activities do not begin until all stakeholders approve the plan. For one thing, a review process must occur to ensure that the data will be collected ethically. Also, data collection grounded in a solid plan allows others to see the credibility of the results reported. Sometimes, data are collected to guide the evaluation plan. In the example of the grant to develop a family violence plan, surveys were conducted with service providers to learn about the prevention activities already offered. This data-collection strategy still needed to be approved by the grant advisory group.

Documents created in the evaluation planning stage can become blueprints guiding and organizing future evaluation decisions. The RFP, the proposal submitted in response to the RFP, and the approved contract may contain the following:

1. *A literature review.* The successful interventions and evaluation procedures identified in that literature can be the jumping-off point for the replication of those procedures.

2. *A logic model.* Keep persons accountable to their stated or implied goals, activities, and expected results until they have documented reasons for changing them.

3. *The values.* If you have decided that clients will serve as advisers to the evaluation, make sure that they participate and feel welcome to give feedback. Ensure that the plan is informed by the SCREAM values by making the decisions outlined in figure 3.14. If you are going to evaluate whether the intervention was delivered in a culturally competent manner, make this clear at the beginning.

4. *The time line.* Establish deadlines for making planning, implementation, and evaluation decisions. Keep people to the time lines they agreed to in the evaluation stakeholder plan.

5. *The resources and contracted personnel.* The SCREAM value *resources* is meant to remind social service workers to conduct evaluations that are within the agency's means. The evaluation stakeholder plan in figure 2.9 can serve as the contract specifying the tasks of each person responsible for the evaluation.

For an example of the original plan for the evaluation of FSIs, see figure 6.1.

DOCUMENTING IMPLEMENTATION OF THE EVALUATION

Evaluators, just like practitioners and planners, are expected to write formal progress reports. In many cases, these reports are expected every three to six months. They summarize the evaluation activities and preliminary findings. Following is one way to organize evaluation progress reports and the eventual final report.

Background Information.   In this section, state the circumstances that gave rise to the current evaluation, such as the evaluator's response to an RFP. Summarize the answers to these questions:

Who authorized the evaluation and for what purposes?

How will the evaluation be used to make program or implementation decisions?

Who was hired to conduct the evaluation, and why were those persons selected?

Who are the key stakeholders overseeing the evaluation?

What is the time line of the evaluation, and how is it connected to the planning and practice time lines?

What were the values, theories, and data-collection expectations prior to beginning the evaluation?

Figure 6.1.   Case example: Documenting evaluation planning decisions for the evaluation of family support interventions.

Original Scope of the Evaluation

The purpose of this externally driven evaluation was to evaluate the implementation of thirty-eight family support interventions (FSIs) employed across the state. The key stakeholders were funders at the state level representing two different funding bodies, the Department of Education and Department of Jobs and Family Services. Local directors of the FSIs became aware of the evaluation after the state contracted with the evaluation team. The two-year, $250,000 evaluation was awarded through a competitive request for proposals (RFP) to a team of university evaluators and researchers. This data-collection team consisted of university social work faculty from seven different universities across the state who conducted site visits to all thirty-eight programs. Another evaluation team conducted the participant telephone survey from one location. An evaluation advisory board of state funders, local FSI stakeholders, and primary evaluators was formed. FSI staff, community members, and consumers were represented on the advisory board. All stakeholders agreed that the evaluation was being conducted to describe the current implementation of FSIs and guide future implementation decisions.

There were two general evaluation questions (one descriptive, the other explanatory) that followed the evaluators' plan documented in the RFP. The descriptive question was, "How do different stakeholders (administrators, direct-care staff, community representatives, and consumers) perceive success of the programs?" The explanatory hypothesis posed was, "Consumers of the FSIs will significantly improve family functioning over an eighteen-month period compared to persons with similar demographics who did not receive the services of the programs."

The seven goals of the evaluation logic model below were written into the RFP and approved by the stakeholders. There were specific objectives, strategies, and time lines listed under each goal:

> *Goal 1.* Provide a collaborative evaluation by organizing an interdisciplinary, cross-regional team of evaluators.
>
> *Goal 2.* Coordinate all evaluation activities in consultation with the state funders, FSI program directors, and parent consumers.
>
> *Goal 3.* Assess current program results by providing qualitative data from FSIs.
>
> *Goal 4.* Analyze the qualitative data by identifying the results that the FSIs collect. These results will be organized according to the four systems described by Kagan (1995).
>
> *Goal 5.* Assess FSI participants' general family functioning by collecting quantitative survey data from consumers of services.
>
> *Goal 6.* Develop an evaluation tool grounded in the qualitative data collection.
>
> *Goal 7.* Disseminate the findings.

(figure continues)

Orginal Adherence to SCREAM Values

The following SCREAM values were stated in the evaluation RFP. *Strengths* of client systems will be captured through open-ended interviews with FSI stakeholders and the use of a standardized instrument that measures family functioning. *Culturally competent* evaluation practices will be followed by conducting interviews with client systems from different backgrounds and including a comparison group that represents the demographics of the participants. *Resources* will be provided from the state funders for the evaluators to complete the agreed-on tasks. The main resource requested from the FSIs will be to provide time for local stakeholders to participate in the site visits and provide documentation requested from the evaluators. The contractual *agreement* for the evaluation is between the funders, representing the state, and the university, as represented by the principal investigators. The evaluators and funders will explain the purpose and procedures of the evaluation to the evaluated program directors through written communication and meetings led by the evaluators and funders. *Multiple* systems will be represented by including consumers, direct-care staff, administrators, community representatives, and funders in the site interviews. The site interview guides will ask how FSIs measure changes in children, families, agencies, and communities.

Original Theory Guiding Evaluation Decisions

The practice logic model written in the evaluation RFP for all FSIs was that healthy families be a short-term result for all programs. The primary desired long-term result for some community-based FSIs was the prevention of child abuse and neglect. The primary desired long-term result for the school-based FSIs was school readiness. There was variation in how local stakeholders perceived the program theory for reaching the short- and long-term results. The literature review guiding the evaluation plan was based on theoretical and descriptive studies of community-based family support programs and evidence-based research and led to the evaluators implementing the Family Assessment Device to measure family functioning, the concept must appropriate to all FSIs.

Original Data-Collection Approaches Guiding Evaluation Decisions

The descriptive evaluation question will be answered through qualitative focus groups conducted with key stakeholders at each of the thirty-eight FSIs. The narrative responses to the interviews, observation notes, and secondary documents gathered will be organized according to changes in child; family; agency; and community. The explanatory evaluation question will be answered through a quantitative telephone survey conducted at three different times over eighteen months with FSI consumers and a comparison group. The survey will contain the twelve-item general functioning scale of the standardized Family Assessment Device.

Evaluation Purpose.   In this section, state the evaluation questions as you see them given your interpretation of the background information. Phrase each set of questions in one of three ways:

1. The exploratory evaluation questions are . . .

2. The descriptive evaluation questions are . . .

3. The explanatory questions are . . .

These three distinctions help clarify to the stakeholders the focus of each type of question. Go back to the discussions in chapters 1, 4, and 5 to review the important relationship between type of question, theory (e.g., theory building or theory testing), and approaches (e.g. qualitative or quantitative) to data collection.

Evaluation Plan.   In this section, describe all aspects of the evaluation according to the decisions outlined at the end of each chapter and summarized in appendix C. Include the statement of values and the place of theory as these influenced the data-collection tasks. Specify who agreed to complete each data-collection task and within what time line. For a case example of a stakeholder plan, see figure 2.8.

Evaluation Progress.   In this section, describe progress toward achieving the tasks outlined in the evaluation design. Describe changes to any aspect of the evaluation, and note which stakeholders approved the changes. Facilitate the public dissemination of a progress report. For a summary of the midpoint review of the evaluation of FSIs, see figure 6.2.

This format is a logic model for conceptualizing evaluations and demonstrating the sequential connection between each component of evaluation. The original background information and the original evaluation questions become the foundation for all other decisions. This format is similar to the working contract used by social service workers in clinical settings. It is flexible, allowing for changes based on feedback from key stakeholders.

Evaluations and the documents resulting from them can be part of a larger grant for program planning or implementation. Be clear about whether the agency report and evaluation report will be mailed to the funders together or separately. Agencies are sometimes requested to submit evaluation reports as part of the periodic program reports. In such cases, distinguish between the evaluation report and the program report, clarifying who authored each.

EVALUATING THE EVALUATION AND DOCUMENTING CHANGES TO THE EVALUATION

The evaluation process itself should be evaluated. This should occur continuously through communication between the primary evaluator and the

Figure 6.2.   Case example: Documenting implementation decisions for the evaluation of family support interventions.

Scope of the Evaluation

Ongoing communication between the primary evaluators and the primary funders occurred weekly by telephone and e-mail and bimonthly through face-to-face meetings. A kickoff forum was held with the evaluation team and funders to clarify the scope and activities of the evaluation. The primary evaluator also attended two meetings with FSI directors to discuss the evaluation.

A formal report, "Results from Year One," was published and distributed to the state funders and directors of the thirty-eight FSIs. This report began with a three-page executive summary of the results from the site interviews and first round of telephone surveys. The main report contained the following sections:

1. Introduction
   a. Evaluation goals
   b. Evaluation design
   c. Use of this report
2. Site visit findings
   a. Child/student measures/desired results
   b. Family environment measures/desired results
   c. Agency/school access measures/desired results
   d. Multiagency collaboration measures/desired results
   e. FSI evaluation activities
3. Telephone survey findings
   a. How to read this section
   b. FSI results
   c. FSI comparison group results
4. Discussion and recommendations
   a. Family support: measures of desired community change and agency change
   b. Family health and stability: measures of desired family change and child change
   c. Recommendations: continued telephone survey and implementation of common evaluation tool
5. Appendixes
   a. Goals and objectives
   b. Glossary of terms
   c. Telephone survey tables
   d. Budget

The report documented that the original goals, objectives, and time lines were met. The original evaluation questions remained relevant from the evaluators' standpoints.

Adherence to SCREAM Values

Strengths of client systems were captured through open-ended interviews with FSI stakeholders. The open-ended, qualitative focus group format gave staff and clients an opportunity to tell their stories of the success of the FSIs even if there was not measurable evidence of these successes. There was some criticism from stakeholders that the instrument used to measure family functioning could actually be perceived as focusing on dysfunction rather than healthy functioning.

Culturally, FSIs located in urban areas had a higher African American population than did the rural FSIs, which had a predominantly white population. There were more female than male participants in the telephone survey. The modal age group represented in the survey was between twenty-five and forty-four. There was a wide range among participants on education and income.

Resources were adequate to complete the evaluation tasks. The one-year report became the basis on which to reexamine the original stakeholder *agreement. Multiple* systems desired results were reported in the focus groups.

Theory Building and Testing

Four different agency practice logic models emerged from the focus group data:

1. *Community Change Model.* The goal is to create change in the communitywide delivery system. Activities are intended to increase service coordination and community involvement. The short-term results are changes in the community that will eventually lead to improved functioning for families and children in the community.

2. *Agency Change Model.* The goal is increased members of families with access to agency services. Activities are intended to increase parent involvement, increase child involvement, expand service capacity, establish positive rapport between staff and families, and provide families with supportive services such as transportation to the agency. The short-term results are changes in the agency's accessibility, which will eventually lead to improved functioning for families and children in the community.

3. *Family Change Model.* The goal is to improve conditions for families. Activities are intended to decrease child abuse and neglect, help families meet their physical needs, increase parent knowledge and positive parenting behavior, reduce stress for parents, and improve health for children and parents. The short-term results are changes in the family that will lead to changes for children and the larger community.

4. *Child Change Model.* The goal is to improve child physical, emotional, educational, and social behaviors. Activities are intended to increase school performance, increase positive social interactions with peers and adults, and promote positive emotional development for children. The short-term results are changes in the child that will eventually lead to improved functioning for families and the larger community.

These four logic models did support the literature review findings about the range of family support programs. At the same time, not all the models identified family functioning as a short-term result. This became a data-collection issue

(figure continues)

because family functioning was being measured by consumers of all FSIs, not just the agencies following a family change model.

Preliminary Results from Data Collection

Results from the two data-collection approaches were reported. The four different types of agency change models emerged from the qualitative focus groups. There was no significant difference on the Family Assessment Device (FAD) between the FSI participants and the comparison group. Both groups were reporting healthy family functioning. The evaluation question addressed by the survey became more of a descriptive than an explanatory question because a true random sample of the FSI participants was not obtained.

---

primary stakeholders authorizing the evaluation. Formal, written feedback about the evaluation should be provided every three to six months, with a major review conducted no later than the midpoint of the evaluation.

All aspects of the evaluation should be reviewed. Below are some questions to consider about the performance of the evaluation team:

Is the evaluation team following the stakeholder agreement plan and any other applicable formal contracts?

Are the evaluators communicating with an agreed-on representative of the funding source or evaluation stakeholder group regarding the progress of the evaluation?

Is the required documentation (e.g., six-month reports, literature reviews, or evaluation training material) following the agreed-on format and content?

Are the evaluators following ethical guidelines in conducting the evaluation?

Is the evaluation team following the agreed-on time line for conducting evaluation tasks and submitting results?

In addition to evaluating the performance of the evaluation team, some stakeholders may want to change the focus and scope of an evaluation after the original proposal is accepted. Evaluation contracts should allow at the latest a midpoint negotiation of the evaluation goals, questions, and tasks based on stakeholder input about the evaluation. Some of the reasons stakeholders may request a change in the evaluation focus are the following:

Sometimes with the clarification of the evaluation process comes the realization that the actual evaluation activities are very different from expectations based on the evaluation proposal. Questions therefore arise that must be addressed.

Ramifications of the evaluation decisions also become clear as the evaluation activities are implemented. Stakeholders and participants often become nervous about how the evaluation findings will affect future program decisions.

Stakeholders may decide that certain evaluation questions need to be added or removed for reasons having nothing to do with the evaluation itself.

Preliminary results may lead to a change in the scope of the evaluation.

Stakeholders may want the evaluation team to play a more active role in training agency staff about the evaluation process. Stakeholders may want the evaluators to serve the role of facilitator or educator rather than the role of outside, objective evaluator. Or the opposite may be preferred. Maybe the stakeholders feel the evaluator has too much influence on agency practices and should be more objective and unobtrusive.

For an example of the process involved in evaluating changes to the two-year evaluation of FSIs, see figure 6.3.

Any changes to the original evaluation plan must be documented and agreed on. This can mean establishing an entirely new contract with the same evaluators or simply making additions to the original proposal. Evaluation is negotiation. All of chapter 2 was devoted to the many issues that influence evaluation stakeholders' decisions. Key stakeholders, including consumers, should be given the opportunity to offer feedback about the evaluation. The evaluators are stakeholders too and need to make their positions on the evaluation decisions clear. If agreement about proposed changes cannot be reached, the option that the evaluation contract can be discontinued should exist.

For an example of the changes agreed on in the evaluation of the FSIs on the basis of the midpoint review, see figure 6.4.

WRITING THE FINAL REPORT

The final evaluation report summarizes all the evaluation activities, results, and analyses of the results. Many stakeholders request that the final report include a recommendations section based on the findings of the evaluation. Clarify from the beginning whether recommendations are expected and, if so, how those recommendations will be utilized. Patton (1997) states that discussing utilization of the evaluation is necessary before the evaluation begins. Scriven (1991) counters that recommendations from evaluators compromise the role of the evaluator.

Evaluation is a teaching and learning opportunity. In some evaluations, stakeholders request structured training materials that they can use once the

Figure 6.3.   Case example: Documenting evaluation of the family service intervention evaluation.

Evaluating the Original Scope of the Evaluation

The first-year report became the basis for evaluating whether changes should be made to the original scope, goals, and activities of the evaluation. The evaluators proposed that a common evaluation tool could be administered with ten FSIs during the second year of the grant. Other stakeholders emphasized the importance of FSIs measuring child outcomes, especially related to school performance. Some stakeholders wanted the evaluators to provide more technical assistance to help FSI staff conduct self-evaluations since very few FSIs had conducted credible evaluations of their programs.

Evaluating the Original Adherence to SCREAM Values

Strengths of client systems were captured in all four types of FSI logic models. All FSIs had embraced the philosophy of the family support movement to encourage positive agency-client interaction. Stakeholders never questioned the evaluation's emphasis on strengths. Some stakeholders did question whether the agency and community change models resulted in short-term changes in families and children. *Culturally competent* evaluation practices were followed. The qualitative focus groups did capture the cultural diversity of the FSI client so stakeholders rightfully pointed out that the telephone survey missed lower-income families with no access to a telephone. *Resources* continued to be appropriate to complete the original evaluation activities. Some stakeholders felt, however, that the resources used for the telephone survey and proposed common evaluation tool could be better spent on helping agencies conduct self-evaluations. The contractual *agreement* for the evaluation was up for negotiation based on feedback from the first-year report. *Multiple* systems were captured in the focus group data. Some stakeholders did not agree that the funding should support change models that do not target short-term child and family results.

Original Theory Guiding Evaluation Decisions

Even though all FSIs had the long-term desired result of improving family functioning, there were two separate, additional long-term results expected across FSIs: (1) improved school readiness and (2) the prevention of child abuse and neglect. There was disagreement among stakeholders about whether it was feasible for FSIs to achieve all three long-term results. The focus from stakeholders for literature reviews also moved toward evidence-based practices to improve school performance.

Original Data-Collection Approaches Guiding Evaluation Decisions

Much descriptive information was learned from the qualitative focus groups. At the same time, several stakeholders wanted to see the FSIs collect more measurable child and family outcomes. There was also discussion about whether to continue the second and third telephone surveys since the original hypothesis was not upheld by the findings to date. The evaluators emphasized that the longitudinal nature of the telephone survey design could still produce significant results in the second and third measures.

Figure 6.4.   Case example: Documenting changes made to the evaluation of family support interventions.

Changes to the Original Scope of the Evaluation

On the basis of the points discussed in figure 6.3, a new evaluation plan was written and approved by the evaluation advisory board. The following were changes to the original scope of the evaluation:

1. Add these descriptive evaluation questions:

   a. Do school-based FSIs report positive changes in school performance?

   b. What are the most valid and reliable instruments that FSIs can implement to measure desired child and family outcomes?

   c. Are parents becoming more involved in their children's school performance?

2. Add these data-collection tasks:

   a. All school-based FSIs must provide actual results of school performance that minimally include pass rates of proficiency scores, attendance, retention, and graduation.

   b. The evaluators will add to the telephone survey questions that ask participants how involved they are in their child's education and whether their child has improved in school.

   c. The evaluators will conduct literature reviews of standardized instruments that measure child health, family health, and parents' involvement in their child's school performance.

3. Omit the original evaluation goal to develop and administer a common evaluation tool across a selected number of FSIs.

Changes to Adherence to the SCREAM Values

Strengths of client systems will be a focus of the instrument critiques listed in item 2 above. Administration of the FAD for times 2 and 3 will continue to measure healthy family functioning. No new qualitative data were collected from the FSI sites during the second year of the evaluation. *Culturally competent* instruments will be a focus of the instrument critiques in item 2. The telephone survey was repeated with the same participants as in time 1. Recidivism among participants did not vary across cultural groups. *Resources* continued to be appropriate to complete the revised evaluation activities. *Ethical* guidelines continued to be followed. Changes to the telephone survey were approved by the university institutional review board.

(figure continues)

Multiple systems measurements were now focused primarily on family functioning as measured by the FAD and child and family outcomes through the instrument critiques. The agency and community-based results emphasized by stakeholders at some FSIs were not being measured in the second year.

Changes to the Theory Driving Evaluation Decisions

The child and family change logic models became the primary focus in the second year. Even more specifically, the logic model that focused on school-based FSIs mandated that the requirement to measure school performance become more important. The literature review shifted toward a critical review of rigorous, credible instruments that measured child health, family health, and parent involvement.

Changes to Data Collection

The administration of the quantitative telephone survey continued during times 2 and 3. The proposal to implement a common evaluation tool across ten selected FSIs was not approved. Rather, this data-collection task was replaced with the tasks involving completing the instrument critiques.

---

evaluation is completed. Examples of such training materials include the following:

- annotated bibliographies and literature reviews related to the evaluation questions
- critiques of standardized instruments that measure the desired outcomes
- a basic outline of evaluation tasks similar to the Evaluation Decision-making Model in appendix C

For an example of material contained in the final report of the FSI evaluation, see figure 6.5. Notice that the final report began with an executive summary, which is a brief (three- to twenty-page) synopsis of the evaluation activities. Some stakeholders, especially policymakers, take the time to read only the executive summary. Make sure, therefore, that it demonstrates the connection between the scope of the evaluation, the evaluation questions, the values driving the evaluation, the theories underlying the evaluation, the methods used to collect the data, and the findings reported. The executive summary should contain any limitations of the evaluation and how the evaluation results can be utilized.

The exploratory research with parents described in this book was not a formal evaluation of an agency intervention. Therefore, there was no contractual agreement related to submission of evaluation reports. The researcher did, however, have an ethical obligation to provide the results to the participants. He informed all participants how they could obtain a copy

Figure 6.5.   Case example: Items contained in the final report of the evaluation of family support interventions.

A formal report, "A Combined Methods Evaluation of Family Support Interventions: Final Report of Results," was published and distributed in hard copy and on CD to the state funders. The printed copy of the report was distributed to the directors of the thirty-eight FSIs. This report began with a twenty-page executive summary of the results from the entire survey that also contained a recommendations for future evaluations section.

The main report contained the following sections:

Section I. Evaluation background and context

Section II. Review of first-year site interview results

Section III. FSI consumer survey findings

Section IV. Discussion

Section V. Recommendations for future evaluations

Appendixes:

    A.   Steps to conducting program evaluation

    B.   Steps to conducting program evaluation applied to the FSI evaluation

    C.   Site interview questions

    D.   Phone survey questions

    E.   Glossary of evaluation terms

    F.   Evaluation resources

    G.   Examples of evaluation questions related to school-based FSI logic models

    H.   Examples of evaluation questions related to the theorized impacts of collaboration

    I.   Promotional indicators for FSIs

    J.   Resources for conducting culturally competent evaluation

    K.   Demographic tables

    L.   Statistical tables for telephone survey (CD-ROM only)

Three separate documents were submitted that contained instrument critiques of

    A.   Child health

    B.   Family health

    C.   Parent involvement

of the final report, which in this case was his dissertation. Expecting that the participants would not request that verbose academic document, the researcher did mail or hand deliver to each participant her narrative, which was about twenty pages long. And, with permission from each participant, he also verbally reported the findings of the research to the agency workers who helped facilitate contact with the participants.

The published reports from this study were the researcher's dissertation (Brun, 1993), a presentation to parents and agency workers of National Head Start, and an article in a journal published by Head Start (Brun, 1997). Head Start parents and staff were chosen as an audience for dissemination because one goal of Head Start is to support the strengths of families. Readers must determine for themselves whether the themes from the dissertation study and excerpts from the parent participants can be applied to similar families they help.

In the evaluation of the Strengths-Based Case Management (SBCM), progress reports were provided to the director of the program. All participants, consumers and social service workers, were informed that they could obtain the results of the evaluation. Only the director requested written results. Be clear about what information you will provide to those requesting the results. Provide a brief summary and information about how a more detailed report can be obtained, for example, by contacting the funder for a copy of the final report, tracking down publications related to the evaluation, or attending conferences at which the evaluation is to be discussed.

The evaluator provided a summary presentation to the staff of the SBCM. The director attended the presentation and discussed ways in which the staff could make program changes based on feedback from the consumer participants. The evaluator mailed or hand delivered the summaries of the interviews to each consumer participant. The director of the agency and the evaluator presented results of the evaluation at an NASW conference and had a cowritten article published in *Social Work* (Brun and Rapp, 2001). Readers of the article can determine how the authors' analysis of the SBCM program can be applied to their own social service setting.

Think of each evaluation as an opportunity to improve practice and contribute to the knowledge base. Consider presenting your results at local, state, national, and international conferences. Consider submitting the findings to professional journals. Work with other stakeholders to accomplish these activities. For more information on report writing and submitting evaluation findings for publication, consult the "Further Readings" section at the end of this chapter.

MAJOR POINTS

We have now come full circle. Documenting the decisions made at each step in the evaluation makes writing the final report much easier and shows the connection between all the decisions. Such documentation also shows the integration of planning, implementation, and evaluation of programs. Documentation of values, theories, and data-collection approaches guiding the evaluation keeps the practitioner accountable. Evaluation, like practice, goes through a cycle of planning, implementing, evaluating, and changing. Material to consider in preliminary and final evaluation reports was discussed. This book ends with the encouragement to share the findings of your evaluation with others at conferences and in professional journals.

FURTHER READINGS

Writing Reports to Qualitative Approaches

Drisko, J. (1997). Strengthening qualitative studies and reports: Standards to promote academic integrity. *Journal of Social Work Education, 33*(1), 185–97.
Padgett, D. (2004). Spreading the word: Writing up and disseminating qualitative research. In D. Padgett (Ed.), *The qualitative research experience* (pp. 285–96). Belmont, CA: Wadsworth/Thomson Learning.

Writing Reports to Quantitative Approaches

Fortune, A., & Reid, W. (1999). *Research in social work* (3rd ed.). New York: Columbia University Press. (See esp. app. 2.)
Marlow, C. (Ed.). (2005). *Research methods for generalist social work* (5th ed.). Belmont, CA: Wadsworth/Thomson Learning. (See esp. chap. 14.)
Royse, D., Thyer, B., Padgett, D., & Logan, T. (2001). *Program evaluation: An introduction* (3rd ed.). Belmont, CA: Brooks/Cole. (See esp. chap. 15.)
Thyer, B. (2002). How to write up a social work outcome study for publication. *Journal of Social Work Research and Evaluation, 3*(2), 215–24.
Westerfelt, A., & Dietz, T. (2005). *Planning and conducting agency-based research: A workbook for social work students in field placements* (3rd ed.). Boston: Allyn & Bacon.

REFLECTIVE JOURNAL ACTIVITIES

1. Now that you have come to the last chapter, have your views about evaluation changed since you first started this book?

2. Are you more optimistic or more pessimistic about the place of evaluation in the social service setting?

3. Are you more confident or less confident in your evaluation skills?

4. Do you see this book helping you with future evaluations?

5. How can you utilize the lists, case examples, and figures in this book for evaluations?

6. As a student, do you see yourself as a future practitioner-evaluator?

7. As a practitioner, do you see yourself as a practitioner-evaluator?

PROCEDURAL JOURNAL ACTIVITY

1. Think of an evaluation in your agency or practicum setting, and complete the Evaluation Decisionmaking Model for reporting results listed in figure 6.6.

Figure 6.6. Evaluation decisionmaking model: Reporting results.

The following *reports* are expected from the evaluation (check all that apply):

____ Written evaluation proposal

____ Written evaluation reports submitted every _____ months

____ Written final evaluation report

____ Presentation on the findings to be given to _____

____ Submission of an article for review in a refereed journal

____ Literature review

____ Logic model

____ Instruments used

____ Human subjects review protocol

____ Other

APPENDIX A

CODE OF ETHICS, APPROVED BY THE NATIONAL ASSOCIATION OF SOCIAL WORKERS, JANUARY 1, 1997, SECTION 5.02, EVALUATION AND RESEARCH

(a.) Social workers should monitor and evaluate policies, the implementation of programs, and practice interventions.

(b.) Social workers should promote and facilitate evaluation and research to contribute to the development of knowledge.

(c.) Social workers should critically examine and keep current with emerging knowledge relevant to social work and fully use evaluation and research evidence in their professional practice.

(d.) Social workers engaged in evaluation or research should carefully consider possible consequences and should follow guidelines developed for the protection of evaluation and research participants. Appropriate institutional review boards should be consulted.

(e.) Social workers engaged in evaluation or research should obtain voluntary and written informed consent from participants, when appropriate, without any implied or actual deprivation or penalty for refusal to participate; without undue inducement to participate; and with due regard for participants' well-being, privacy, and dignity. Informed consent should include information about the nature, extent, and duration of the participation requested and disclosure of the risks and benefits of participation in the research.

(f.) When evaluation or research participants are incapable of giving informed consent, social workers should provide an appropriate explanation to the participants, obtain the participants' assent to the extent they are able, and obtain written consent from an appropriate proxy.

(g.) Social workers should never design or conduct evaluation or research that does not use consent procedures, such as certain forms of naturalistic observation and archival research, unless rigorous and responsible review of the research has found it to be justified because of its prospective scientific, educational, or applied value and unless equally effective alternative procedures that do not involve waiver of consent are not feasible.

(h.) Social workers should inform participants of their right to withdraw from evaluation and research at any time without penalty.

(i.) Social workers should take appropriate steps to ensure that participants in evaluation and research have access to appropriate supportive services.

(j.) Social workers engaged in evaluation or research should protect participants from unwarranted physical or mental distress, harm, danger, or deprivation.

(k.) Social workers engaged in the evaluation of services should discuss collected information only for professional purposes and only with people professionally concerned with this information.

(l.) Social workers engaged in evaluation or research should ensure the anonymity or confidentiality of participants and of the data obtained from them. Social workers should inform participants of any limits of confidentiality, the measures that will be taken to ensure confidentiality, and when any records containing research data will be destroyed.

(m.) Social workers who report evaluation and research results should protect participants' confidentiality by omitting identifying information unless proper consent has been obtained authorizing disclosure.

(n.) Social workers should report evaluation and research findings accurately. They should not fabricate or falsify results and should take steps to correct any errors later found in published data using standard publication methods.

(o.) Social workers engaged in evaluation or research should be alert to and avoid conflicts of interest and dual relationships with participants, should inform participants when a real or potential conflict of interest arises, and should take steps to resolve the issue in a manner that makes participants' interests primary.

(p.) Social workers should educate themselves, their students, and their colleagues about responsible research practices.

AMERICAN EVALUATION ASSOCIATION, GUIDING PRINCIPLES FOR EVALUATORS

The American Evaluation Association (AEA) strives to promote ethical practice in the evaluation of programs, products, personnel, and policy. AEA has developed these principles to guide evaluators in their professional practice:

THE PRINCIPLES

A. Systematic Inquiry

Evaluators conduct systematic, data-based inquiries and thus should:

1. Adhere to the highest technical standards appropriate to the methods they use.

2. Explore with the client the shortcomings and strengths of evaluation questions and approaches.

3. Communicate the approaches, methods, and limitations of the evaluation accurately and in sufficient detail to allow others to understand, interpret, and critique their work.

B. Competence

Evaluators provide competent performance to stakeholders and thus should:

1. Ensure that the evaluation team collectively possesses the education, abilities, skills, and experience appropriate to the evaluation.

2. Ensure the evaluation team collectively demonstrates cultural competence and uses appropriate evaluation strategies and skills to work with culturally different groups.

These Guiding Principles are an abbreviated version of the full principles that were developed and endorsed by the American Evaluation Association in 1994 and reviewed and revised in 2004. A full text of the original Guiding Principles is available online at www.eval.org.

3. Practice within the limits of their competence, decline to conduct evaluations that fall substantially outside those limits, and make clear any limitations on the evaluation that might result if declining is not feasible.

4. Seek to maintain and improve their competencies in order to provide the highest level of performance in their evaluations.

C. Integrity/Honesty

Evaluators display honesty and integrity in their own behavior and attempt to ensure the honesty and integrity of the entire evaluation process and thus should:

1. Negotiate honestly with clients and relevant stakeholders concerning the costs, tasks, limitations of methodology, scope of results, and uses of data.

2. Disclose any roles or relationships that might pose a real or apparent conflict of interest prior to accepting an assignment.

3. Record and report all changes to the original negotiated project plans and the reasons for the changes, including any possible impacts that could result.

4. Be explicit about their own, their clients', and other stakeholders' interests and values related to the evaluation.

5. Represent accurately their procedures, data, and findings, and attempt to prevent or correct misuse of their work by others.

6. Work to resolve any concerns related to procedures or activities likely to produce misleading evaluative information, decline to conduct the evaluation if concerns cannot be resolved, and consult colleagues or relevant stakeholders about other ways to proceed if declining is not feasible.

7. Disclose all sources of financial support for an evaluation and the source of the request for the evaluation.

D. Respect for People

Evaluators respect the security, dignity, and self-worth of respondents, program participants, clients, and other evaluation stakeholders and thus should:

1. Seek a comprehensive understanding of the contextual elements of the evaluation.

2. Abide by current professional ethics, standards, and regulations regarding confidentiality, informed consent, and potential risks or harms to participants.

3. Seek to maximize the benefits and reduce any unnecessary harms that might occur from an evaluation and carefully judge when the benefits from the evaluation or procedure should be foregone because of potential risks.

4. Conduct the evaluation and communicate its results in a way that respects the stakeholders' dignity and self-worth.

5. Foster social equity in evaluation, when feasible, so that those who give to the evaluation may benefit in return.

6. Understand, respect, and take into account differences among stakeholders, such as culture, religion, gender, disability, age, sexual orientation, and ethnicity.

E. Responsibilities for General and Public Welfare

Evaluators articulate and take into account the diversity of general and public interests and values and thus should:

1. Include relevant perspectives and interests of the full range of stakeholders.

2. Consider not only immediate operations and outcomes of the evaluation but also the broad assumptions, implications, and potential side effects.

3. Allow stakeholders access to, and actively disseminate, evaluative information and present evaluation results in understandable forms that respect people and honor promises of confidentiality.

4. Maintain a balance between client and other stakeholder needs and interests.

5. Take into account the public interest and good, going beyond analysis of particular stakeholder interests to consider the welfare of society as a whole.

APPENDIX C

Evaluation Decisionmaking Model Outline

What is the *scope* of the evaluation?

> How will the evaluation guide practice decisions?
>
> How will the evaluation guide planning decisions?
>
> How will the evaluation guide future evaluation decisions?
>
> Which type of evaluation questions are being asked—*exploratory, descriptive,* or *explanatory?*

Who are the *stakeholders* driving the evaluation decisions?

> Who are the authorizing stakeholders?
>
> Who are the persons on the advisory board?
>
> Who are the persons responsible for conducting the evaluation activities?
>
> How will the stakeholders utilize outside resources to guide the evaluation?
>
> What are the reports of the evaluation expected by the stakeholders?

How are *values* driving the evaluation?

> What *values* are expected by stakeholders?
>
> How will *strengths* of participants be measured?
>
> How will the *culture* of stakeholders and participants be respected?
>
> How will the evaluation be conducted feasibly within the available *resources?*
>
> How will *ethical* guidelines be met?
>
> How will *agreement* on evaluation activities be reached among stakeholders?
>
> How will *multiple* systems be measured?

How are *theories* driving the evaluation?

> How will a *literature review* of other relevant evaluations and research be completed to answer exploratory, descriptive, and explanatory evaluation questions?

What is the *logic model* of program goals, strategies, and results and how will it guide the activities of the current evaluation?

How are *data* driving the evaluation?

How are appropriate data-collection methods chosen to answer exploratory, descriptive, and explanatory evaluation questions?

How are appropriate data-analysis methods chosen to answer exploratory, descriptive, and explanatory evaluation questions?

How is credibility for the evaluation achieved?

How are the evaluation decisions reported?

What are the evaluation products, including the final report?

How do the reports show the connection between all the previous evaluation decisions made?

GLOSSARY

abstract database. A compilation of brief summaries, called *abstracts,* of published scholarship.

advisory board. Those stakeholders overseeing the planning and implementation of the evaluation.

classic experimental design. An evaluation or research study in which participants are randomly selected and assigned to intervention and comparison groups and pre- and postintervention ordinal level and higher measures of results are given to both groups.

comparison group. Persons who do not receive the intervention.

credibility. The rigorous and systematic collection of qualitative and quantitative data according to the most widely accepted procedures cited in the research and evaluation literature.

culture. The values, beliefs, customs, language, and behaviors passed on among individuals, families, communities, and societies.

data. Information systematically collected for specific evaluation and research purposes.

data analysis. Making sense and meaning out of the information gathered in an evaluation.

descriptive evaluation questions. Questions posed about the demographics, attitudes, behaviors, and knowledge of clients, workers, and community members and aspects of an intervention that will lead to program improvement and knowledge building.

descriptive statistics. The numerical meaning attributed to the distribution of data collected quantitatively.

empirical research. The published, peer-reviewed dissemination of the results of studies that applied credible data-collection methods.

ethics. An organization's written statement of the values, principles, and behaviors expected of all members.

evaluation audit. Review of the evaluation decisions by a person not connected to the evaluation.

evidence-based practice. Those interventions that have been demonstrated to be effective on the basis of the most rigorous data-collection feasible for the practice setting.

explanatory evaluation questions. Questions posed to test whether an intervention produced the desired results for clients, workers, or members of the larger community that will lead to program improvement and knowledge building.

exploratory evaluation questions. Questions posed to clients, workers, or community members about their experiences or circumstances that will lead to program improvement and knowledge building.

external validity. The ability to generalize evaluation results to the larger population.

focus groups. Interview conducted with more than one person at a time.

goals. General, abstract statements about the desired processes, outcomes, or results of an intervention or program.

hypothesis. Statement predicting a causal relationship between the intervention or program and desired results.

inferential statistics. The numerical meaning attributed to the relationship between data collected quantitatively.

internal validity. The ability to attribute results to the evaluated intervention or program.

interview guide. A set of general questions that allow the participants to describe their experiences about a subject in their own words.

levels of measurement. The variables used for statistical analysis grouped by the ability to make inferences from the data, including nominal, ordinal, interval, and ratio values.

leveraging. Allocation of funds and other resources by organizations other than the primary funder.

literature review. Summarization and analysis of other evaluations or research studies relevant to the current planning, implementation, or evaluation activities.

logic model. A clarification of the connection between intervention or program strategies, goals, and desired results.

measures of central tendency. Statistics that illustrate how data are distributed including mean, mode, and median.

measures of variability. Statistics that illustrate how spread out data are, including range, variance, and standard deviation.

member checking. Seeking feedback from the participants about the evaluator's reporting, and, in some cases, interpretation, of the information collected.

multiple systems. The individuals, families, groups, organizations, and communities that are the targets for change and the sources for creating change.

objectivity. Identifying evaluator biases and influences that distort the data-collection process.

participants. Those persons from whom data are collected through interviews, surveys, observations, and documents to answer evaluation questions.

peer debriefing. Consultation about the evaluation process from persons selected for their expertise.

peer-reviewed research article. A printed article for which two or more researchers or practitioners have approved the academic and practice contributions.

purposive. Selecting participants on the basis of specific criteria addressed in the evaluation question, that is, not randomly.

qualitative approaches. The gathering of information using open-ended questions, the answers to which will build theory to answer exploratory and descriptive evaluation questions.

quantitative approaches. The gathering of information using closed-ended questions, the answers to which will test theory to answer descriptive and explanatory evaluation questions and statements.

random sample. Participants chosen in such a way that every member of the larger population has an equal chance of being selected.

reliability. The consistent measurement of the same concept.

resources. The time, materials, and training needed to complete evaluation tasks.

response rate. The number of persons who complete an evaluation survey or instrument divided by the number of persons who were given the survey or instrument.

results. Desired changes related to specific strategies.

secondary documents. Sources of information recorded by someone else prior to the current evaluation that are used to answer the current evaluation questions.

single system design. An evaluation or research study in which the desired results are measured both before and after an intervention has been delivered to a single system, i.e., an individual, family, group, organization, or community.

social service evaluation. Systematic collection and analysis of information about one or more social service interventions and clients to improve social service practice, planning, and accountability and to contribute to knowledge building.

social service programs. One or more social service interventions delivered to achieve specified goals and results among identified client systems.

stakeholders. Those persons affected by the intervention or program and the process, results, and reports of the evaluation.

standardized instrument. Evaluation and research data-collection tool tested and reported in the literature.

statistical significance. Existence of a relationship between the intervention or program and results outside an acceptable level for chance.

strategies. The actual interventions employed to reach the stated goals.

strengths. Behaviors and beliefs that help individuals, families, agencies, and communities reach their optimal level of social functioning.

survey. Set of questions developed by the evaluation stakeholders to collect locally specific information.

themes. The meaning attributed to narrative data collected qualitatively.

theme redundancy. The repetition of conceptual ideas when persons possessing the same characteristics are selected.

theory. A description or explanation of the relationship between a social service intervention or program and desired results for clients.

theory building. The process of exploring or describing what one learns while gathering information.

theory testing. The process of gathering information to describe or explain the relationship between interventions and client change.

triangulation. Implementing multiple data-collection methods in an evaluation.

trustworthiness. The accurate description of the concepts and realities as intended by the evaluation participants.

validity. The accurate measurement of concepts learned from evidence-based theory intended for the current evaluation.

values. Preferences, beliefs, cherished ideas, worldviews, assumptions, traditions, and morals that consciously and unconsciously shape and influence decisions of individuals and groups.

References

Babbie, E., Halley, F., & Zaino, J. (2003). *Adventures in social research: Data analysis using SPSS 11.0/11.5 for Windows*. Chicago: Pine Forge.

Benson, P. (1997). *All kids are our kids: What communities must do to raise caring and responsible children and adolescents*. San Francisco: Jossey-Bass.

Bisman, C., & Hardcastle, D. (1999). *Integrating research into practice: A model for effective social work*. Belmont, CA: Brooks/Cole.

Bloom, M., Fischer, J., & Orme, J. (2003). *Evaluating practice: Guidelines for the accountable professional* (4th ed.). Boston: Allyn & Bacon.

Brode, R. (1990). *Public child welfare professionals: Those who stay*. Unpublished doctoral dissertation, Ohio State University.

Brun, C. (1993). *A naturalistic inquiry into the lives of six women labeled "at-risk" for child neglect*. Unpublished doctoral dissertation, Ohio State University.

Brun, C. (1997). A model to assess parental strengths of Head Start consumers: Results from a qualitative study of the lives of six women labeled "at-risk" for child neglect. *National Head Start Association Research Quarterly, 1*(2), 74–83.

Brun, C., Dockery, J., Sweet-Holp, T., O'Connor, M., & Brannon, C. (1998). *A combined quantitative/qualitative evaluation of the results of two Ohio family support programs: Final report*. Dayton, OH: Wright State University.

Brun, C., & Giga, S. (1999). Organizing on behalf of families: Facilitating a community application to a state block grant to prevent teenage pregnancies. *Child and Adolescent Social Work Journal, 16*(1), 23–26.

Brun, C., & Rapp, R. (2001). Strengths-Based Case Management: Individuals' perspectives on strengths and the case manager relationship. *Social Work, 46*(3), 278–88.

Campbell, D., & Stanley, J. (1963). *Experimental and quasi-experimental designs for research*. Chicago: Rand McNally.

Clasen, C., Meyer, C., Brun, C., Mase, W., & Cauley, K. (2003). Development of the Competency Assessment Tool—Mental Health, an instrument to assess core competencies for mental health care workers. *Psychiatric Rehabilitation Journal, 27*(1), 10–17.

Cook, T., & Campbell, D. (1979). *Quasi-experimentation: Design and analysis issues for field settings*. Chicago: Rand McNally.

Corcoran, K., & Fischer, J. (2003). *Measures for clinical practice: A sourcebook* (3rd ed., Vols. 1–2). New York: Free Press.

Denzin, N., & Lincoln, Y. (Eds.). (1994). *Handbook of qualitative research*. Thousand Oaks, CA: Sage.

Donaldson, S. (2003). Theory-driven program evaluation in the new millennium. In S. Donaldson & M. Scriven (Eds.), *Evaluating social programs and problems: Visions for the new millennium* (pp. 109–41). Mahwah, NJ: Erlbaum.

Donaldson, S. & Gooler, L. (2002). Theory-driven evaluation of the work and health initiative: A focus on winning new jobs. *American Journal of Evaluation, 23*(3), 341–46.

Drisko, J. (1997). Strengthening qualitative studies and reports: Standards to promote academic integrity. *Journal of Social Work Education, 33*(1), 185–97.

Drisko, J. (2004). Qualitative data analysis software: A user's appraisal. In D. Padgett (Ed.), *The qualitative research experience* (pp. 189–210). Belmont, CA: Wadsworth/Thomson Learning.

Dunst, C., Trivette, C., & Deal, A. (Eds.). (1994). *Supporting and strengthening families: Methods, strategies, and practices.* Cambridge, MA: Brookline.

Epstein, N., Baldwin, L., & Bishop, D. (1982). *Family Assessment Device.* Providence, RI: Brown University/Butler Hospital Family Research Program.

Evans, C., & Fisher, M. (1999). Collaborative evaluation with service users: Moving towards user-controlled research. In I. Shaw & J. Lishman (Eds.), *Evaluation and social work practice* (pp. 101–17). Thousand Oaks, CA: Sage.

Fetterman, D. (2001). *Foundations of empowerment evaluation.* Thousand Oaks, CA: Sage.

Fink, A. (2003). *The survey handbook* (2nd ed.). Thousand Oaks, CA: Sage.

Fitzpatrick, J. (2002). Dialogue with Stuart Donaldson. *American Journal of Evaluation, 23*(3), 347–65.

Fong, R., & Furuto, S. (Eds.). (2001). *Culturally competent practice: Skills, interventions, and evaluations.* Boston: Allyn & Bacon.

Frechtling, J., & Sharp, L. (1997). *User-friendly handbook for mixed method evaluations.* Washington, DC: National Science Foundation.

Gambrill, E. (1997). *Social work practice: A critical thinkers' guide.* New York: Oxford University Press.

Gambrill, E. (1999). Evidence-based practice: An alternative to authority-based practice. *Families in Society: The Journal of Contemporary Human Services, 80,* 341–50.

Gambrill, E. (2003). From the editor: Evidence-based practice: Sea change or the emperor's new clothes? *Journal of Social Work Education, 39*(1), 3–23.

Gibbs, L. (1990). Using online databases to guide practice and research. In R. Reinoehl & T. Hanna (Eds.), *Computer literacy in human services* (pp. 97–116). New York: Haworth.

Gibbs, L. (2003). *Evidence-based practice for the helping professions: A practical guide with integrated multimedia.* Pacific Grove, CA: Brooks/Cole.

Gibbs, L., & Gambrill, E. (1999). *Critical thinking for social workers: Exercises for the helping professions.* Thousand Oaks, CA: Sage.

Gibbs, L., & Gambrill, E. (2002). Evidence-based practice: Counter-arguments to objections. *Research on Social Work Practice, 12,* 452–76.

Gilbert, D., & Franklin, C. (2001). Developing culturally sensitive practice evaluation skills with Native American individuals and families. In R. Fong & S. Furuto (Eds.), *Culturally competent practice: Skills, interventions, and evaluations* (pp. 396–412). Boston: Allyn & Bacon.

Ginsberg, L. (2001). *Social work evaluation: Principles and methods.* Boston: Allyn & Bacon.

Glicken, M. (2004). *Using the strengths perspective in social work practice: A positive approach for the helping professions.* Boston: Allyn & Bacon.

Guba, E., & Lincoln, Y. (1989). *Fourth generation evaluation.* Thousand Oaks, CA: Sage.

Hess, P., & Mullen, E. (1995). Collaborative considerations in practitioner-researcher knowledge-building partnerships. In P. Hess & E. Mullen (Eds.), *Practitioner-researcher partnerships: Building knowledge from, in, and for practice* (pp. 1–39). Washington, DC: NASW Press.

Hood, S. (2004). A journey to understand the role of culture in program evaluation: Snapshots and personal reflections of one African American evaluator. *New Directions for Evaluation, 102,* 21–38.

Joint Committee on Standards for Educational Evaluation. (1994a). *The program evaluation standards* (2nd ed.). Thousand Oaks, CA: Sage.

Joint Committee on Standards for Educational Evaluation. (1994b). *What the program evaluation standards say about designing evaluations.* Thousand Oaks, CA: Sage.

Kagan, S. (1995). *By the bucket: Achieving results for young children* (Issue brief for the Governors' Campaign for Children). Washington, DC: National Governors' Association.

Kibel, B. (1999). *Success data as hard data: An introduction to results mapping.* New York: Kluwer Academic/Plenum.

King, J., Stevahn, L., Ghere, G., & Minnema, J. (2001). Toward a taxonomy of essential evaluator competencies. *American Journal of Evaluation, 22*(2), 229–47.

Kretzmann, J., & McKnight, J. (1993). *Building communities from the inside out: A path toward finding and mobilizing a community's assets.* Evanston, IL: Asset-Based Community Development Institute, Institute for Policy Research, Northwestern University.

Krueger, R., & Casey, M. (2000). *Focus groups: A practical guide for applied research* (3rd ed.). Thousand Oaks, CA: Sage.

Lather, P. (1991). *Getting smart: Feminist research and pedagogy with/in the postmodern.* New York: Routledge.

Lather, P. (2003). Issues of validity in openly ideological research: Between a rock and a soft place. In Y. Lincoln & N. Denzin (Eds.), *Turning points in qualitative research: Tying knots in a handkerchief* (pp. 185–218). Walnut Creek, CA: Alta Mira.

Leviton, L. (2003). Commentary: Engaging the community in evaluation: Bumpy, time consuming, and important. *American Journal of Evaluation, 24*(1), 85–90.

Lewis, L. (2001). Program evaluation with Native American/American Indian organizations. In R. Fong & S. Furuto (Eds.), *Culturally competent practice: Skills, interventions, and evaluations* (pp. 412–25). Boston: Allyn & Bacon.

Lincoln, Y., & Guba, E. (1985). *Naturalistic inquiry.* Thousand Oaks, CA: Sage.

Mark, R. (1996). *Research made simple: A handbook for social workers.* Thousand Oaks, CA: Sage.

Marsh, J. (2002). What knowledge is relevant to social work practice? The case of TANF reauthorization. *Social Work, 47*(3), 197–200.

Marsh, J. (2003). Chewing on cardboard and other pleasures of knowledge utilization. *Social Work, 48*(3), 293–94.

Matsuoka, J. (2001). Evaluation and assessment in Hawaiian and Pacific communities. In R. Fong & S. Furuto (Eds.), *Culturally competent practice: Skills, interventions, and evaluations* (pp. 438–53). Boston: Allyn & Bacon.

McClintock, C. (2003). Commentary: The evaluator as scholar/practitioner/change agent. *American Journal of Evaluation, 24*(1), 91–96.

McKnight, J., & Kretzmann, J. (1997). Mapping community capacity. In M. Minkler (Ed.), *Community organizing and community building for health* (pp. 157–72). New Brunswick, NJ: Rutgers University Press.

Mertens, D. (2003). The inclusive view of evaluation: Visions for the new millennium. In S. Donaldson & M. Scriven (Eds.), *Evaluating social programs and problems: Visions for the new millennium* (pp. 91–108). Mahwah, NJ: Erlbaum.

Meyer, C., Brun, C., Yung, B., Clasen, C., Cauley, K., & Mase, W. (2004). Marketing outreach efforts to enroll children in the Medicaid Expansion Children's Health Insurance Program (CHIP). *Journal of Nonprofit and Public Sector Marketing, 12*(2), 87–104.

Meyer, C., Yung, B., Ranbom, L., Cauley, K., Brun, C., Fuller, B., et al. (2001). *Medicaid outreach expansion evaluation* (Final research report submitted to the Ohio Department of Jobs and Family Services). Dayton, OH: Wright State University.

Miles, M., & Huberman, A. (1994). *Qualitative data analysis: An expanded sourcebook* (2nd ed.). Thousand Oaks, CA: Sage.

Morris, M. (2003). Ethical challenges: You want to ask them what?!?!?! *American Journal of Evaluation, 24*(1), 81–84.

Netting, F., & Rodwell, M. (1998). Integrating gender into human service organization, administration, and planning curricula. In J. Figueira-McDonough, F. Netting, & A. Nichols-Casebolt (Eds.), *The role of gender in practice knowledge: Claiming half the human experience* (pp. 287–322). New York: Garland.

Neuman, W., & Kreuger, L. (2003). *Social work research methods: Qualitative and quantitative applications.* Boston: Allyn & Bacon.

Nichols-Casebolt, A., & Spakes, P. (1995). Policy research and the voices of women. *Social Work Research, 19*(1), 49–55.

O'Neill, T. (2000). The dream catcher and the universality of grief. In J. Morgan (Ed.), *Meeting the needs of our clients creatively: The impact of art and culture on caregiving* (pp. 277–88). Amityville, NY: Baywood.

Padgett, D. (Ed.). (2004a). *The qualitative research experience.* Belmont, CA: Wadsworth/Thomson Learning.

Padgett, D. (2004b). Spreading the word: Writing up and disseminating qualitative research. In D. Padgett (Ed.), *The qualitative research experience* (pp. 285–96). Belmont, CA: Wadsworth/Thomson Learning.

Patrizi, P., & McMullan, B. (1998). *Evaluation in foundations: The unrealized potential* (Report prepared for the W. K. Kellogg Foundation Evaluation Unit). Battle Creek, MI: Kellogg Foundation.

Patton, M. (1997). *Utilization-focused evaluation: The new century text* (3rd ed.). Thousand Oaks, CA: Sage.

Patton, M. (1999). Enhancing the quality and credibility of qualitative analysis. *Health Science Research, 34*(5), 1189–1207.

Patton, M. (2002). *Qualitative evaluation and research methods* (3rd ed.). Thousand Oaks, CA: Sage.

Pecora, P., Fraser, M., Nelson, K., McCroskey, J., & Meezan, W. (1995). *Evaluating family-based services.* Hawthorne, NY: Aldine De Gruyter.

Posavac, E., & Carey, R. (2003). *Program evaluation: Methods and case studies* (6th ed.). Upper Saddle River, NJ: Prentice Hall.

Potocky-Tripodi, M., & Tripodi, T. (2003). Twelve steps for quantitative analysts anonymous: On recovery from dependence on statistical significance testing, or (effect) size matters. *Journal of Social Work Research and Evaluation, 4*(2), 139–44.

Richards, L. (1999). Data alive! The thinking behind Nvivo. *Qualitative Health Research, 9*(3), 412–28.

Ristock, J., & Pennell, J. (1996). *Community research as empowerment: Feminist links, postmodern interruptions.* New York: Oxford University Press.

Robson, C. (2000). *Small-scale evaluation.* London: Sage.

Rodwell, M. (1995). Constructivist research: A qualitative approach. In P. Pecora, M. Fraser, K. Nelson, J. McCroskey, & W. Meezan, *Evaluating family-based services* (pp. 191–214). Hawthorne, NY: Aldine De Gruyter.

Rodwell, M. (1998). *Social work constructivist research.* New York: Garland.

Rodwell, M., & Woody, D. (1994). Constructivist evaluation: The policy/practice context. In E. Sherman & W. Reid (Eds.), *Qualitative research in social work* (pp. 315–27). New York: Columbia University Press.

Royse, D., Thyer, B., Padgett, D., & Logan, T. (2001). *Program evaluation: An introduction* (3rd ed.). Belmont, CA: Brooks/Cole.

Saleebey, D. (Ed.). (1992). *The strengths perspective in social work practice.* New York: Longman.

Saleebey, D. (1997). The strengths perspective: Possibilities and problems. In D. Saleebey (Ed.), *The strengths perspective in social work practice* (2nd ed., pp. 231–45). White Plains, NY: Longman.

Saleebey, D. (Ed.). (2002). *The strengths perspective in social work practice* (3rd ed.). Boston: Allyn & Bacon.

Sawin, K., Harrigan, M., & Woog, P. (Eds.). (1995). *Measures of family functioning for research and practice.* New York: Springer.

Schön, D. (1983). *The reflective practitioner.* New York: Basic.

Scriven, M. (1991). *Evaluation thesaurus* (4th ed.). Thousand Oaks, CA: Sage.

Smith, M. (1995). Utilization-focused evaluation of a family preservation program. *Families in Society, 76*(1), 11–19.

Stanfield, J. (1999). Slipping through the front door: Relevant social scientific evaluation in the people of color century. *American Journal of Evaluation, 20*(3), 415–31.

Strauss, A., & Corbin, J. (1998). *Basics of qualitative research: Techniques and procedures for developing grounded theory* (2nd ed.). Newbury Park, CA: Sage.

Stufflebeam, D. (2000). Professional standards and principles of evaluation. In D. Stufflebeam, G. Madaus, & T. Kellaghan (Eds.), *Evaluation models: Viewpoints on educational and human services evaluation* (2nd ed., pp. 439–56). Boston: Kluwer.

Thyer, B. (Ed.). (2001a). *The handbook of social work research methods.* Thousand Oaks, CA: Sage.

Thyer, B. (2001b). What is the role of theory in research on social work practice? *Journal of Social Work Education, 37*(1), 9–25.

Thyer, B. (2002). How to write up a social work outcome study for publication. *Journal of Social Work Research and Evaluation, 3*(2), 215–24.

Tingler, P. (2000). *Building bridges to stability: A qualitative study that investigates what happens after a family leaves a homeless shelter.* Unpublished honors thesis, Wright State University.

United Way of America. (1996). *Measuring program outcomes: A practical approach.* Alexandria, VA: United Way.

United Way of America. (1998). *Community impact. A new paradigm emerging: A white paper on change in the United Way movement.* Alexandria, VA: Author.

Unrau, Y., Gabor, P., & Grinnell, R. (2001). *Evaluation in the human services.* Belmont, CA: Brooks/Cole.

U.S. Department of Health and Human Services (USDHHS). (1993). *Measurements in prevention: A manual on selecting and using instruments to evaluate prevention programs.* Rockville, MD: Author.

U.S. General Accounting Office (USGAO). (1998). *Program evaluation: Agencies challenged by new demand for information on program results* (GAO GGD Publication No. 98-53). Washington, DC: USGAO, General Government Division.

Villa, R. (2001). Social work evaluation with Mexican Americans. In R. Fong & S. Furuto (Eds.), *Culturally competent practice: Skills, interventions, and evaluations* (pp. 370–84). Boston: Allyn & Bacon.

Weiss, C. (1998). *Evaluation: Methods for studying programs and policies* (2nd ed.). Upper Saddle River, NJ: Prentice Hall.

Weitzman, E. (1999). Analyzing qualitative data with computer software. *Health Services Research, 34*(5), 1241–62.

Weitzman, E., & Miles, M. (1995). *A software sourcebook: Computer programs for qualitative data analysis.* Thousand Oaks, CA: Sage.

INDEX

ABA designs, 154
Abstract databases, 99
Abstracts, 99
Academic research. *See* Research
Accountability, evaluation and, 3–5
Advisory boards, evaluation, 31–32, 41–44
Agencies
 committees that support evaluation activities of, 33f
 evaluation advisory boards for, 31–32
 integrating evaluation into daily operations of, 29–31
Agency evaluation values, 49–50
Agreements, 77
 case example of adherence to ethical guidelines and, 78–79f
Analysis. *See* Data analysis; Statistical analysis
Analysis of variance (ANOVA), 172
Applied research, evaluation as, 5–6
Articles, peer-reviewed research, 99
Asset mapping, community, 77
Assets, economic, 77
Audit committees, 33f
Audits, evaluation, 177

Baseline data, 179
Bivariate analysis, 171
Boards, advisory evaluation, 31–32, 41–44

Campbell Collaborative, 93
Categories, 162–163
Change agents, evaluators as, 26
Child Welfare League of America, 77
Chi-square, 172
Classic experiment design, 178
Clean sample rates, 135
Clients, 24. *See also* Consumers; Participants
Codebooks, 168

Code of Ethics, for evaluation and research, 205–209
Codes, 162–163
Coercion, evaluations and, 65–73
Committees, for supporting evaluation activities of agencies, 33f
Community asset mapping, 77
Community members, defined, 25
Community values, 50–51
Comparison groups, 136
Compensation, for participation, 72–73
Computerized descriptive statistics, 168–171
Confidentiality, of participants, 73
Conflicts of interest, evaluation and, 75
Consent forms, 72–73
Constructed surveys, 146–151
Consultants, 61
Consumers. *See also* Participants
 defined, 24
 levels of involvement in evaluation decisionmaking by, 25
Contingency tables, 171
Coordinators, of evaluations, 36
Coping with Life's Demands, Interactive Model of, 95, 96f
Correlations, 171
Credibility, 123. *See also* Data credibility
Cross-tabulations, 171
Culturally competent evaluation, 57–59
 case example of, 58–59
Cultural respect, evaluations and, 74–75
Culture, 55–57
Cycles, of evaluations, 91, 91f

Data
 defined, 120
 myths about, 121–124, 121f
 transforming information into, 120–124